W9-CIG-590

PUERTO RICO

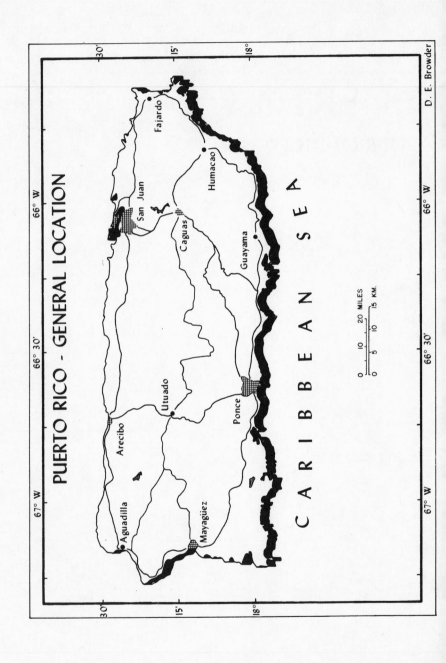

PUERTO RICO - GENERAL LOCATION

67° W   66° 30'   66° W

30'
15'
18°

Aguadilla
Arecibo
Utuado
Mayagüez
Ponce
San Juan
Caguas
Humacao
Guayama
Fajardo

CARIBBEAN SEA

0   10   20 MILES
0   5   10   15 KM.

67° W   66° 30'   66° W

30'
15'
18°

D. E. Browder

PUERTO RICO
A PROFILE

Kal Wagenheim

Second Edition

Foreword by Piri Thomas

PRAEGER PUBLISHERS
New York

FERNALD LIBRARY
COLBY-SAWYER COLLEGE
NEW LONDON, N. H. 03257

F
1958
W3

70163

Published in the United States of America in 1975
by Praeger Publishers, Inc.
111 Fourth Avenue, New York, N.Y. 10003

This is the revised edition of a
book originally published in 1970 by
Praeger Publishers, Inc.

© 1970, 1975 by Praeger Publishers, Inc.

All rights reserved

Library of Congress Cataloging in Publication Data

Wagenheim, Kal.
    Puerto Rico.

    Bibliography: p. 279
    Includes index.
    1.   Puerto Rico.
F1958.W3   1975   972.95   74-30999
ISBN 0-275-33670-0
ISBN 0-275-85250-4 pbk.

Printed in the United States of America

To Olguita and our children

Contents

A SECTION OF PHOTOGRAPHS FOLLOWS PAGE 80.

Maps

Foreword

By Piri Thomas

When I was asked to write an introduction to this book, my initial reaction was to say no because it had been written by a non–Puerto Rican. I remembered with pain and bitterness several books and articles by non–Puerto Ricans that had presented a distorted and stereotyped image of my people here on the mainland and in Puerto Rico. Like many other Puerto Ricans, I consider these works especially harmful when they appear cloaked in sociological authenticity and reality. But Léon King of Praeger Publishers persuaded me at least to take a look at Kal Wagenheim's book.

Even so, I approached *Puerto Rico: A Profile* with more than a little skepticism. But, when I began reading it, I soon realized that this was a book of another sort entirely. It is an objective, comprehensive, carefully researched study of the island—its people, history, culture, geography, economics, politics, and beauty. It is not meant to titillate, to debase, to derogate. It presents a credible picture of what modern-day Puerto Rico and Puerto Ricans are all about; at the same time, it gives adequate and relevant attention to the past. When I finished the book, it was clear to me that this was the work of a man who had written from the heart and with great feeling for the beauty of all peoples.

This book fills a tremendous need in the vast desert of ignorance about Puerto Rico and Puerto Ricans. We Puerto Ricans on the mainland have gone through whole lifetimes with almost no opportunity to learn about our roots, our history, our culture, our unique contributions to the history of the world's peoples. We—and I include myself—have been taught in school about the greatness of the English, the French, the Italians, the Russians, the Germans, but the great contributions of Puerto Ricans have been singularly ignored or known only to a small intelligentsia.

As a young boy growing up in the poverty of Spanish Harlem during the Depression, I often wondered what Puerto Rico, my people's island, was all about. I remember my father patiently teaching all the children—myself, my sister, and my brothers—to speak Spanish, our native tongue. He didn't have much formal education, but he had a fine mind and he wanted us to be proud of our Puerto Rican heritage even if he didn't fully know what it was.

Many times I would ask my mother, "Mommy, where are we from? Ain't we from some place great?" My mother would look puzzled. "Mommy, they keep calling me 'spic' and 'nigger.' They call me 'bodega' (Spanish grocery store) and tell me that I'm nothing and how great they are. I have nothing to come back to them with. Do we have any great people, in *música,* in *arte,* like some kind of heroes? Is this all we got, this place called *El Barrio* in Harlem?"

My mother would say, *"Sí,* I'm sure we have great people." Because she had never had the opportunity to learn, she couldn't come up with any real answers to my questions. But what she couldn't answer she made up for in her love for Puerto Rico and its children.

It was not until I was an adult that I had a chance to visit Puerto Rico. When I got off the plane, I was overwhelmed by the feeling that I had come home and lost in amazement at the beauty of the island of my blood. I had grown up a stranger to it physically but not emotionally or spiritually. From my mother, I had heard much about its beautiful mountains, its rivers, the emerald waters of the sea and ocean, the palm trees, the acres and acres of sugarcane, of coconuts with sweet water inside, of mangoes, *aguacates, quenepas,* and *lechón asado.* From my mother, I had also learned of the poverty amidst all this beauty that had led many Puerto Ricans to migrate to the United States in the hope of bettering their lives.

During the past few years, I have had many opportunities to

speak with young American-born Puerto Ricans in our communities, schools, and universities. They have developed an awareness of, and identity with, the land of their heritage and a strong desire to preserve its language and culture. They have told me that they are tired of the stereotyped picture of Puerto Ricans as a meek, submissive, or sexually immoral people. They are tired of reading books in English about Puerto Ricans written from a politically or sociologically up-tight viewpoint that they consider to be a "put-down." These young people, among others, will certainly welcome *Puerto Rico: A Profile.*

Also, this book should be read and studied by the many Americans who have had no previous exposure to the history and culture of Puerto Rico, except perhaps for a brief tourist's visit to the Emerald Island. The author of this book is an excellent guide for anyone who would understand the struggles, hopes, aspirations, and beauty of a people.

I have never met Kal Wagenheim, but, while reading his book, I could not help feeling the undercurrent of his love for Puerto Rico, *La Isla Verde.* I say to him here, *"Adelante. Tienes un hermano más."*

> *Somos gentes, somos almas,*
> *Somos una parte de la humanidad.*
>
> *Sí,* at last, *yo entiendo lo que es*
> *ser puertorriqueño.*
>
> (We are a people, we are souls
> We are a part of humanity
>
> Yes, at last, I understand what it means
> to be Puerto Rican.)

—From a poem by PIRI THOMAS

Preface

The first edition of this "Profile," in 1970, coincided fortuitously with the growth of Puerto Rican studies in many high schools and colleges on the U.S. mainland.

At the time, I lamented the "gap in the five-foot shelf of books about Puerto Rico," because no up-to-date survey in the English language was available to the student, journalist, or general reader.

I'm pleased to say that my perception was correct, because there was a very gratifying response to this book, which has been adopted as a text in many schools and has served as an introduction to the island for many non–Puerto Rican readers. As I had hoped, *Puerto Rico: A Profile* also served as a springboard from which students have gone on to other books that focus upon particular aspects of Puerto Rico's history, economy, and culture. (See the annotated bibliography at the conclusion of this book.)

Perhaps the key reason that encouraged me to write this book in the first place was a comment in Praeger's invitational letter, which explained that the firm was preparing a series of books that "profile" different nations of the world, and "although Puerto Rico is not an independent nation, it does have many unique characteristics that might justify our including it in such a series." That statement beckons forth a tidal wave of controversy, which will be discussed in the coming pages.

This book is laced with my own opinions but has no grand design or narrow thesis to prove. It is a "mini-encyclopedia" of Puerto Rico, which attempts to transmit some flavor of island life and discusses the problems and prospects that Puerto Rico faces. In this new edition, I have (with the kind help of readers) corrected some errors and updated many statistics. I trust that observations on traits and trends will have a' longer effective life. The critiques by other observers of the Puerto Rican scene are most welcome; if there are future editions, I shall try to incorporate other views that appear meritorious.

A few critics have argued that this book is too "indecisive," and should be more "committed" to some solution for Puerto Rico's problems. I have tried, on the other hand, to describe the island as it *is,* not as it *should be.* I doubt that I have achieved a high enough plateau of wisdom to tell people what they ought to think. Furthermore, I happen to feel quite indignant about outsiders—no matter how sublime their motives—who barge into other people's homes and begin to rearrange their furniture. The sad, lilting strains of *La borinqueña* have brought chills to my spine, too, and wetness to my eyes; but I shall never forget that in Puerto Rico I am just a friendly spectator—not a member of the orchestra.

When I moved from New Jersey to Puerto Rico in 1961, my work as coeditor with Augusto Font of the *San Juan Review* (1964–66, R.I.P.), as translator-researcher for Oscar Lewis, and as local correspondent for *The New York Times* took me into many corners and levels of Puerto Rican life. By marrying into a Puerto Rican family, I have been privileged to acquire insights that might never have occurred to me in a century of library research. When I moved back to the U.S. mainland in late 1970, I learned a great deal about the large, emerging Puerto Rican community in "the diaspora." Thus, much of this book is based on personal experience. But I have also borrowed extensively from the scholarly work of other authors.

I owe a special debt to the following persons, whose written works or personal communications have been indispensable: Rafael Picó, Gordon K. Lewis, Lidio Cruz Monclova, Luis Vivas, Robert Hunter, Hubert Barton, René Marqués, Manrique Cabrera, Leopold Kohr, Henry Wells, Arturo Morales Carrión, Sidney Mintz, Nilita Vientós Gastón, Ricardo Alegría, Francisco Watlington, William Laidlaw, Elmer Ellsworth, José Guzmán, Tomás Blanco, the late Antonio S. Pedreira, the late Manuel Zeno Gandía, and the late

Oscar Lewis (who gave me a rare opportunity to assist him in his studies of the subculture of poverty).

I also owe thanks to Praeger editors Fredric Kaplan and Léon King; to Barry Levine (my former coeditor on the *Caribbean Review* quarterly), for his encouragement and advice; to my father-in-law, *don* Santos Jiménez, and brother-in-law Luis Muñiz, for the many pleasurable talks that heightened my appreciation of Puerto Rico's way of life, and also taught me the meaning of the word *jaibería* (which every poor gringo like me must slowly learn for himself); to novelist Pedro Juan Soto, for his friendship and his example; to my children, for keeping very quiet; and, finally, to my wife, Olga, a student of Puerto Rican history herself, for her help in too many ways to mention.

San Juan, Puerto Rico, and Maplewood, New Jersey
February, 1975

PUERTO RICO

1 Introduction

Puerto Rico is a small, warm, crowded, Spanish-speaking island in the Caribbean, situated roughly midway between North and South America in terms of geography, culture, and living standards. The U.S. flag has flown there since 1898. The Puerto Rican flag—a single white star on a triangular blue field, with three red and two white stripes—has shared the breeze since 1952, when the island, once an outright U.S. colony, entered a commonwealth form of association, which Puerto Ricans call the *Estado Libre Asociado* (Associated Free State).

Puerto Rico is growing in importance to the United States. Over 1.5 million Puerto Ricans—by birth or parentage—live on the mainland (compared with 3 million on the island), most of them clustered in a few large American cities. The Spanish language prevails in many neighborhoods of these cities. After Canada, Japan, West Germany, and England, Puerto Rico is America's largest trade partner. In strategic terms, the island is the site of an immense U.S. naval base that shields America's southern coast.

But the United States is even more important to Puerto Rico. Most of the investment dollars and expertise for new industry, and credit for housing and consumer goods purchases, come from U.S. mainland financial circles. Tourists, most of them from the United States, spend over $300 million yearly. United States Federal agencies provide vital subsidies for education, public housing, highway and hospital construction, and relief for the poor and aged.

3

Puerto Rico is somewhat like a small independent nation, locked within the U.S. sphere. It also bears a considerable resemblance to a state of the Union. Puerto Ricans have been U.S. citizens since 1917, but, unless they reside on the mainland, they may not vote in U.S. elections. Nor do they pay taxes to the Federal Treasury. They do, however, serve in the U.S. armed forces, which is paradoxical because they cannot elect the legislators who declare wars, or the President, who is commander-in-chief of America's military. Puerto Ricans elect their own governor and local legislature, as well as a resident commissioner, who represents their interests in the U.S. Congress but has no vote there. The island's post offices, radio and television licensing, and customs service are all under Federal control.

This unique midway relationship (critics have called it "perfumed colonialism," while advocates have claimed that it is a sensible, pragmatic arrangement) merits attention. But this is not the only intriguing feature. Puerto Rico also happens to be one of the fastest-changing places in the world. The velocity of change after World War II, particularly in the past decade, has been vertiginous, and it seems to be accelerating.

As recently as 1940, Puerto Rico was dismally poor (yearly per capita income, $118), mostly agricultural (sugarcane, coffee, tobacco, and citrus crops were the major products), and more or less ignored by the rest of the world (in 1940, only twenty-three thousand visitors came to the island). It was also overpopulated with 1.8 million persons (over five hundred per square mile), and health conditions were so poor that life expectancy was only forty-six years.

Today, despite a population boom to 3 million, per capita income has multiplied to over $1,800 a year. This is below the income level in the poorest U.S. state, but Puerto Ricans are wealthier than the citizens of any Latin American republic, even oil-rich Venezuela. The "Operation Bootstrap" industrial development program, with tax exemption and other lures to manufacturers, has attracted 1,800 new plants, which employ more than 110,000 workers. In the 1950's, manufacturing replaced agriculture as Puerto Rico's number one industry. On an island famed for its smooth cane rum (still a major revenue source, despite a worsening crisis in the sugarcane industry), milk consumption per capita has quadrupled and is higher than that on the U.S. mainland.

The pace of change is startling. Over 675,000 cars (compared with 26,000 in 1940) clog new roads soon after the inaugural ribbons are cut. In one recent month, 347 ships pulled into San Juan's harbor, belching forth camera- (and peso-) laden tourists; sacks of rice from California; dried codfish from Nova Scotia; cars from Detroit, Japan, and Germany; and thousands of other commodities. San Juan's bustling *Aeropuerto Internacional* handles 5 million in- and outgoing travelers yearly.

Today, acres of crop- and pastureland are covered with ranch-style bedroom communities, which house Puerto Rico's large, growing middle class. In the shadow of rural wood shacks, sturdy pastel-colored cement homes, adorned with television antennas, dot the steep hillsides—so steep, it seems the cows are nailed to the slopes for grazing. Buses, free lunches, and cash allowances for shoes help 97 per cent of the young children to enter the first grade of school. Free public health clinics are found in the smallest towns, and a large government medical center in San Juan treats patients with more serious ailments from all over the island. (Recently, a Puerto Rican heart specialist, chatting with a visitor in his office, exclaimed with a smile and a glint of pride: "Do you know that today in Puerto Rico heart disease is now the number one killer?" No doubt there was a touch of chauvinism for his own specialty, but he really meant that the many infectious diseases once rampant in Puerto Rico have by now been largely controlled and that more and more citizens have the "luxury" of growing old enough to become cardiac cases.)

The middle class suburbs, or *urbanizaciones,* would be familiar to most Americans. *"Juan del Pueblo"* (the Spanish equivalent of John Doe) buys his gas at the corner Gulf, Mobil, or Esso station; shops at Sears, J. C. Penney's, or Woolworth's; pushes a cart through air-conditioned supermarkets, which display all the familiar U.S. products; and takes his wife to theaters in town (when he isn't watching "Kojak" on television), which often show first-run films simultaneously with New York (about three hours and $75 away by thrift-flight jet).

But there are a number of ominous cracks in what has been hailed as "The Showcase of America in the Caribbean." Over *two-thirds* of Puerto Rico's families are still poor. Family income doubled in each of the past three decades, but this is deceiving, because income distribution is inequitable. There is depressing evidence that the poor are falling farther behind. The poorest 45 per cent of Puerto Rico's families earned only 18.2 per cent of total income in 1953, when the island's developmental push was just gathering steam. Today, although the income "pie" has expanded, the slice earned by the poorest 45 per cent has dropped to 16 per cent. Development has been lopsided; one family in four still earns less than $1,000 per year. Nearly one-fifth of Puerto Rico's mothers still queue up monthly to receive U.S. surplus food. Packages of rice, beans, powdered milk, and canned beef are crucial supplements to the groceries that a meager weekly salary can buy, especially when price levels surpass those of New York City.

Unemployment wavers between 10 per cent and 17 per cent, despite a shortage of skilled and semiskilled workers. If one includes the nearly one million adults and young school dropouts who are not even in the labor force, the unemployment figure soars closer to 30 per cent, twice as high as the U.S. rate during the Depression of the 1930's.

Poverty and the rapid flux of unskilled rural workers to the cities and to urban America have helped generate an appalling drug addiction problem. In 1961, Puerto Rico had 1,600 addicts. Today, there are closer to 15,000, about one for every 250 men, women, and children on the island. Thefts have increased tremendously, and police attribute at least half of this type of crime to addicts.

Housing is another serious dilemma. Most families live in their own homes, but many of these are "deteriorating, dilapidated, or inadequate," according to the U.S. Census Bureau. Nine of every ten families in substandard housing do not earn enough to pay today's prices for a home on the private market, largely because of soaring land costs. Squatter slum shacks spring up at a clip of a thousand a year. The point where supply and demand converge is "a long way off," government officials say.

In the field of education, Puerto Rico's humane goal of providing each child with a chance to attend school has taken its toll in qualitative terms. Classrooms are overcrowded, and many children attend less than a full day. Most teachers are undertrained, since they were rushed through to attend to the exploding student population; they are also undermotivated because of low pay and crowded classrooms. In rural areas, as many as 40 per cent of the children drop out before sixth grade, and the drop-out rates are also serious in the cities, though not as high.

"Change" (which is a more accurate term than "progress") has meant different things to different people. For a large part of the population, who before lived at substandard levels in terms of nutrition, health, and shelter, these basics have now been supplied. Even the harshest critic of Puerto Rico's "peaceful revolution" will grudgingly admit this. For those who always enjoyed the basics, life is gaudier and more comfortable, thanks to the cement, chrome, Formica, and cellophane of modern urban and suburban life. But gone are the pleasant two-hour luncheons at home and other vestiges of "the good old days." Today, many middle-class Puerto Ricans live in suburbs far from their jobs. They fight through nerve-jangling traffic jams twice daily and feel the constant pressure of keeping up the payments on the house, car, TV set, washer, and so forth—bought on easy, high-interest credit. Another large chunk of the populace, those whom anthropologist Oscar Lewis identifies as living in the generation-after-generation culture of poverty, has seen progress pass it by. Although in the 1940's, many were landless peons (*agregados*), toiling for pennies a day in the fields—and sinking ever deeper into debt when there was no work—today, they live in urban shanties, sometimes within the shadows of sleek new office buildings, surviving on meager relief payments and odd jobs.

There are acute psychological pressures on all these groups. Those who have "made it"—the middle-class consumers, who live in new suburban homes—often have rural roots and are adjusting to a city that is larger and more hectic than their birthplace, and where knowledge of a foreign tongue (English) is, sometimes, essential to get ahead in one's job. Those who still live in poverty see prosperity spring up all around them—new homes, cars, home appliances—but beyond their reach.

Most of this change—the good and the bad—is largely because

Puerto Rico (which is within the U.S. tariff barrier and, also, enjoys fiscal autonomy) has been open to massive infusions of investment and modernization capital from the United States. The influx was accompanied by the policies of a basically decent (and slightly bewildered) liberal government, trying to spread the new wealth equitably. But, physical and social planning has lagged behind action, and huge discrepancies have occurred; in contrast with impressive strides in manufacturing, agriculture has collapsed—to the point of near morbidity. Cost-conscious management found automated ways to produce goods (in a society where more labor-intensive production would provide more people with the dignity of a job). Urban sprawl has scarred the countryside and polluted some of the island's most beautiful scenic resources. Near the new petrochemical plants on the south coast, which promise so much for the island's economy, new slums spring up, as more rural poor flock to the place where "the action is."

Few of Puerto Rico's leaders feel that they can—or should—halt the tide of change. To do so without providing some adequate alternative would, they contend, be equally disastrous. It appears that Puerto Rico's "establishment" believes in further accelerating change, bringing in more investment, inflating the income "pie" to such a degree that even the poorest of the poor will receive a slice large enough to satisfy their basic needs.

This philosophy was summed up well in March, 1966, when former Governor Roberto Sánchez Vilella spoke at his alma mater, Ohio State University:

> We [in Puerto Rico] stand at the threshold of development and success . . . a demi-developed society. The alternative to stop is no longer ours. We are already beyond the point of refusal. If we put on the brakes, we are going to crash. And so we must continue to change, to improve, to alter, to succeed.

Concern over the cultural and psychological impact of such change was also summarized by Sánchez' predecessor, Luis Muñoz Marín, Governor from 1948 through 1964, who is considered the "architect" of modern Puerto Rico. Muñoz wrote the following in 1928 in the *American Mercury,* when he was a thirty-year-old journalist (he is now in his seventies). Although his tone is now more philo-sophical, he and his countrymen still share the same preoccupations:

> Saving a culture, even an inferior one, from becoming the monkey of another, even a superior one, is a good in itself. And in the present case it is by no means certain that the heritage shared by Porto Rico is to be unfavorably compared with the heritage to which the blind forces of production and exchange now seek to hook it up. . . . Whether the island is to be semi-independent, like Cuba, or autonomous under some special dispensation of Congress, is a question to be determined by the interplay of political and economic interest. But it is certain that it will never be incorpo-rated into the Union as a State save through the operation of cultural forces: that is, not unless, and until, our manner of life and thought has been respectably Americanized. Will this ever come about? Will the island retain its historical personality? An unqualified answer to either of these questions would necessarily fall short of the possibilities. Perhaps a more absurd fate is in store for us. Perhaps we are destined to be neither Porto Ricans nor Americans, but merely puppets of a mongrel state of mind, suscep-tible to American thinking and proud of Latin thought, subservient to American living and worshipful of the ancestral way of life. Perhaps we are to discuss Cervantes and eat pork and beans in the Child's restaurant that must be opened sooner or later. Perhaps we will try not to let mother catch us reading the picaresque verses of Quevedo. Perhaps we are going to a singularly fantastic and painless hell in our own sweet way. Perhaps all this is nothing but a foretaste of Pan-Americanism.

The conflict between cultural identity and the search for economic survival has been the crux of Puerto Rico's political status dilemma; it has perplexed the island for the past century.

Even when Puerto Rico was a Spanish colony, different factions favored assimilation, independence, and a form of autonomy from the *madre patria*. In 1897, the autonomists (led by Muñoz' father, Luis Muñoz Rivera), won an autonomic charter from Spain, but this was nullified the next year when the island passed into U.S. hands as a result of the Spanish-American War.

In the past seventy years, the same three factions—those in sup-port of U.S. statehood, independence, and autonomy—have continued to struggle. Autonomists ruled from the 1940's until 1968, when a pro-statehood government won a shaky mandate, largely due to a split in the autonomist forces. In 1972, the autonomists regained power, but were more concerned with surviving the impact of severe economic recession. While nothing drastic is expected in the immediate future, Puerto Rico's political relationship with the United States remains uncertain. All three alternatives remain alive (even independence, despite small voting turn-outs in recent years). Much depends upon how the changes sweeping over Puerto Rico today affect the attitudes and loyalties of tomorrow's voters— the youth (the island is very "young"; the median age is twenty-one).

Reading of the island's past and present in subsequent chapters will provide some clues to the future, but no scholar, journalist, or politician with an ounce of sense is making any confident predictions.

2 The Caribbean Setting

If, as a philosopher once said, "every man believes he is the center of the universe," it helps to understand a man—and his country— by viewing the universe from the particular vantage point that he occupies.

In Puerto Rico, "the Deep South" means the city of Ponce, not America's Dixieland; "the Wild West" (if such a term were used there) might mean Haiti or the Dominican Republic; "cold weather" means somewhere around 60 degrees Fahrenheit; and "leaving the country" always involves a voyage by ship or plane, since "home" is surrounded by water.

Puerto Ricans are islanders. And insularity makes people view the world through lenses quite different from those of the Chicago clerk, the Argentine gaucho, the Tibetan peasant, or the Italian auto-worker. In addition to language, religion, and other cultural factors, an island's geography—its size, climate, topography, and distance from other lands—plays a dominant role in defining what we might call its "personality."

Climate dictates at least one major difference between the islanders of northern Europe and those in the tropics. The influence of other cultures makes tropical islanders in the Pacific different from those in the Caribbean. Historical pressures have molded the insularity of Puerto Ricans into something quite distinct from that of Jamaicans, Haitians, Arubans, and even Dominicans and Cubans, who share the same Hispanic roots and language. The Caribbean is a mosaic of many cultures, or personalities, and Puerto Rico occupies its own unique place in that design.

First, it would be helpful to see the island in geographical context. Puerto Rico lies on the northeast periphery of the Caribbean Sea, part of an elongated cluster of 7,000 tropical islands of various shapes and sizes, which are called the West Indies. These islands occupy an area called the Antilles, or, simply, the Caribbean.

All three names—West Indies, Antilles, and Caribbean—date back to the European discovery of the New World. The first two stem from Christopher Columbus' mistaken notion that sailing westward offered a direct route to India.

"West Indies" was coined because the natives of the islands were first thought to be inhabitants of outlying regions of India. Very old accounts say that during Columbus' first voyage, when the Spaniards asked the Indians the name of their capital and were told "Cubanacán" (the original name of Cuba), this sounded enough like the fabled Kublai Khan to convince them that they had, indeed, reached the Asian continent. It was not until Columbus' third trip that he knew he had found, not India, but a strange new wilderness. The name "Antilles" is believed to come from "Antilia," which appears on fifteenth-century maps and means anterior or previous; Columbus believed that en route to India there was an island where he could stop for fresh provisions.

"Caribbean" derives from "Carib," the name of the bellicose tribe that inhabited parts of South America and some islands south of Puerto Rico. The fierce Caribs overran the more pacific tribes of the region; their northward thrust was checked only by the arrival of the colonizers from Europe, whose armor, firearms, and greed proved invincible.

The Sea

The Caribbean Sea is one of the larger branches of the Atlantic Ocean. It stretches 1,800 miles east-west and 900 miles north-south, with a total area of 750,000 square miles; roughly the size of western Europe, if you subtract the extremities of Scandinavia, Spain, and Italy. But only one-eighth of the Caribbean—about 87,000 square miles—is dry land. The islands describe a 2,500-mile arc, which begins at Florida's southern tip and ends near the northeast coast of Venezuela. Vast areas of blue water separate the archipelago from Mexico to the west and from the Isthmus of Panama to the south.

The Caribbean's rocky bottom is an enormous basin, divided into three valleys that rise gradually to a massive submerged mountain range, which would be among the world's tallest were its base at sea level. The exposed tops of these mountains are the islands of the West Indies. Between the mountains, even steeper precipices form channels that link the water of the Caribbean and the Atlantic.

The Islands

The West Indies may be divided into three main geographical groupings: the Bahamas, the Greater Antilles, and the Lesser Antilles. The Bahamas, an archipelago of 4,403 square miles, fractured into nearly 700 small islands and islets, are in the Atlantic Ocean, just north of where it meets the Caribbean. The Greater Antilles form the major land mass of the West Indies and include Cuba, Jamaica, Hispaniola (shared by Haiti and the Dominican Republic), and Puerto Rico. The Lesser Antilles, curving southeast from Puerto Rico, include: the Leeward Islands (U.S. and British Virgins, Guadeloupe, St. Eustatius and Saba, St. Martin, Antigua, St. Kitts–Nevis–Anguilla, Montserrat); the Windward Islands (Martinique, Dominica, St. Lucia, St. Vincent, Grenada, the Grenadines); Barbados; the A–B–C Dutch islands (Aruba, Bonaire, and Curaçao); Trinidad-Tobago; and Venezuela's Margarita Island. Sprinkled among these are thousands of smaller islands, islets, and cays, many of them uninhabited.

Geographical Similarity

The Caribbean islands are generally similar in topography, climate, and flora and fauna. Except for Cuba all of the Greater Antilles are traversed by an east-west spinal column of mountains. None have remarkably high peaks; the tallest, in the Dominican

Republic, measures 10,200 feet. Summery climate prevails all year round, with only slight temperature variations as the seasons change. Rainfall is quite high; in some of the southernmost islands, it rains 300 days a year, although a completely sunless day is rare, since rain often falls in brief cloudbursts. Yet some areas, such as Puerto Rico's south coast, resemble the dry American Southwest, complete with cacti. Most Antillean rivers are short, fast-flowing, and navigable only along brief stretches. The longest rivers are the Yaque del Norte in the Dominican Republic and the Cauto in Cuba, each of which measures about 250 miles. Some of the lesser Antillean islands have no rivers at all; but springs, waterfalls, and streams are fairly abundant. Other islands must depend upon mountainside rain catches and deep wells (and, more recently, salt water conversion plants) for at least part of their fresh water supply. Despite the volcanic origin of the Caribbean islands, they have only two active volcanos—Mont Pelée on Martinique and Souffrière on St. Vincent—both of which last erupted in 1902. But several islands have thermal and sulphur springs, which indicate previous volcanic activity.

There is also a marked similarity in the economies of the islands, which are heavily dependent upon agriculture. Sugarcane is a key crop in many islands, as are its by-products: rum, molasses, and bagasse (the discarded cane fiber, which is used to make paper and other fiber products). Also common are coconuts, bananas, citrus, fruits, coffee, and tobacco (the Caribbean Indians enjoyed smoking cigars long before Columbus' arrival).

Some of the islands have unique resource endowments. Jamaica, for example, has very rich bauxite deposits. Trinidad's economy is bolstered by a large supply of asphalt. Mining keeps increasing in importance as once unexplored tracts of land yield surprisingly rich ore deposits. In Puerto Rico, for example, a billion-dollar lode of copper was discovered about a decade ago, although it has not yet been mined. Other islands have created their own resources through a combination of initiative and propitious marketing situations. The barren Netherlands Antilles, for example, are now booming since they got into the business of refining and trans-shipping Venezuelan oil. A few areas have become important manufacturing centers by offering tax exemption and other incentives to foreign investors.

The People

Over four centuries ago, Columbus called the West Indies "a paradise on earth." Today a tourist sipping rum beneath a graceful palm, where the loudest noise is the lapping of the blue sea against white sand, would have little reason to disagree. Even for the more blasé West Indian, there is something paradisiacal about the gentle climate, the year-round profusion of flora, and the prevailing *suavidad* of its people, in comparison with those who march to the drumbeats of the more "developed" regions of the world.

However, another interesting—and quite different—perspective of the West Indies can be gained from a careful study of its history. To Adolph Berle, former Assistant Secretary of State for Latin American Affairs, the West Indies are "a patchwork of separate nations, languages, races and cultures."

"Patchwork" is an apt description. Over 26 million West Indians live in a land area about the size of Oregon, yet twelve times more thickly populated. Many of the 7,000-odd islands, such as the Grenadines, are either bare of human life or sparsely inhabited. Others, such as Barbados, with 1,250 persons per square mile, literally swarm with humanity.

The people cover a broad spectrum of races, cultures, and religions. There are Indians (from India), Orientals, Negroes, and Caucasians. Intermarriage over the centuries has wrought racial amalgams that defy categorizing. In Trinidad, they once tried such labels as "mulatto" for a person with one Caucasian and one Negro parent, "quadroon" for the child of white and mulatto, "octoroon" for the offspring of white and quadroon, "mustee" for a combination of white and octoroon, and "mustefino" for a mix between white and mustee. But the crosses between hybrids were so profuse (and a large influx of East Indians further complicated the situation) that most Trinadadians gave up trying.

Some West Indian historians estimate that about 40 per cent of the region's population is "white," with the remainder split roughtly between mulatto and black. But "white" by some criteria could range from blue-eyed blond Scandinavian types to brown-skinned persons with thin lips and straight hair. Although there is little overt racism in the West Indies (there are too few persons without at least a drop of African blood to cast the first stone), the fact that the area has been dominated for centuries by white European or North American political and economic power has imparted an aura of prestige to "whiteness." This could account for ascribing "whiteness" to some sectors of the population which, in other areas of the world, might be considered colored.

Racial composition varies from island to island and within different regions of each island. Haiti, for example, is predominantly black. In the Dominican Republic, Cuba, and Puerto Rico, mulattoes and dark-skinned "whites" form a larger group than the pure African community, and the pure white (in the European or North American sense) sector is also large. There are noticeable traces, too, of Antillean Indian blood, although the Indians, as a civilization, were wiped out centuries ago by the conquistadores. Enough of them survived, however, in hidden mountain enclaves to intermarry with blacks and whites, leaving a unique—and often strikingly handsome—racial imprint.

The British- and French-influenced islands have larger ratios of black citizens than do the areas once controlled by Spain, where more mixed marriages took place. The Spanish attitude toward the darker races is quite complex. In the Spanish Caribbean, for example, "black" in a certain sense is "beautiful." The word *negro* ("black") is often used as a term of endearment. It is not uncommon for a white-skinned Puerto Rican to affectionately refer to his white-skinned wife as *"negrita,"* which literally means little black one. On the other hand, *"pelo malo"* ("bad hair") refers to kinky hair. The Dutch, French, Spanish, British, and North American concepts of beauty with respect to skin color appear to be reflected in the racial mixtures of the islands that they colonized. It is no mere coincidence that the first Black Power groups in the Caribbean were formed in the British (and to a lesser extent in the Dutch) islands, or that the recent murders of white tourists and residents by black terrorists occurred on the U.S.-controlled island of St. Croix.

As for language, each Caribbean island reflects the nation that colonized it. But strictly "native" languages have emerged to become the lingua franca. Creole (a blend of French, Spanish, and African languages), for example, is far more common in Martinique, Guadeloupe, and Haiti than is French. Papiamento (a mixture of Spanish, Portuguese, Dutch, and English) rivals Dutch in the Netherlands Antilles. Spanish prevails in Cuba, the Dominican Republic, and Puerto Rico (although English is making strong inroads in the last owing to the island's relationship with the United States since 1898); English predominates in the U.S. and British islands, but thick regional accents and local idioms often make it incomprehensible to the visitor (two Virgin Islanders, for example, can insult the dickens out of a tourist standing next to them in a bar, without the poor fellow having the vaguest idea of what they are talking about).

Religions, too, are well represented. There are all manner of Christians (from Roman Catholics to Holy Rollers), Buddhists, Moslems, Jews, and many spiritualist sects, as well as the blend of Catholicism and West African religions in Haiti called *vodum,* or voodoo.

Standards of living vary. The Dutch islands of Aruba and Curaçao enjoy the highest per capita income (higher than in the Netherlands) due to their petroleum processing industry, which involves skilled, well-paid labor. Haiti, 500 miles northward, far larger and wealthier in natural resources, has the area's lowest yearly personal income, about $70. (In Haiti's drought-ridden northwest region, mothers were reported, in 1968, to be selling their children to strangers for as little as 40 cents in the hope of giving them a better life).

The political picture, too, is kaleidoscopic. There are British colonies and dependencies, such as Antigua, Dominica, Grenada, St. Lucia, and the British Virgin Islands. There are colonial territories, such as the U.S. Virgin Islands. The Dutch Caribbean islands are self-governing integral units of the homeland in Europe. Guadeloupe and Martinique are overseas *départements* (somewhat like states) of France. Puerto Rico is a commonwealth associated with the United States. There are long-established republics, such as Cuba, the Dominican Republic, and Haiti; there are new nations, such as Barbados, Jamaica, and Trinidad-Tobago, which became independent members of the British Commonwealth system in the 1960's. In all the former colonies, the trend since World War II has been toward more self-government.

In this region of contrasts, it is not surprising to note that, while the French and Dutch have peacefully shared tiny St. Martin for 300 years, the Haitians and Dominicans have continually squabbled over border locations in the far more spacious confines of Hispaniola. Some islands have been models of internal tranquillity, while governmental coups or other outbursts of violence have occurred with almost monotonous regularity in others.

With so many islands represented, one needs a high-speed calculator to figure the relative value of U.S. dollars, British West Indian dollars, Dominican pesos, Jamaican and British pounds, Cuban pesos, Haitian gourdes, French francs, and Dutch guilders, which makes interisland commerce a sometimes exasperating enterprise.

Political philosophies range from the free-wheeling tax exempt capitalism of St. Martin to the homespun socialism of Martinique, to the native Marxism of Cuba, to the feudal-style dictatorship of Haiti.

It is no wonder, then, that of the several billion dollars in imports and exports generated by the West Indies, more than 96 *per cent* of this trade either comes from or is directed to countries *outside* the West Indies. The Caribbean, then, is a region only in the geographical sense, because each small component of the area is attracted, as though by an irresistible magnet, to the colonial power (past or present) with which it has been related throughout history. Puerto Rico, with the largest import-export volume in the region, does only 2 per cent of its business with its Caribbean neighbors. Most of the remainder is with the United States. The Netherlands Antilles, second to Puerto Rico in import-export volume, does only about 1 per cent of its business in the Caribbean.

Though many West Indian islands are figuratively (and, sometimes, literally) just a stone's throw from each other, they are distant in other respects. The average Puerto Rican, for example, is far more aware of developments in New York—1,600 miles away—than of those in Trinidad, less than half the distance, or even of those in St. Thomas, a next-door neighbor.

Not many years ago, the most convenient way to travel from San Juan, Puerto Rico, to nearby Port-au-Prince, Haiti, was on a steamship, which first made a "slight detour" to New York. Today, interisland radio and postal communication and air and sea transportation are far better, but these services are still slow and erratic.

Many Caribbean leaders have dreamed of uniting the region, but the big obstacles must still be overcome if this long-cherished idea is to become a reality. In addition to awkward transportation and telecommunications, the tariff structures of the various Caribbean islands are perplexing, even to the trained economist. Traditional ties with "mother countries" are not easily severed, or even relaxed. There is only a limited interchange of data on the availability of, and market for, commodities produced within this area.

Trying to open the door for more trade (the precursor of cultural and political relationships) between the islands is like an Alphonse-Gaston act. Exporters ignore markets because transportation is either nonexistent or overly expensive. Transporters cannot improve service or reduce rates because there is not enough demand on the part of exporters.

Even when a trade agreement is obviously beneficial, since many of the islands are governed from abroad, negotiations may be complex and maddeningly slow, with the prospective traders acting as powerless messengers between their respective "mother countries."

If, by some miracle, the present situation were reversed and most of the Caribbean's import-export trade were circulated within the region, the financial impact would be staggering. But such a turnabout is unlikely.

The Caribbean Free Trade Association (CARIFTA) has tried to establish a common market concept among a few of the islands, but its impact thus far has been minimal. One nagging problem is that most islands produce similar crops and must ship them to areas of the world where demand exists. This dependence upon distant markets and the exchange of low-priced foodstuffs and raw materials for expensive manufactured goods from abroad perpetuate dependence in cultural and political affairs.

Tourism—which attracts cash in exchange for inexhaustible resources such as sunshine—has not been a uniting factor, because the islands compete for the same tourist dollar. Also, tourism is viewed with a mixture of zeal and apprehension. Many islands at first welcomed tourism as the panacea for their economic doldrums. Now there are second thoughts, and some feel that tourism has deteriorated the quality of life in their communities. Tiny Anguilla, for example, which declared itself independent in 1967, has expressed concern that a massive influx of visitors might convert its youth (who are black) into "a nation of waiters and busboys."

Thus, most Caribbean islands remain insular in several respects, and their world view focuses narrowly upon a distant, more powerful nation. Puerto Rico is no exception.

3 Geography and Ecology

It [Puerto Rico] is one of the finest islands I ever saw, and I verily believe not any one island is more capable of improvement than this; but through the pride and sloth of its inhabitants it is the far greater part of it a wilderness. It abounds in oranges, lemons, citrus, limes, etc. in such plenty that they are not worth gathering. There are prodigious quantities of bananas, plantains, coconuts, pineapples, mountain cabbage; with a great many fruits and vegetables. In short, there is not anything for the support of human nature but may be found here and cultivated.

—JOHN GEORGE, a British sailor imprisoned in Puerto Rico after being captured by a Spanish privateer in 1748

Just one lifetime ago, when the people were fewer, and most of them lived from the land, Puerto Rico's natural beauty seemed eternal. The landscape was colored many shades of green, complemented by the brilliant silver of ripe sugarcane tassels, the flame-orange of *flamboyán* trees, and the yellow, crimson, pink, and violet hues of tropical blossoms. There were also, to be sure, masses of poverty-stricken people, weakened by disease and malnutrition, who lived in flimsy shacks.

Today, in an era of unprecedented (but still not equitable)

prosperity, the people of Puerto Rico have multiplied, and more than half of them live in the cities. The face of the island has been changed by new roads and homes and by the refuse of new factories. Much of the countryside remains idyllic, but the cities and suburbs are expanding so quickly that the hundred-mile north coast, for example, may soon blend into a megalopolis of homes, factories, drive-in restaurants, gas stations, and junkyards, linked by a six-lane superhighway.

A recent report says that all of Puerto Rico's "surface water and some underground reserves are being polluted." Bird populations have been "greatly reduced," and river shrimp and other fresh water fish have been "nearly extinguished." At least 2.5 million tons of air pollutants are now generated each year from cars, garbage dumps, thermoelectric plants, sugar mills, and other industries. In thirty years, the report predicts, Puerto Rico will be "no fit place to live in."

The prophecy has already been fulfilled in some parts of the island. On the south coast, a burgeoning petrochemical industry has upset an ecological harmony that went undisturbed for, perhaps, millions of years. Now, says one observer, the Guayanilla-Peñuelas area has been turned into "a foul valley of stench and smoke," and the harbor, once one of the most beautiful in Puerto Rico, is "a giant cesspool." In Yabucoa, which was nearly a ghost town ten years ago, new oil refineries built by Sun Oil and Union Carbide spurred an economic boom. But now residents complain that their town is "unlivable." Said one woman, "The smell from the Sun Oil plant never goes away. . . . You can see the children coming home from school some days, vomiting in the streets." Respiratory ailments among local residents are said to have risen sharply. In Guayanilla in 1972, three hundred persons required hospital treatment when lethal chlorine gas leaked from a PPG petrochemical plant. La Parguera's Phosphorescent Bay, which attracts thousands of tourists yearly to view the spectacular "glowing water," at night, grows slowly dimmer; new industry and weekend vacation cabins near the shore have killed many of the microorganisms that give the bay its nocturnal sparkle. In sectors of San Juan, Bayamón, and Carolina, heat shimmers from concrete drives and parking lots that have displaced shade trees and pastures. In the mountainous northwest, near Adjuntas and Utuado, pending strip copper mining projects could, unless strict guidelines are observed, poison not only the local air and water but also beaches several miles north, where refuse from the copper mines will be dumped. Already there are warning signs along stretches of the Condado beach (San Juan's equivalent of Miami) alerting swimmers that the sewage-contaminated water does not meet minimum pollution standards.

Ever since ecology became a global issue in the early 1970's, Puerto Rico has tried to stem the tide of pollution. Strict regulations against air, water, and solid waste contamination have been issued. Enforcement actions have been taken. But, on an island with such widespread poverty, environmentalists are cautious to tread lightly lest they scare away jobs.

"The easiest way would be to close down every factory; pollution would stop overnight," says Cruz Matos, former head of the island's Environmental Quality Board. "But a man with an empty belly, with kids with empty bellies, doesn't care if that tree is saved or not." Puerto Rico, he insists, "must develop a technique of co-existence with industry."

Puerto Rico, the easternmost of the Greater Antilles, is shaped like a parallelogram and measures 111 miles east-west by thirty-six miles north-south. Together with its smaller offshore islands—Vieques, Culebra, and Mona, as well as several tiny keys and islets—Puerto Rico's land area is 3,435 square miles, about the size of Connecticut. Compared with its Greater Antillean neighbors, Puerto Rico is one-sixth the size of the Dominican Republic and one-thirteenth as large as Cuba.

The island's north coast faces the Atlantic Ocean, the Caribbean Sea bathes its eastern and southern shores, and the Mona Channel separates it from the Dominican Republic to the west. It lies 1,662 miles southeast of New York, 1,050 miles southeast of Miami, 550 miles north of Caracas, Venezuela, and 480 miles east of Cuba. Its central location between North and South America, at the entrance to the Caribbean Sea, gives it strategic importance. In the sixteenth century, during the conquest of the New World, Spain used its island colony as a fortress at the gateway to the Caribbean. During World War II and throughout the cold war of the 1950's, large military installations (particularly Ramey Air Force Base on the west coast and Roosevelt Roads Naval Station on the east) made Puerto Rico an important link in the U.S. global defense system.

Puerto Rico sits on the crest of a massive underwater mountain, which was volcanic in origin. A shallow submarine shelf, which skirts the shore in an irregular pattern, extends seaward from two to seven miles. Just two miles from the north coast, the sea floor drops 600 feet from the surface; forty-five miles north is the Milwaukee Deep, one of the world's largest chasms, plunging 28,000 feet downward.

It is said that when Queen Isabella of Spain asked Christopher Columbus to describe Puerto Rico, he crumpled a piece of paper, dropped it to the table, and replied: "It looks like this." The story may be apocryphal, but it conveys the truth. Three-fourths of Puerto Rico's terrain is mountainous or hilly. For so small an island, there is an astonishing variety of landscape and geological formations. In half a day by car, one passes from flat coastal plains to tightly knotted mountains; from strange limestone "haystacks" and "sinkholes" on the north coast to desert land, replete with cacti, on the south; from serene forests to cacophonous cities.

Puerto Rican author-educator Margot Arcé de Vázquez once wrote: "The island's surface undulates like a green lake whipped by the breeze. The entire coastal plain begins to crumple as one moves inland, with a gentle wave-like rhythm, ascending gradually to the Central Cordillera." It is as if the Cordillera, a mountain range that stretches east-west, were the island's spinal column, varying from 1,000 to 3,000 feet high. Puerto Rico's best-known peak is El Yunque ("The Anvil") in the Luquillo Mountain Range, which measures 3,483 feet above sea level. But its tallest mountain is Cerro de Punta, near Jayuya: 4,398 feet high.

Puerto Rico's shoreline is quite regular. The largest inlet is San Juan Bay, a major shipping center, on the north coast. The south coast is the least regular, with several small bays.

Puerto Rico has few natural lakes. When sugarcane production grew in the early 1900's, the need for better irrigation prompted the building of several artificial lakes, which also helped to power hydroelectric plants. By 1936, over 80 per cent of the island's electricity was generated by water power. There are now sixteen of these lakes, which have been stocked with striped bass, catfish, and other species. However, demand for electricity from factories and new homes has outstripped hydroelectric capacity; today, over 95 per cent of the island's power is supplied by thermoelectric plants. Nuclear energy is viewed as a future power source.

Because of abundant, frequent rain in most sectors of the island, Puerto Rico has over 1,000 water courses, only fifty of which are large enough to be called rivers. All the rivers are short; none are navigable with large ships. The strongest rivers flow down from the Cordillera to the north coast; the longest, the Río de la Plata (forty-six miles), weaves northward from Cayey to Dorado on the Atlantic shore. Perhaps the river best known to tourists is the Loíza, which empties muddily into the Atlantic just east of San Juan in a very scenic beach area. Here, people and cars, a few at a time, are crossed on an old wooden ferry, propelled by men wielding long poles.

Though Puerto Rico is in the torrid zone, its distance from the equator and steady trade winds from the northeast keep temperatures at about 85 degrees in summer and in the low 70's in winter. The lowest temperature ever recorded in Puerto Rico is 39 degrees (in a mountain zone during winter), and the highest is 103 degrees (in August of 1906 in the town of San Lorenzo). San Juan's heat record, 96 degrees, was set in June, 1972. On a typical summer day in San Juan, it may reach 90 degrees at noon but slip back to the 70's in the evening. The residents of Old San Juan, a hilly islet, enjoy brisk sea breezes through most of the day, while persons living a few miles inland, in the low, flat residential sectors of Santurce, Río Piedras, and Hato Rey, have frequent need of air conditioning (if they can afford it). The south and west of Puerto Rico are generally warmer, since the Cordillera Central blocks off the trade winds. Mountain towns are from five to ten degrees cooler than the coast; every 500 feet of altitude means a one degree drop in heat. Some wealthier families from the coast keep summer residences in towns such as Lares and Aibonito.

The months of December through March are noticeably cooler, and if one takes to the hills during the Christmas holidays (as many urban families do, to visit relatives), a sweater is often welcome after sundown.

There is an old saying that "Puerto Rico is the product of water and wind." Some 3,600 billion gallons of water bathe the island each year, but a completely sunless day is rare. Rain falls rather evenly throughout the year, although May through November is generally damper, and brief dry spells in January through April are not uncommon. Though rainfall averages seventy-seven inches a year, this varies from twenty-nine inches in the parched south to 108 inches in the highlands. El Yunque's 30,000-acre National Rain Forest, in the east central sector, lives up to its name; 1,600 showers a year deposit 180 inches of rain, dousing the slopes, where tree ferns grow to heights of thirty feet, orchids bloom profusely, and birds dart through the dense foliage, which contains more species of trees (about 250) than any national forest in the United States.

Sometimes the rainfall turns erratic. Heavy downpours in October, 1970, caused floods that took several lives, destroyed hundreds of homes, and swept away bridges, isolating six island towns. On the other hand, severe droughts in 1967 and 1974 forced emergency rationing of water.

In the pre-Columbian era, one of the gods worshiped by Puerto Rico's Taíno Indians was *Juracán,* who, when angered, made the sky darken and created tremendous winds. The hurricane is often mentioned in Puerto Rican folktales, poetry, and music. Older *campesinos* still note important events, such as the birth or death of a relative, not by citing a date on the calendar, but by recalling how long before or after a particular storm.

The Caribbean hurricane season is from June through December. Puerto Rico has been hit by seventy-three hurricanes since 1508—when record-keeping commenced—the last being Donna in September, 1960, which claimed more than 80 lives. The incidence of hurricanes has been sporadic; ten were recorded in the sixteenth century, four in the seventeenth, twenty-two in the eighteenth, thirty-three in the nineteenth, and only eight, thus far, in the twentieth. Two of these—San Felipe (1928) and San Ciprián (1932)—caused many deaths and serious damage to crops and property. August 16 has been a favorite hurricane date; San Roque has paid visits in 1508, 1788, and 1893. The same name was given to three different hurricanes because, until a few years ago, Puerto Ricans baptized these storms with the name of the saint corresponding to the date on the Catholic Church calendar. Today, the U.S.

system of using the first names of women (Anna, Betty, Clara, and so forth) prevails.

In the past decade, there have been several close calls, as hurricanes swept past Puerto Rico's coast and slammed into Cuba and the U.S. continent. Today, radar and hurricane hunter planes warn islanders several days in advance of approaching storms. Hurricane watching has almost developed into a national pastime. Radio and television stations announce frequent status reports; some companies, as a public service, give away Caribbean maps on which the populace can trace an advancing storm's path. In August, 1969, when one such hurricane approached (Hurricane Camille, which caused over $1 billion in damage to Cuba and the U.S. Gulf Coast), Puerto Ricans dutifully charted it on their maps, after having boarded up windows and taken other precautions. The storm came close, but the island's avocado growers released a statement to the press, insisting that "there is nothing to worry about." Folkloric superstition in Puerto Rico contends that when avocadoes are plentiful, there will be no hurricanes. The "avocado theory" may sound far-fetched, but the *aguacateros* (as they are known in Spanish) have been uncannily accurate weathermen.

River flooding, caused by heavy rains or strong coastal waves and stirred up by distant tropical storms, has also caused severe damage on occasion. In 1967, high waves battered old San Juan's La Perla slum in the middle of the night, sweeping away several dozen seaside shacks. Fortunately, the waves had grown in crescendo over a few hours and the families escaped, but the water washed away most of their furniture, as well as a number of pigs and chickens kept in the back yards. (The only near-casualty was an eager documentary filmmaker, who rushed down early in the morning to record the scene in his camera. As he stood on a rock near the water's edge, a huge wave gobbled him up, while his companions watched, horror-stricken. A moment later, the wave returned him to land, soaked but unharmed, without his camera.)

Although the entire Caribbean area is in the zone of an active fault movement, there have been no strong earthquake shocks near Puerto Rico in the last half-century. The worst earthquake recorded in Puerto Rico occurred on October 11, 1918, in the Mona Channel off the island's northwest corner. Vibrations and tidal waves took

116 lives and did $4 million worth of damage. In 1867, an undersea shock, seventy-five miles off the east coast, caused damage island-wide. About 100 tiny shocks are recorded each year in Puerto Rico, but only two or three cause even the slightest tremor.

Historians say that the only domestic animal found in Puerto Rico when the Spaniards came was a multicolored mute dog (now extinct), which the Indians liked to fatten up and roast. They had no cows, pigs, or horses. Their meat diet consisted chiefly of birds (which they raised in cages), iguanas, *jutías* (a large rodent still found in Cuba and the Dominican Republic), *coríes* (a type of guinea pig), oysters, clams, turtles, and various kinds of fish. There were no really dangerous animals. Even today, the most vicious creature is the mongoose, which was imported years ago from India to combat poisonous reptiles, which once existed here. The mongoose has since multiplied, and while it is no threat to human life, it loves to gnaw away at certain crops and is considered a nuisance by farmers.

If Puerto Rico can be said to have a national mascot, it is the *coquí,* an indigenous, seldom seen, very small amphibious frog, which enjoys lounging on lily pads or in the moist leafage of large plants. The name *"coquí"* is onomatopoeic with its call: a musical, high-pitched ko-*kee!* ko-*kee!* There are similar frogs in the Caribbean and other parts of the world, but the *coquí* is truly local; its scientific name is *Eleutherodactylis portoricensis,* which means, literally, Puerto Rican free-fingered one, since its toes are not webbed together.

Nilita Vientós Gastón, a literary critic, once told the following anecdote:

> Yes, our little *coquí* is really one hundred per cent Puerto Rican. A few years ago, when Juan Bosch [former President of the Dominican Republic] was resident writer at our university and he had to return to Santo Domingo, he decided to take a *coquí* with him, because he had come to enjoy its music. Bosch later wrote to me that the *coquí* was alive and well, but it had stopped singing altogether.

Puerto Rico has over 200 species of bird life. Also, birds from the U.S. continent spend the winter there or continue farther south.

Year-round inhabitants include thrushes, orioles, grosbeaks, hummingbirds, doves, owls, pigeons, and—one of the most common —the *reinita* ("little queen"), which loves sweets and flies through kitchen windows to snatch sugar grains from the table. Also very typical is the small *pitirre* (*Tyrannus dominicensis*), whose name is also onomatopoeic with its shrill call. The El Yunque Rain Forest is a refuge for many colorful species of birds, including a small flock of very rare parrots, which are nearly extinct.

Insects also flourish on this tropical island. Cockroaches, for example, are so much larger than the kind found in New York City apartments that one wag has suggested they be required to carry license plates. Mosquitoes are a nuisance in damp, flat areas, as are *mimes,* tiny sand flies, which are the scourge of the beach after sundown. There are several frightening, but harmless, species of spiders. One, for example, is called the *araña boba* ("silly spider") because it is so innocuous despite its menacing mien. Another, the giant crab spider, prefers roaches to humans. Perhaps the most menacing insect is the giant centipede, measuring fifteen inches or more, which deals out a painful, but rarely fatal, bite that can keep a man bedridden for a day or two. Workers in the cane fields often tie strings around their trouser legs to prevent such bites. The poisonous black widow spider is extremely rare in Puerto Rico. Although crocodiles are not indigenous to Puerto Rico, an increasing number have made the journey from pet shops to homes to local rivers and appear to be flourishing.

Off Puerto Rico's north and west coasts are reefs with colorful marine life. Through boats' glass bottoms or swimming goggles, one can watch sea horses, sea cucumbers, sea porcupines, many kinds of crabs, starfish, a wide variety of tropical fish, and coral. Sharks also inhabit the waters in some parts, but death or injury from these man-eaters is rare. More common are stings from jellyfish, known in Spanish as *agua viva* ("living water"). In 1969, a specimen of deadly jellyfish known as the sea wasp (most frequently found in the Pacific near Australia) was reported near the Humacao Public Beach, but no fatalities from jellyfish bites have been documented.

From the air, Puerto Rico offers every conceivable shade of green. Due to differences in soil and climate, there are five well-defined areas of natural vegetation: humid sea forest (marshland); humid wood forest (coconut palm groves and seashore shrubs); humid tropical forest (in the island's center); subhumid forest (along the northwest coast, where one finds satinwood and mahogany trees); and horny dry forest (on the south coast, from Patillas to Hormigueros, with cactus, spiny plants, and drought-resistant trees, such as the *ceiba,* or West Indian silkcotton, tamarind, mastic, and carob).

Despite this seeming abundance of verdure, and the presence of 1,000 tree species, the island's mature timberland is exceedingly scarce, which aggravates problems of erosion and flooding. Three-fourths of the island was covered by trees a century ago, compared with one-fourth today. The original trees were long ago felled for home-building and charcoal, once the most common cooking fuel. The few remaining stands of hardwoods—nutmeg, satinwood, Spanish elm, Spanish cedar, and candletree—make excellent furniture, but they are rare. Particularly lamented is the virtual extinction of the *ausubo* tree, a type of ironwood. The *ausubo,* used for beams to span the ceilings in Old San Juan's colonial era homes, resists rot and termites. It is so valued that when houses in the old city are demolished, the Institute of Puerto Rican Culture stores the old beams for use in future restoration projects.

Far more plentiful in Puerto Rico are flowers; the best known is the *flamboyán.* Along the coastal plains and in the mountains, the landscape is alive with scarlet, orange, lavender, yellow, and pink blossoms.

But, as mentioned before, industry, commerce, the expansion of housing developments, and unwise farming methods have taken a serious toll. Today, perhaps 1 per cent of Puerto Rico's surface is in a virgin, or pre-Columbian, state.

Although the island's climate is excellent for agriculture, only one-third of the topsoil is considered of good or medium quality. Much of the land has been abused by poor crop rotation practices or by the decimating of trees. Much of the rich, deep soil is near the coast, in the path of new housing.

In pre-Columbian days, the Indians cultivated corn, yucca, sweet potatoes, yams, peanuts, *ají* (a kind of hot pepper), *yautía* (a starchy potato-like root), tobacco, and cotton. Many of the fruits and vegetables that are considered native Puerto Rican, because they have been grown here so long, are not. The coconut was brought from Cape Verde to Dutch Guiana, and then to Puerto Rico by Canon Diego Lorenzo in 1549. Sugarcane, bananas, plantains, mangoes, oranges, lemons, and grapefruits were all introduced to America by the conquistadores. Coffee was brought from the French island of Martinique in 1755.

There are, however, a number of purely American products, such as the pineapple, the guava, the tamarind, the papaya, and the cashew. Puerto Rico also has a number of fruits unknown to most North Americans. These include the *mamey,* ("mammee-apple"), *guanábana* ("custard apple"), *guamá, níspero* ("sapo-dilla"), *caimito* (star apple), *jobo* ("hogplum"), and the *jagua* ("genipap"). Particularly delicious is the *quenepa* ("Spanish lime"), known in Cuba as the *limoncillo* (or "tiny lemon"). About the size of a large walnut, the *quenepa* has a brittle, green skin, which is cracked open to reveal a large white pit, surrounded by pinkish fruit, with a delicate bittersweet citrus flower. Few, if any, of these native fruits are grown commercially. They are not available in Puerto Rico's urban supermarkets, or *colmados* ("grocery stores"), but are found in the countryside, sometimes at roadside stands. Also commonly grown today in Puerto Rico are several varieties of beans, tomatoes, peppers, squash, breadfruit, and watermelon. Agricultural innovators have also grown peaches, strawberries, and wine grapes in cool mountain regions.

Puerto Rico first attracted the Spaniards because of its gold. But the deposits gave out early in the sixteenth century, just when most of the Taíno Indians—enslaved to mine the precious metal— had either fled or died out. The island has deposits of copper, iron, manganese, cobalt, nickel, and titanium, but none are being mined today (see chapter on the economy). There is also a possibility of petroleum and natural gas deposits on the north coast.

Common minerals play a more important role in Puerto Rico's economy, especially in its booming construction industry. Clay, limestone, sand, and gravel—the essential ingredients for cement —are plentiful. Extraction of sand from beaches, however, has created serious conservation problems in some north coast areas. Also in good supply are silicate for glass, marble for household tiles, and blue limestone for highway building. Salt, for table and industrial use, is not mined, but "farmed" from the ocean on flat evaporation beds in the south.

On a world map, Puerto Rico is a small dot. But the island's varied topography gives it a complexity equal to that of much larger land areas. In his book *Nueva Geografía de Puerto Rico,* Rafael Picó divides the island into several distinct regions.

The north coast plain is a level strip 100 miles long by five miles wide. Within 13 per cent of the island's land area, it holds more than half of the urban population, including the capital city of San Juan, which was founded in 1521. (In 1970, San Juan had 463,242 residents, and the total San Juan metropolitan area had a population of 851,247.) About half of Puerto Rico's net income is generated from San Juan, which holds 40 per cent of the island's commerce and factories. Sugarcane, once a key product on the north coast, has declined. But dairy farming and cultivation of pineapples and other fruits continues. Most of Puerto Rico's hotels and tourism facilities are clustered on the north coast plain, in or near San Juan.

The east coast valley stretches south from Fajardo (the largest town in the area, with 23,032 people) to Cape Mala Pascua. Mostly agricultural (cane, coconuts, fruits, domestic animals), it is growing as a tourism center because of its fine beaches and pleasure-boating facilities.

The Caguas Valley, in the island's east central area, has sugar cane, tobacco, cattle, poultry and dairy products. Caguas, the island's largest inland city, is twenty-two miles south of San Juan. A modern highway connecting to San Juan has boosted Caguas' population by 47 per cent (to 95,661) in a decade.

The west coast, from Aguadilla (population 51,355) to Cabo Rojo (population 26,060) is also heavily rural. The island's third largest city, Mayagüez (85,857) has tuna-packing canneries, numerous factories, a good port, and a branch of the University of Puerto Rico.

The semiarid south coast produces one-fourth of Puerto Rico's sugarcane and is the site of the island's new petrochemical complex. Ponce (population 158,981), the island's second largest city, is its urban focal point.

The southern hill country, also semiarid and sparsely populated, is devoted largely to sugar cane, coffee, fruits and dairy farming.

The humid north hills, with about 25,000 people, are planted in tobacco, coffee, corn, and beans.

The humid eastern mountain area is Puerto Rico's tobacco growing center and has large cigar factories, as well as a large poultry-raising and processing industry in Aibonito (population 20,044).

The rainy western mountain sector has 35,000 people spread among seven small towns. Coffee is a key product.

Least populated is the rain-soaked Luquillo Sierra, whose scenic forests attract many tourists.

Puerto Rico's largest offshore island is Vieques (the Indian word "bieque" means small land), which lies nine miles east and has an area of fifty-one and one-half square miles. A series of small mountains rambles east-west across the island, which has several streams. Its only town, Isabel Segunda, was founded in 1843. Ferries and small aircraft link it with Puerto Rico. The U.S. armed forces carry out large maneuvers on Vieques. During World War II, a long pier was built to shelter the British Fleet in the event that England fell to Germany. Because more than 70 per cent of the land is held by the U.S. Government, agriculture and tourism have been discouraged, and the population has held steady at under 8,000. Some sugarcane is exported to the main island, but Vieques' main export is its people, who have migrated to Puerto Rico, to the American mainland, or to nearby St. Croix, in the U.S. Virgin Islands.

Culebra, seven miles long and four wide, located twenty-two miles east of Fajardo, is very dry and warm, has neither mountains nor rivers, and is populated by about 700 persons, most of whom live in the town of Dewey, founded in 1898. The U.S. Navy uses parts of Culebra for aerial and naval target practice, limiting its meager chances for agriculture or tourism. Fishing and cattle raising are other sources of income.

Mona Island, nineteen and one-half square miles large, is forty-two miles southwest of Puerto Rico. Hot, flat, and uninhabited, it is a good hunting area for wild birds, goats, and pigs.

Other tiny islands are Desecheo ("Castaway"), Isla de Cabras ("Goat Island"), and Caja de Muertos ("Dead Man's Chest").

70163

FERNALD LIBRARY
COLBY-SAWYER COLLEGE
NEW LONDON, N. H. 03257

No section on geography would be complete without some comment on Puerto Rico's population "problem."

TABLE 1. PUERTO RICO'S POPULATION GROWTH

Year	Population	Percent Increase
1765	44,883	—
1775	70,250	56.5
1800	155,426	121.2
1815	220,892	42.1
1832	330,051	49.4
1846	447,914	35.7
1860	583,308	30.2
1877	731,648	25.4
1887	798,565	9.1
1899	953,423	19.4
1910	1,118,012	17.3
1920	1,299,809	16.3
1930	1,543,913	18.8
1940	1,869,255	21.1
1950	2,210,703	18.3
1960	2,349,544	6.3
1970	2,712,033	15.4
1973	2,912,000	7.3

SOURCES: 1970 U.S. Census, Number of Inhabitants, Puerto Rico. P.C.(1)-A53 P.R. Table 1, pp. 53–59 Also Puerto Rico Planning Board, "Socio-economic Characteristics of Puerto Rico: Fiscal Years 1940, 1948, 1950, 1960 to 1973," p. 4.

If every human being on earth (minus those in India) were crammed into the United States, its population density would be about equal to Puerto Rico's, which is nearly 900 persons per square mile. (The Dominican Republic has a density of 159, while Cuba's is about 140.) Between 1899 and 1970, Puerto Rico's population tripled to 2.7 million. Since the end of World War II, and despite mass migrations to the United States, Puerto Rico has added enough people to create two more San Juans.

But even more dramatic than population growth has been the shift from rural to urban areas. Between 1960 and 1970, while the island's population grew by 15 per cent, the countryside lost 13 per cent of its people. At the same time, urban populations grew by 51 per cent, and in what census officials refer to as "the urban fringe" (suburbs to the layman) the population exploded by 213 per cent.

The size and drift of Puerto Rico's population, intimately connected to social problems, culture, economic development, and planning—even to the island's political destiny—will be dealt with in more detail later on.

4 History

You shall not be the all-powerful ship,
Armed for war, daring hurricanes,
Conquering ports, dauntlessly
And bravely dominating waves and men.

But you shall· be the placid little boat
Which, nudged by the perfumed breeze,
Reaches the calm of the white shore;
This, fatherland, is your destiny,
To conquer liberty, science, and fortune,
Without leaving in the brambles along
   The path
Even a shred of your white vestment.

             —Fragment translated from
                 "Puerto Rico,"
           by José Gautier Benítez

Historians often divide Puerto Rico's past into four major stages: (1) the sixteenth through the eighteenth century, marked by the island's discovery, conquest, and colonization; (2) the nineteenth century, when Puerto Ricans expressed themselves as a people, or a well-defined ethnic group, and won home rule from Spain; (3) the early twentieth century, marked by the return of undiluted colonialism, with the U.S. invasion of 1898, and the slow, Sisyphus-like fight for political dignity; and (4) the period beginning with World War II, when the island began to industrialize and the extent of home rule was expanded.

The Sixteenth Through the Eighteenth Century

The first stage, lasting for about 300 years, is classified by Puerto Rican historian Eugenio Fernández Méndez into five cycles: (1) the Indian culture, 1493–1508; (2) the conversion to a mining economy, 1508–35; (3) the first sugar cycle, 1535–1640; (4) the growth of cattle raising and contraband, 1640–1750; and (5) the agrarian reform period, when varied crops were planted and large Spanish mercantile companies were established, 1750–1815.

The Indian Culture (1493–1508)

After Christopher Columbus found the New World in 1492, he returned to Spain with several Indians, as well as plants, fruits, birds of many colors, and gold samples. King Ferdinand and Queen Isabella had him prepare immediately for a second voyage, to colonize the new lands. The second voyage, less familiar to North American readers, was an imposing project. Seventeen ships bore 1,200 men, including astronomers, cartographers, artisans, laborers, and criminals whose pardons required them to leave Spain, plus various domestic animals. The fleet left Cádiz, Spain, on September 25, 1493. With Columbus was Juan Ponce de León, a soldier who had distinguished himself in the wars against the Moors and who would play a major role in Puerto Rico's history.

Columbus reached the Caribbean on November 3. After discovering Dominica and other islands, he landed at Santa María de Guadalupe, where he found twelve Indian women and two young boys, who said that they were prisoners of the man-eating Caribs. They told him that they lived on another island called Boriquén, and asked to go with him, in the hope of returning home.

On November 19, after sailing through a multitude of tiny islands, which Columbus christened the Eleven Thousand Virgins, they reached a larger, very lovely body of land, whereupon the

Indians leaped overboard and began to swim ashore. This was
Boriquén.

Columbus called the island San Juan Bautista ("St. John the
Baptist") in honor of Don Juan, son of the King and Queen. His
fleet sailed along the south coast to a bay on the western shore,
where it remained for two days, while they took on water, fished,
and gathered tropical fruits. In his *History of the Indies,* Padre
Bartolomé de las Casas (who had access to Columbus' documents)
writes:

> Columbus arrived at another large island, which he called San
> Juan Bautista, which we now call San Juan, and which, as we said
> before, was called Boriquén by the Indians, in a bay of this island,
> towards the west, where all the ships caught many kinds of fish, such
> as shad and large sardines, and, in great quantities, skates, because
> there is a great abundance of these in the Indies, in the sea and in
> the rivers. Several Christians went ashore and walked to some houses
> that were artfully made, although of straw and wood; and there
> was a plaza, with a road leading to the sea, very clean and straight,
> made like a street, and the walls were of crossed or woven cane; and
> above, beautiful gardens, as if they were vineyards or orchards or
> citron trees, such as there are in Valencia or Barcelona; and next
> to the sea was a high watchtower, where ten or twelve people could
> fit, also well made; it must have been the pleasure-house of the lord
> of that island; or of that part of the island.

But Boriquén was ignored for several years as Columbus crossed
the Mona Passage westward to Hispaniola; the new city of Santo
Domingo, founded in 1496, was to be the center of Spain's government in the New World.

The Taínos. Life, meanwhile, passed tranquilly in Boriquén, which
was inhabited by the Taínos, a peaceful tribe who inhabited a good
part of what are today Puerto Rico and the Dominican Republic.

Archaeological diggings indicate two Indian cultures prior to the
Taínos. The first, called the Arcaicos ("Archaics") by local in-
vestigators, appears to have come from southern Florida, probably
first by primitive raft to Cuba, then to the other Antillean islands.
The Arcaicos knew nothing of agriculture and made no arrows or

boats. They seem to have been primitive fishermen, since their remains are found near the beaches. The Arcaicos were apparently conquered by the Igneris (a subculture of the Arawaks), who rowed their canoes from Venezuela along the chain of Lesser Antillean islands. The Igneris have left examples of multicolor ceramics. They, in turn, were dominated by the Taínos (also an Arawak subculture), who were adept at stone-carved religious objects and arms. The Taínos lived in small tribes, bound together by a larger federation. Authoritative estimates put the Taíno population in Puerto Rico at 30,000 when the Spaniards came.

The Taínos were short, strong, copper-colored, with straight black hair and prominent cheekbones. Since they considered a back-sloping forehead a sign of beauty, they deformed the craniums of their children with tightly wrapped cotton. They went naked, except for the married women, who wore a small cotton wrap known as the *nagua* (which is the root of the Spanish word *"enagua,"* meaning slip). They painted themselves with red vegetable dyes and wore adornments fashioned from shell, bones, clay, and gold.

The Taínos located their *yucayeques* (or "villages") near salt or fresh water and lived in small wood and thatch homes called *bohíos*. They enjoyed relaxing in the *hamaca* ("hammock"), which they wove from cotton fibers. The women tended the crops in the fields, while the men hunted. The men smoked or sniffed *tabaco* during magical-religious rites. The Taínos used hooks, nets, and traps to fish in the sea and rivers; they also employed certain plants in the river waters to narcotize the fish. They raised some animals (including a now-extinct species of mute dog), and caught wild birds and rodents. One task of the young boys, part play and part work, was to cover themselves with leafy branches and pose as "trees," whereupon they would seize any bird that came to perch upon them.

The Taíno chieftains, or caciques, wore a golden disc called the *guanín,* which hung from their necks. When a cacique died, power passed along the maternal line to his sister's son. One rather advanced aspect of their culture was the Taíno belief in a supreme creator ("Boriquén" in their language meant Land of the Noble Lord) called Yukiyú, who lived in the misty heights of the mountain known today as El Yunque. They recognized a devil, or evil spirit, known as *Jurakán,* who could unleash the fury of nature against them with violent storms. They also worshiped lesser deities known as *cemíes.* Each village and each family had its own protecting *cemí,* and the Taínos made carvings of these in wood, stone, clay, or gold. Since the Taínos believed in a hereafter, they buried their dead with great care, together with water, food, arms, and adornments. A cacique's burial was quite elaborate—and dramatic; his favorite woman was buried alive with him.

The Taíno villages had plazas called *bateyes,* where they celebrated religious ceremonies known as *areytos,* danced, sang, and —since they had no form of writing—passed along their history by telling tales. They made music by drumming hollow tree trunks with sticks, shaking a type of gourd known as the *maraca,* or scratching the notched surface of another type of gourd, called the *güiro.* Human bones were also used for flutes. A game that involved a rubber ball was played in some regions, and, although the game appears to have had some religious connotation, it was also considered a pastime. The game was somewhat like soccer and volleyball combined. The two teams hit the heavy ball back and forth with the head, shoulders, elbows, hips, or with a heavy stone ceremonial belt. The team that let the ball fall to the ground and remain immobile lost the point.

The Taínos were ill-prepared for the invasion of the Spaniards. Their only weapons were bows, arrows, a type of hardwood sword known as the *macana,* and wood-handled stone axes. When the Taínos first saw metal swords, they cut the palms of their hands as they ingenuously stroked the razor-sharp blades.

It was the gentle Taíno Indian culture that gave the European his first contact with such products as corn, tobacco, and rubber. Also, many Taíno words were later absorbed into Spanish, English, and French. A few are *canoa* ("canoe"), *tabaco* ("tobacco"), *maíz* ("maize," or corn), *sábana* ("savanna"), and *cayo* ("key," or islet).

Colonization Begins.   In the year 1500, Vicente Yáñez Pinzón (who commanded the caravel La Niña in Columbus' first voyage) discovered Brazil. On his return to Europe, he stopped at the island of San Juan and obtained some gold samples. Five years later, King Ferdinand gave Yáñez permission to colonize the island. But Yáñez never went back to Puerto Rico; in 1508, he sold his rights to Martín García de Salazar, who let a year pass and also lost his rights. By then, the colonization was begun by Juan Ponce de León, who lived with his family in a villa in Hispaniola, after helping to extinguish an Indian revolt there in 1504. In the middle of 1508, Governor Nicolás de Ovando, Governor General of the Indies, agreed that Ponce de León should colonize the nearby island of San Juan, build a fort, and reside there as its commander.

On August 12, 1508, Ponce de León set sail with fifty men, reached an Indian settlement on the south coast, and was received by the island's main cacique, Agüeybana the Elder. Observing the native custom, Ponce de León exchanged names with the cacique (the Taínos believed that by taking a man's name, one acquired his virtues). After exploring the island, he gathered some gold samples, ordered that plantings of yucca be made (the Indians happily obliged), and returned to Hispaniola with his invited guest Agüeybana, who, according to the accounts, was most impressed with the European-style settlement being built there.

Ponce de León returned to San Juan in March, 1509. (Students of Afro-American history may be interested to know that he was accompanied by a black freeman, Juan Garrido, born in Angola, who had lived for some years in Seville, emancipated himself, and become a Christian. Garrido later sailed with Ponce de León when he discovered Florida, and was, thus, possibly the first black man in North America. Historical accounts say that Garrido later went to Mexico with Hernán Cortés and, also, was the first man to plant wheat in that country.)

By August, King Ferdinand had named Ponce de León Governor of San Juan and ordered him to assign land and Indians to the colonizers and to thirty other persons who were en route from Seville to inhabit the island. The colonization of Puerto Rico had begun.

The Conversion to a Mining Economy (1508–35)

That same year, Diego Columbus, the son of the discoverer of America, claimed his father's inheritance, which included the right to govern the new lands. The King named him Governor of the Indies, and removed Ponce de León from San Juan. After a power struggle, Ponce de León was again named head of San Juan, but the vengeful Diego confiscated the stone house in Hispaniola. Franciscan friars arrived to teach religion to the Taínos. Cattle and horses were shipped in, and a small gold smelter was set up. On October 25, 1510, the first smelting yielded 100,000 pesos' worth, one-fifth of which was sent to the King; and Ponce de León sent for his wife and children, to live in the large house he built in Caparra, near the south shore of San Juan Bay, which also served as a fortress and government headquarters.

On November 8, 1511, the Caparra settlement was renamed Puerto Rico ("Rich Port"), and the King granted the island its coat of arms, which is the oldest in use in the Western Hemisphere.

Since, despite the fact that they had been caring for themselves for thousands of years, it was "obvious" that the simple, good-natured (and weaker) Indians needed help, the Spaniards created a welfare system for them. This system was known as the *encomienda,* and was a thinly disguised form of slavery. From 30 to 300 Indians, under the command of a cacique, were assigned to each Spanish colonizer, whom they would serve in the mines or at other tasks. The Spaniard, in return, taught them the Christian religion, as well as to adapt themselves to Spanish culture.

With the death of Agüeybana the Elder (who preached co-operation with the white "gods"), his nephew, Agüeybana II, a valiant young warrior, rose to prominence. Under the *encomienda* system, Ponce de León had assigned the younger Agüeybana and his people to a Spanish settler named Sotomayor, whose crude treatment of the cacique exacerbated the situation. Only the Indians' ingenuous belief that the Spaniards were immortal had prevented an armed revolt.

The Indians Rebel. Finally, a skeptical old chieftain named Urayoán, whose village was on the west coast near the Guaorabo River, decided to test the immortality theory. In November, 1510, a young Spaniard named Diego Salcedo was passing through the region and asked Urayoán for some men to guide him and help carry his baggage across the river. The Indians carried Salcedo to midstream, halted, and dropped him. They held him under—for several hours. They were taking no chances. They carried him to shore and, still fearful that he might be alive, begged his pardon. After watching over his bloated corpse for three days, they ran to Urayoán with the news that the Spaniards were, indeed, as mortal as themselves.

Acts of rebellion soon erupted. Agüeybana and other caciques, such as Aymamón and Guarionex, went to war. A number of bloody skirmishes occurred, and many Spaniards who lived isolated on small plantations near the mines were killed.

But when the Indians tried a major assault against Ponce de León in the Yagueca region, Agüeybana the Brave, who led the charge, was shot down by one of the Spanish harquebusiers. The warriors fell back in disorder. Ponce de León offered amnesty to those caciques willing to live in peace, and two of them accepted (Caguax, who commanded the region near the present city of Caguas, and another from Utuado, who came to be known as *don* Alonso after he was baptized). Other Indians fled to the mountains or rowed to neighboring islands. Many others, in captivity, unable to face the rigors of slave labor, killed their young children and committed suicide. From this time on, Indian resistance in Puerto Rico was limited to scattered encounters. So many Taínos left the island that Ponce de León asked the King for a ship to pursue them. If they were not brought back, there would be no one to work the mines. The conquistadores combed the hills, capturing numerous rebel Indians and attacking several small villages.

Not all the settlers were indifferent to the way the Indians were treated. The first to protest were the Dominican friars of Hispaniola. Fray Antonio de Montesino, for example, in a sermon delivered one Sunday in 1511 before Diego Columbus, warned the settlers that they would live and die in mortal sin because of their unjust wars and because of the servitude they imposed upon the Indians. Columbus and the royal officials demanded a retraction, but, the next Sunday, the dauntless friar repeated his words. The Dominican order supported him and sent him to Spain to report to the King, who called a meeting of jurists and theologians in Burgos in 1512. At this time, the principle of freedom for Indians was established: The settlers were ordered to reduce working hours, tend to the sick Indians, and baptize them. Each Spaniard was obliged to teach at least one of the Indians in his charge to read and write. Married Indian women were exempted from work in the mines, and children under fourteen could not be assigned hard labor. But the edict of Burgos was difficult to enforce from distant Spain, and abuses continued.

In 1514, Sancho Velázquez took a census of Puerto Rico and reported that "counting all of your Highness's Indians, there are not even 4,000." He warned the King that the settlers were unhappy because many had been left without a single Indian. An armada was organized to pursue the Caribs on the nearby islands.

When the island's gold resources no longer seemed limitless, agriculture was proposed as a means to bolster the economy; this led to the importation of African slaves, who were considered stronger and more skillful than the Indians. In 1519, an epidemic of smallpox—apparently transported to the island by newly arrived African slaves—killed nearly one-third of the Indians and a goodly number of Spanish settlers. Two years later, Emperor Charles V ordered the freedom of all Indians assigned to the crown, to persons not living on the island, or whose owners had died. They were rounded up, all 600 of them, and assigned to a type of "pacified village"—the royal farm in Toa, which Ponce de León had founded years before as an agricultural experiment station, where plants and animals from Europe and the Canary Islands were acclimated. The Indians there were allowed to work in agriculture under the tutelage of the clergyman.

By now, Ponce de León's ambitions had far exceeded the limited scope of Puerto Rico. In 1513, he sailed from San Germán on the island's west coast—and during this voyage he became the first European to set eyes on the North American mainland (Florida) and the Yucatán peninsula of Mexico. The name "Florida," in fact, stems from the coincidence that Ponce de León sighted the place during the flowery Easter holidays. On a second voyage, in 1521, Ponce de León sailed from Puerto Rico's Caparra port and remained in Florida for five months. During his stay, he was wounded by an Indian arrow and sailed to Havana for treatment. But the leg became gangrenous, and he died at the age of forty-seven.

(Nearly a century later, Ponce de León's grandchild, who became the island's first native colonial governor, moved his remains

from Havana to San José Church in San Juan. In 1913, his remains were moved a few blocks to San Juan Cathedral, where they
rest beneath a marble slab that is inscribed: "Here lies the very
illustrious Señor Juan Ponce de León, first provincial governor of
Florida, first conquistador and governor of this island of San Juan.")

By 1521, the city of Puerto Rico had been moved across the bay
from mosquito-infested Caparra to a breezy site overlooking the
Atlantic Ocean. Its name was changed to "San Juan," and the
island became "Puerto Rico."

The ensuing years were harsh. Caribs attacked San Germán,
killing five friars; French pirates called at the same town, sacking
and burning it; and the daring Caribs even rowed into San Juan
Bay beneath the Spanish cannon and attacked a town on the far
shore. The year 1530 was particularly critical. The gold was nearly
exhausted, and the Indians were almost all gone. Three storms
lashed the island, and many of the settlers, who had bought African
slaves on credit, were deeply in debt. A census was taken, showing
426 Spaniards, 1,148 Indians (including free and slave), and 2,077
African slaves; these figures did not include young children, nor
all the Indians, many of whom hid deep in the mountains. There
were only seventy-one married Spaniards; others who were not
clergy lived with Indian or Negro mistresses. Two years later,
when emissaries of Francisco Pizarro came from Peru to buy
horses and told of the fabulous riches of the Inca empire, the
settlers in Puerto Rico looked around and found their home to be
a rather drab, unpromising place. "May God take me to Peru!"
became a familiar cry, and many islanders left to seek their fortune.
So many left, in fact, that Governor Francisco Manuel de Lando
declared emigration a serious crime and meted out harsh punishments: Anyone caught trying to leave risked amputation of a leg.

The First Sugar Cycle (1535–1640)

As the gold sources petered out, some miners hiked to the
mountainous interior in search of new lodes. There was a brief
burst of optimism in 1532, when 20,000 pesos' worth of gold was
mined from the highlands, but the next year's haul was barely
6,000 pesos. Governor Lando asked the crown to help set up a new
economy based on agriculture, primarily sugarcane.

Puerto Rico and Hispaniola were ideal places to cultivate sugarcane. The weather was excellent, and the African slaves were a source of cheap labor. Puerto Rico's first sugar mill had been set up in 1523 in the Añasco region by Tomás Castrillón. Within the next two decades, several more mills were established. Experts in sugarcane-processing were called in from the Canary Islands, and more slaves were imported from West Africa.

The nature of Puerto Rico's society changed: The first generation, dominated by adventurers and miners, made way for a new class of landholders seeking a comfortable, wealthy life. Income from sugar-generated commerce on the island rose, and a class of shopkeepers and artisans began to emerge in San Juan. Charles V proclaimed general freedom for all the Indians. Only sixty Indians were found to be slaves; other small groups were scattered in the mountains, but the Indian population, estimated at nearly thirty thousand half a century before, had been practically eradicated.

By now, Spain had built a rich empire in the Americas. Two convoys left Spain each year: One loaded Mexican silver at Vera Cruz and the other took on pearls at Cartagena and Peruvian treasure at Puerto Bello on the Isthmus of Panama. The two fleets converged at Havana and sailed home through the Caribbean waters, where they were constantly attacked by roving French, English, and Dutch corsairs.

Because of this, in 1539 Spain authorized the fortification of San Juan; otherwise, enemies of Spain would seize the island and use it as a base from which to attack the treasure fleets. Construction of El Morro castle began, a process that would continue for 350 years. The name *morro* refers to the rocky headland, or promontory, at the west end of San Juan islet, where the harbor fortifications began.

Puerto Rico's era of prosperity from sugar was short-lived. The non-Hispanic Antillean isles adopted new methods of production and lured away most of the island's markets. The influx of slaves diminished; the sugar mills, now considered obsolescent, languished; and continual pirate attacks limited shipping. In 1572, a newly arrived bishop found such poverty that there was "neither oil for the lamps of the church, nor wax for the candles." Twelve months passed without a ship entering harbor.

In 1586, when Sir Francis Drake's fleet devastated the Caribbean ports of Santo Domingo, Cartagena, and St. Augustine, Spain dispatched military engineers to San Juan to strengthen the port defenses. By 1591, four hundred laborers were at work, constructing the enormous rock and limestone hornwork walls that converted El Morro into a citadel. The work was subsidized by an economic aid system known as the *situado* (allowance), whereby Puerto Rico received 2.6 million *maravedíes* from the treasury of the Viceroyship of Mexico, which became the island's principal source of revenue. Other small forts were also built (a military governor had been ruling the island for some years now) and San Juan became one of Spain's key defense centers in the New World.

The new fortifications helped repel an attack by Sir Francis Drake's fleet in 1595, but three years later, George Clifford, the Count of Cumberland, headed a large force that took San Juan for England. But the Englishmen were helpless against the "invisible weapons of the tropics." They suffered in the hot sun and rain and were ravaged by dysentery. Clifford decided to leave. Twenty-seven years later, the Dutch laid siege to the city and burned a good part of it, but Spain's flag was still flying when the Dutchmen sailed away. Now Spain began to build a massive system of walls (some fifty feet high) around the entire city, and a new fort (San Cristóbal) to protect the land approach to the east.

Cattle and Contraband (1640–1750)

With the island's sugar aristocracy impoverished, emphasis was given to cattle, ginger, and tobacco. As a colony of Spain, Puerto Rico's commerce was limited to trade with a single Spanish port. But maritime traffic slackened; during one seven-year period, not a single vessel from Europe stopped at San Juan. Unable to buy or sell goods by legal means, enterprising islanders developed a bustling contraband business with the neighboring French, British, and Dutch islands, which were willing customers for Puerto Rico's cattle and foodstuffs. Government officials looked the other way or dipped their own hands into the brimming till of the smuggling industry, which became Puerto Rico's economic mainstay. The coast villages of Aguada, Cabo Rojo, Arecibo, and Fajardo became thriving small communities, visited by an international set of rogues, pirates, and assorted picaresque characters. Without wars to fight, the Spanish soldiers garrisoned in Puerto Rico led an easy-going life, whose most arduous effort was pursuit of the island's attractive creole women. It was a colorful period in Puerto Rico's history. But the government's treasury was empty (smugglers paid no taxes), and the Caribbean waters were infested with pirates.

The Reform Period (1750–1815)

While life slipped uneventfully by in Puerto Rico, the world was shaken by a chain reaction of revolutions, whose repercussions would reach the island. During this period, Spain tried to reform agriculture and commerce to combat the smuggling industry; the population was swelled by a large influx of foreigners fleeing revolutions elsewhere; San Juan was attacked by the British; and the city's defenses were enlarged to massive proportions.

In 1750, Puerto Rico had fourteen towns (compared with five towns in 1690), and other settlements were being formed as Catholic priests opened small hermitages in rural areas, which served as nuclei for urban growth. Governor Felipe Ramírez de Estenós recommended agrarian reform and broke up the large cattle ranches into smaller farms. Coffee was brought in from the nearby French islands and was soon being cultivated in the mountainous central regions. A Barcelona trading company was given a royal franchise to deal with Puerto Rico, Hispaniola, and Margarita Island (now part of Venezuela) via the Spanish ports of Cádiz and Barcelona. But, as the agrarian reform lagged, the trading company was soon engaged in a lucrative smuggling racket with St. Thomas, Curaçao, and Jamaica.

In 1765, Spain sent Field Marshal Alejandro O'Reilly, an authoritarian, no-nonsense Irishman with a splendid war record, to investigate the military situation. Puerto Rico's governor at the time was Ambrosio de Benavides, a genial, pleasure-loving soul. He often invited the prettiest *mulata* girls of the region to frolic in La Fortaleza mansion, after first discreetly removing the King's somber portrait from the wall. When the governor was unable to answer numerous questions, O'Reilly undertook an intensive investigation of the entire island. He also prepared a census, showing 39,846 Spaniards and 5,037 slaves. Whites mixed with blacks and mulattos "without any repugnance whatsoever," he reported, with apparent disdain. In the country, he said, many of the people, called *jíbaros* (see chapter on culture), lived Indian-style in small huts furnished with hammocks, subsisting on native fruits and vegetables and planting meager cash crops of coffee, cane, and tobacco. Smuggling was still the prime industry; trade with Spain was limited to a few food products, and taxes remitted to Europe barely reached 10,000 pesos a year.

O'Reilly recommended major reforms: Sugar should be revived as the bulwark of agriculture; Spain should invest in a large sugar mill, to insure that the raw cane was processed; commerce regulations must be liberalized; and artisans and farmers should be brought from Spain and given uncultivated land to work. He also called for reform of the military. Many of the soldiers lived in huts with creole mistresses, barely subsisting on four pesos a month, often lacking even a proper uniform in which to drill. Corrupt sergeants and officers often advanced the soldiers their meager wages and charged usurious interest on payday.

San Juan was declared to be a defense station of "the first order," and O'Reilly's engineer, Thomas O'Daly, set about to strengthen the city's fortifications. (By the end of the century, San Juan, which occupied about 62 acres, sat within a 200-acre area surrounded by forts and walls that mounted more than 450 guns.)

A decade after O'Reilly's visit, a wave of revolution was touched off in the Americas when the thirteen U.S. colonies rebelled against England. (Not long after that war, Puerto Rico was nearly traded to England in exchange for Gibraltar, which the British had snatched from Spain in 1704, but the negotiations floundered.) When the vengeful British closed the ports of Jamaica and Barbados to the American republic, it expanded its trade with the Spanish Antilles. Soon, U.S. ships were anchoring at San Juan, laden with slaves and breadstuffs from Philadelphia in exchange for farm produce, including molasses, which the Americans made into rum and shipped to Africa to buy more slaves for the Antilles. Spain relaxed some trade restrictions and permitted Puerto Rico to trade with nine different ports in the mother country, as well as with friendly nations. A large Spanish trading house, La Real

Factoría Mercantíl, opened a prosperous tobacco export business. And a census in 1787, which showed 103,000 inhabitants (compared with 45,000 in 1765), revealed the rather surprising fact that there still remained over 2,000 pure-blooded Indians in Puerto Rico (some of these, however, may have been imported from nearby islands).

In April, 1797, after Spain and France declared war on England, sixty British frigates sailed past Loíza on the north coast, headed for San Juan. Aboard were Admiral Sir Henry Harvey and General Abercromby, in command of 7,000 troops. Shortly before this incursion, they had taken Trinidad. The British blockaded San Juan and landed their men in the flatlands of Santurce, three miles east. But after a series of skirmishes, the Spanish troops and creole militia curbed their advance. Two weeks later, the frustrated invaders sailed away. To show his gratitude for this defense of the island, Spain's King Carlos IV declared Puerto Rico a tariff-free port for twenty years and ordered promotions among the military. During the next four years, lesser British attacks were repelled at Cabo Rojo, Aguadilla, and Ponce.

The Nineteenth Century

As the nineteenth century began, Puerto Rico was poorer than fifty years before, mainly due to the loss of the *situado* funds when Mexico became independent from Spain. Over 70 per cent of the populace was illiterate; and although many of its leading citizens were "schooled," they were far from educated. In the early years of the century, a Frenchman brought in a small printing press, the island's first. Governor Montés bought the press and, in 1807, inaugurated *La Gaceta Oficial,* a government newspaper. But, with such a high degree of illiteracy and only two public and a few private elementary schools (the few persons aspiring to higher education traveled to Santo Domingo, Spain, or Venezuela), the circulation of this paper was quite limited.

Puerto Rico was given a sudden dash of civil rights after Napoleon invaded Spain and deposed Fernando VII in 1808. The Spanish provinces rebelled and formed juntas under the Supreme Junta of Cádiz. A few Spanish leaders convened to rule in the name of the King, thus giving birth to the Spanish Cortes. The Cortes asked Spain's colonies to elect and send representatives to help draft a new constitution. Puerto Rico, one of the few colonies to cooperate, chose Ramón Power y Giralt, a liberal reformer who had traveled extensively and studied in France and Spain.

Meanwhile, Spain tried to recruit Puerto Rico's militia for attacks against rebels in Venezuela. But one night, Antonio Cortabarría, a Spanish official sent to the island for that purpose, found a paper nailed to his door that read: "This people, although docile enough to obey authority, will never permit one single American to be taken off to fight against its brothers in Caracas."

The letter, written by Puerto Rican separatists, showed, by the use of the word "American," the growing schism between Puerto Rico's creoles and the powerful minority of Spaniards who ruled the island's military and commercial affairs. Insular politics, although lacking official parties, already showed three distinct groups: the conservatives, who were avid Spanish loyalists; the liberals, who demanded reform and more local autonomy as part of Puerto Rico's union with Spain; and the separatists, who argued for divorce. The reformers complained that, since 1691, Puerto Rico was ruled by the Code of Law of the Indies, which provided for a nearly omnipotent Spanish military governor and even required that people seek permission before traveling from one town to another.

Spain, fearful that the island might be tempted to go the way of Mexico, Venezuela, and the other defiant colonies, appeared willing to negotiate reforms. Ramón Power was even named a vice president in the Cortes; the Puerto Rican demands that Power took with him to Spain included reforms for public schools, the establishment of a university, the right to form labor guilds, the right to distill rum, the reduction of burdensome taxes and duties, and preference for native Puerto Ricans in public posts. He also asked that if Spain were conquered by France, the island have the right to independently decide its political destiny. Few of these reforms were granted, but Spain approved a new, more liberal constitution and in March, 1812, declared it valid in Puerto Rico. According to the new constitution, Puerto Ricans were no longer colonial subjects; they were full-fledged citizens of Spain. Customs offices were opened. Machinery and tools were declared tariff-free. Immigrants from the Canary Islands poured in. Farmers were given seeds for planting. The island's first lottery was inaugurated, and a nongovernment newspaper, *El Diario Económico,* was founded. Government income tripled. Ramón Power, still seeking reforms in Cádiz, died suddenly of yellow fever in 1813.

The following year, when Napoleon retired his troops from Spain and King Ferando VII returned to the throne, the liberal constitution was discarded, and there was a return to absolutist colonial government. Perhaps to sugarcoat this setback, Spain granted a *cédula de gracia* (royal decree) in 1815 with measures to improve the economy. Immigrants to the island were offered large tracts of land: six acres for each member of the family and three acres per slave. Settlers were granted Spanish citizenship after five years of residence. Free maritime traffic was allowed between Spain and other friendly nations, and tools (manufactured in Spain) were admitted tariff-free. The spurt in the economy placated the spirit of separatism, which had flared when the 1812 constitution was revoked.

Puerto Rico was, by now, a true melting pot. There were Spaniards; Canary Islanders; Dominicans; Haitians; French from Louisiana, who had fled when that territory was bought by the United States; Venezuelans; African slaves; Indians; and mulatto creoles. There were also representatives from different social strata: nobles, priests, thieves, merchants (who were sometimes thieves), planters, artisans, religious and political heretics banned from Spain, and numerous soldiers. Puerto Rico also attracted many *segundones* ("second heirs") from Spain, where the eldest son inherited the family fortune, and the second in line often came to the New World to seek his own fortune.

The Struggle for Home Rule

This was an era of struggle and progress, as Puerto Rico, long isolated, moved into the currents of Western culture. There was a promising nascence in literature, art, and music. And, for the first time, political parties were formed, although their fortunes rose and fell in accord with events in Madrid. Two basic themes prevailed; a large, and growing, segment of the population (which exploded from 150,000 to almost 1 million by 1900) felt Puerto Rican, not Spanish; and the logical outcome of this sentiment was a demand for more civil and political rights.

The chain of events was set off in Spain, when a revolution in 1820 forced Fernando VII to restore the 1812 constitution. Puerto Rico's small separatist groups were encouraged to do their own plotting when Bolívar won independence for Venezuela and the Dominicans also rebelled against Spain. The separatists persuaded a Frenchman who had been a follower of Bolívar's, General Luis Guillermo Lafayette Doucoudray Holstein, to help direct a rebellion. His brother-in-law, Pedro Dubois, who lived on the island, was to recruit followers. But Dubois was found out and taken to El Morro castle, where he was shot, and Holstein's small invading fleet was held up in Curaçao, on orders of the Spanish government. Meanwhile, in 1823, the King regained power in Spain and, once again, revoked the 1812 constitution, making Puerto Rico a colony once more.

When it was feared that Spain might try to reconquer its lost colonies, the U.S. government proclaimed the Monroe Doctrine, declaring it would permit no further colonization of the Americas by any European power. (That same year, the U.S. Congress decided to stamp out piracy in the Caribbean and sent a fleet headed by Commodore David Porter. One of those arrested was Roberto Cofresí Ramírez de Arellano, known as "Cofresí," a thirty-three-year-old Puerto Rican who had become somewhat of a seafaring Robin Hood, since he often shared his booty with the poor in the villages of the south and west coasts. Cofresí and ten of his companions were brought to San Juan and shot.)

The Little Caesars. Also in 1823, a change took place in Puerto Rico's political strategy. With the support of Cuba, José María Quiñones, the island's deputy to Spain, presented a bill to the Cortes, seeking more autonomy for the Antillean colonies. Madrid responded in 1825 by subjecting the island to perhaps its worst colonial period: forty-two consecutive years, under fourteen Spanish military governors, who were often brutish and almost without exception ill-equipped for civil administration. They assumed complete power and abolished all civil rights. Historian José Luis Vivas in *Historia de Puerto Rico* calls them "the little Caesars."

The first in this parade of "Caesars" was Miguel de la Torre, fresh from defeat against Bolívar's rebels in Venezuela and hating all revolutionaries. He prohibited meetings after dark and declared a 10 P.M. curfew. Then, in an apparent change of heart, he decided to make Puerto Ricans enjoy themselves so much that they would not possibly want to rebel. He encouraged cockfights, horse races, dice, and cards. His regime was called "the three B's": *baile, botella, baraja* ("dance, drink, and gambling").

When Fernando VII died in 1833, he left his infant daughter as heir. His widow, María Cristina de Borbón, became Regent and permitted Puerto Rico to send two representatives to Spain. But when the delegates—José Saint Just and Esteban Ayala—traveled to Madrid and asked for reforms, they were denied. Thus, in 1835, the discontented liberals joined with the Granada military regiment in an unsuccessful revolt to restore the 1812 constitution. Again, there was short-lived joy on the island when the Spanish crown fell to a military coup, which restored the 1812 constitution. But when a delegate from Puerto Rico went to Spain in 1837, he discovered to his dismay that the new constitution did not apply to Puerto Rico and Cuba, which were to be ruled by special laws. In 1838, a group of Puerto Ricans united once more with the Granada regiment and tried to proclaim a republic. But the plan leaked out; some of the plotters were exiled, others were killed, and one of the leaders, Buenaventura Quiñones, was shut into a cell in El Morro castle, where, one day, he was found hung by the neck. (A new governor, Miguel López de Baños, went so far as to prohibit beards and goatees, since he felt they were too suggestive of revolution.)

The arrival of another governor, Marshal Juan Prim, Count de Reus (a Liberal in Spain), coincided with a slave uprising—not in Puerto Rico but in Martinique. This prompted Prim to decree the *Bando Negro* ("Black Edict"), which proclaimed that any black man who attacked a white would be executed; if he attacked a free black, he would lose his right hand; if he insulted a white, he would receive five years in prison; if two blacks were caught fighting, they would get twenty-five lashes and fifteen days in jail; and if a black was caught thieving, he would be given two hundred lashes and a fine.

Prim was succeeded in 1848 by Lieutenant General Juan de Pezuelas, who felt that too much education spoiled Spain's colonists and made them subversive. He blocked the founding of a junior college. He also passed a law requiring any person without means to carry a passbook (*"libreta"*) showing where he worked, his salary, and the date when his employment ceased. Anyone found without the passbook was put at forced labor for eight days at half pay. Pezuelas prohibited people from moving their residence, from traveling between cities, and from having parties without permission. He even banned the horse races. The passbook requirement lasted for nineteen years in Puerto Rico, indicating how submissive the island's populace was to the military regime.

In one subsequent five-year period, there were seven governors, all of them soldiers. During this time, a terrible cholera epidemic struck down 30,000 people, and a doctor by the name of Ramón Emeterio Betances became well-known for his efforts to alleviate the people's suffering. In 1856, Betances was exiled for his separatist tendencies. Not long afterwards, two other reformers, Román Baldorioty de Castro and José Julián Acosta, were prohibited from working as professors at the School of Commerce.

In 1862, a rebellion in the Dominican Republic moved Puerto Rico's separatists to act. Soon a proclamation was circulated, calling Puerto Ricans to arms. Betances, who had returned from exile two years before, was ordered to El Morro, where Governor Félix María de Messinas threatened to hang him. Betances' reply shows why he is a hero to Puerto Ricans today. He is reputed to have said: "Hear me well, General Messinas. The night of that day I shall sleep far more peacefully than your excellency."

Again, Betances was banished, this time to St. Thomas, where he proclaimed "Ten Commandments," demanding the abolition of slavery and the granting of fuller civil rights for Puerto Rico.

In 1865, as revolutionary ferment grew in Cuba, Spain invited committees from Cuba and Puerto Rico to report on their needs, which would be considered in drafting a Special Law of the Indies. One request was for a type of autonomy based on the Canadian formula. Although Spain barred the question of slavery from the agenda, the Cubans and Puerto Ricans insisted upon its abolition. They also demanded freedom of speech and of the press. Again, their requests were ignored. And back in Puerto Rico, Governor José María Marchessi, angered over the agitation by these reformist "troublemakers," claimed that they were involved in a revolt of local artillerymen; he exiled several of their leaders, including Betances, who was back on the island again. Betances and his companion, Segundo Ruiz Belvis, ignored the governor's order that they report to Madrid. They fled to Santo Domingo, then to New York, where they joined a proindependence union of Cubans and Puerto Ricans. Ruiz Belvis later went to Chile, to muster support, but died the next year, alone in his hotel room. Betances, however, continued the struggle.

The "Grito de Lares." When Marshal Julián Juan Pavia, a mild-mannered administrator, replaced Governor Marchessi in 1867, his predecessor's tyrannical ways had borne fruit. In December, Ramón Emeterio Betances sailed from New York to Santo Domingo and founded the Puerto Rico Revolutionary Committee; branches sprouted in several towns of Puerto Rico. Members communicated by code and greeted each other with secret handshakes, after which they pronounced the password letters "l" and "m," which stood for *libertad o muerte* ("liberty or death"). The center of the conspiracy was Mayagüez, where the leader of the local junta, a U.S.-born resident named Matías Brugman, owned a farm and other property. The Mayagüez junta secretary was Baldomero Bauren, who had been born in the Dominican Republic. The Lares junta chief was farm owner Manuel Rojas, born in Venezuela, the son of a Puerto Rican doctor who had fought under Bolívar. In Camuy, the junta chief was Manuel María González, also Venezuela-born, while in Ponce, a Puerto Rican, Carlos Elio Lacroix, led the junta.

From Santo Domingo, the exiled Betances tried to persuade Puerto Rico's Liberals to join the movement, but they declined; reforms, they said, were obtainable through firm petitions and legal pressures. Undismayed, Betances bought 500 rifles, six cannon, and a small ship, *El Telégrafo.* He also exacted promises of help from several South American nations, provided he carried off the coup.

However, the plot soured in mid-1868 when one of the rebels, while trying to collect funds, was caught with a list of subversives in his pocket. Another rebel tried to recruit a relative, who warned the Spanish military in Arecibo. When a search was ordered of the home of Manuel María González in Barrio Palomar, Camuy, several conspiratorial documents were found. Rather than be arrested, some of the rebel leaders decided to risk an attack, although others warned it was premature. Betances' weapons were embargoed in Santo Domingo, and *El Telégrafo* was detained in St. Thomas port.

The night of September 23, 1868, the rebels—estimates range from 400 to 1,000 men—held a mass meeting on Manuel Rojas' farm in Barro Pezuelas, Lares. Some bore firearms, but most had only knives or machetes. A new white flag was unveiled, with the words: "Liberty or Death. Long Live Free Puerto Rico. Year, 1868." At midnight, they marched into Lares and took it easily, arresting the Mayor and some well-known Conservatives. The lone casualty was a rebel, who was accidentally shot by one of his companions. That morning, the Republic of Puerto Rico was declared, with Francisco Ramírez Medina as Provisional President. A proclamation called Puerto Ricans to arms, offered freedom to all slaves who joined the revolt, and invited foreign residents to participate as patriots. Then, everyone attended a mass, reluctantly celebrated by parish priest José Vega.

Later in the day, the news reached Aguadilla, and the government sent troops to defend the San Sebastián zone. When the rebels tried to take San Sebastián, they were stymied in several skirmishes and put to flight when troop reinforcements arrived. During the next month, small guerrilla battles took place in the mountains of the region, as the rebels were hunted down. Many were killed, others were jailed in Aguadilla and Arecibo. The two Mayagüez leaders, Brugman and Bauren, were caught hiding in a thicket near Adjuntas and killed by a hail of bullets. In the government's search for the rebels, a few hundred innocent people, including Liberals who had declined to take part in the insurrection, were jailed.

The *Grito de Lares* had failed. Historians disagree as to the importance of this revolt. Governor General Pavía, in his report to Spain, described it as a "mere tomfoolery," which proved "easy to overcome." Another critic called it "the work of four foreigners, surrounded by several poorly armed campesinos." But, in leafing back through the histories of successful revolutions elsewhere, one finds that many began in a similarly inauspicious manner. The "four foreigners" were residents of the island, not globe-hopping agitators; and the several hundred men who risked their lives for freedom were all Puerto Ricans.

(At any rate, the event today has become symbolic for Puerto Ricans of many persuasions. In the past few years, proindependence groups have flocked to the picturesque mountain town to praise the valor of their countrymen a century before. In 1969, Governor Luis A. Ferré, who advocates U.S. statehood, declared September 24 as a holiday, to mark the *Grito de Lares*. Even the Exchange Club of Puerto Rico said it would sponsor an entourage to Lares; this so enraged radical independence groups, who considered it insulting to the memory of the rebels, that the Exchangers reneged, in order to avoid possible violence.)

After Lares, it was "business as usual" in the colony, although there followed an imperceptible, but sure, trend toward reform. In 1869, for the second time, Spain gave the island the right to send representatives to the Cortes. Local elections were held, and four Liberal Party candidates and seven Conservatives won seats. Governor Baldrich relaxed press censorship and several newspapers emerged. By 1871, Isabel II had been ousted, Spain was in Liberal hands, and Puerto Rico's Liberals won fourteen of fifteen seats in the Cortes. The Conservatives, their strength threatened, incited several violent episodes which provoked the Spanish governor to declare martial law.

Between 1871 and 1874, five different governors ruled the island, as the Liberals and Conservatives engaged in a tug-of-war for a voice in Spain. In the 1872 elections, the Liberals were angered when the governor favored the Conservative forces, and Spain's Overseas Minister even named several nonresidents to speak for the island in Madrid.

In November, 1872, King Amadeo I de Saboya abolished slavery in Puerto Rico, and the law became effective on the island on March 22, 1873. Typical of other affairs in Puerto Rico, even abolition was enforced by gradual means. The freed slaves had to work for three more years with their masters; after five years, they won full civil rights. About 30,000 slaves were freed; but half of them remained in the employ of their masters. That same year, the hated passbook law was also revoked. But two years later, things took a turn for the worse, when a coup felled the Spanish republic; press censorship was imposed once again, and public meetings were prohibited. As the war for independence raged in Cuba, a new Spanish constitution provided for the two Antillean colonies to be run in accordance with civil rights criteria different from those in the Spanish provinces.

There was considerable confusion among Puerto Rico's young political parties. The Liberals, pushing for civil rights, were divided on the island's political destiny. Some wanted autonomy, while others said the best road was assimilation with Spain, since they felt close ties with the Hispanic language and culture. The Conservatives considered talk of autonomy treasonous; some of them warned that an autonomous island would be swallowed up by the United States.

In 1887, an assembly of Liberal leaders in Ponce called for self-government and permanent union with Spain. The Conservatives, feeling threatened, demanded a new military governor. Lieutenant General Romualdo Palacios González caused 1887 to be known as "the year of terror." Convinced that the Liberals were plotting acts of subversion, he instituted a series of harsh punishments, known as the *compontes*. The civil guard arrested hundreds of persons, many of whom were tortured or bludgeoned to death. The Liberals' efforts to reach Spain with complaints about this barbaric treatment were almost tragi-comic; even bottles with notes inside were cast into the sea. In November of that year, Palacios locked sixteen autonomist leaders in the cells of El Morro and planned to execute them, but a Liberal in St. Thomas got word to Spain and the governor was removed; even the Conservatives had been moved to deplore his excesses.

The autonomists met in Mayagüez, four years later. Their meeting epitomized the autonomist dilemma: Luis Muñoz Rivera, a liberal journalist, proposed that they fuse with the Spanish Liberal Party in Spain, headed by Mateo Práxedes Sagasta; José de Diego, a young Aguadilla lawyer, favored a link with the Spanish Republicans, headed by Spanish Prime Minister Antonio Cánovas del Castillo. And José Celso Barbosa, a prominent doctor, was against any fusion at all with Spain.

When José Martí led another revolt in Cuba in 1895 and Puerto Ricans in New York formed a Borinquen chapter of the Cuban Revolutionary Party, separatist feelings were stirred in Puerto Rico. Muñoz Rivera, hoping to avoid an armed revolution, went to Spain and elicited a promise from Sagasta, now head of Spain's monarchic Liberal Party, that, once in power, he would grant autonomy for the island.

In 1897, the Autonomist Party met in San Juan and, after a close vote, agreed to a pact with Sagasta, whereupon the party changed its name to the Fusionist Liberal Party. Barbosa and his followers walked out and formed the Pure and Orthodox Liberal Party. When a Spanish terrorist killed Prime Minister Cánovas del Castillo in August, 1897, Sagasta rose to power and fulfilled his promise. He signed a royal decree on November 28, granting autonomy to Puerto Rico; and the warring autonomists on the island united to form the Liberal Autonomist Union Party.

The Return of Colonialism

Now, at least on paper, Puerto Rico had more political freedom than ever before in its history. The reforms this time were unprecedented. Puerto Rico elected voting delegates to both houses of the Spanish Cortes. It also elected all thirty-five members of the local House of Representatives and eight out of fifteen members of the insular Administrative Council (which was equivalent to a Senate). The governor general, appointed by Spain, chose the other seven senators. The governor could also suspend civil rights in emergencies or refer legislation to Madrid if he felt it unconstitutional, but his powers were weaker than ever before. Puerto Rico's legislature could pass on all matters of insular importance, fix the budget, determine tariffs and taxes, and accept or reject any commercial treaties concluded by Spain without local participation.

The cabinet of the new autonomous government was appointed in February, 1898; general elections for legislators were held in

March; and in July the government officially began to function. But the rules of the game had changed. That April the Spanish-American War broke out. The United States, plagued by a savage depression and growing anarchy at home, sought to expand its markets and influence abroad. Part of America's "Manifest Destiny," it was declared, was to rid the Western Hemisphere of all European influence and to seek a foothold in Asia. It was not a new idea. The United States had long contemplated expansion beyond its continental borders. In 1853, it had threatened to annex Cuba (and possibly Puerto Rico). In 1895, U.S. Senator Henry Cabot Lodge, referring to the threat of a British attack against the Atlantic seaboard, said, "We should have among these islands [of the West Indies] at least one strong naval station." In 1898, when hostilities broke out, letters from American businessmen to the State Department urged the annexation of Puerto Rico as "a garden spot" that would boost U.S. commerce. On July 11, 1898, an article on the editorial page of the *New York Times* said there was "no question" about "the wisdom of taking possession of the Island of Puerto Rico and keeping it for all time." The island was "the real gem of the Antilles," it continued, explaining that its "prolific" soil would be an asset, and it would make a fine naval station with a "commanding position between the two continents."

Noting that the Cubans had long been engaged in a bloody war of independence from Spain, the article said: "We are not pledged to give Puerto Rico independence, and she will have done nothing to entitle her to it at our hands. Besides, it would be much better for her to come at once under the beneficent sway of the United States than to engage in doubtful experiments at self-government."

On July 21, the eminent Puerto Rican educator Eugenio María de Hostos arrived in the United States and sought an audience with President McKinley, to ask that Puerto Ricans be allowed to decide their political future by popular vote if the U.S. occupied the island. "It looks as if my native land is destined to become American territory whether the inhabitants desire it or not," he told reporters. "If Cuba is to be free and its people their own masters," he asked, "are not Puerto Ricans entitled to the same privilege?" McKinley granted a brief audience but ignored the request for a vote on political status.

The same day that Hostos arrived in the States, a government statement (described as "practically official" by the press) declared: "Puerto Rico will be kept. . . . That is settled, and has been the plan from the first. Once taken it will never be released. . . . Our flag, once run up there, will float over the island permanently."

At dawn on July 25, 1898, General Nelson A. Miles landed with the first contingents of 16,000 American troops at the southcoast town of Guánica. "Our Flag Raised in Puerto Rico," said the front-page headline of the *New York Times*.

In the first skirmish, at Yauco, the Americans beat back the Spanish troops. Two days later, three U.S. ships stood offshore at Ponce and won the surrender of the defenseless city without a shot. On July 31, General John R. Brooke landed at Arroyo, to meet with General James Wilson's troops, who were marching east to San Juan. Early in August, General Teodoro Schwann overcame light resistance and took Mayagüez. General Wilson was stopped for three days near El Asomante, a high area where the Spaniards were firmly entrenched. On August 13, as the Americans prepared to attack, orders came to stop hostilities. Spain had surrendered.

"It wasn't much of a war, but it was all the war there was," Teddy Roosevelt said later. It lasted only 115 days, with bloody fighting in Cuba and the Philippines. But the Puerto Rico campaign lasted only seventeen days; of the 16,000 American troops who landed, only four were killed and forty wounded. Flamboyant American correspondent Richard Harding Davis called it "a picnic, a *fête de fleurs*." In his dispatch to *Scribner's Magazine* at war's end, he wrote:

Peace came with Porto Rico occupied by our troops and with Porto Ricans blessing our flag, which must never leave the island. It is a beautiful island, smiling with plenty and content . . . and it came to us willingly, with open arms. But had it been otherwise, it would have come to us. The course of empire to-day takes its way to all points of the compass.

America's famed poet Carl Sandburg, then a twenty-year-old private from Galesburg, Illinois, had landed with the invasion force. Years later, in his memoirs, he recalled:

For four hundred years this island had been run by a Spanish government at Madrid. Now it was to be American and it was plain that the island's common people liked the idea and had more hope of it. More than once we saw on the roadside a barefoot man wearing only pants, shirt and a hat, eating away at an ear of parched corn. We saw kneehigh children wearing only a ragged shirt and their little swollen bellies told of something wrong with their food, not enough food, and not the right kind.

Few Puerto Ricans had resisted the U.S. invasion, and many received the new troops cordially. The peasants knew little about the United States, but harbored no love for the price-gouging Spanish merchants, who controlled the island's commerce. Others, in the cities, knew that the United States was a wealthy country, and a democratic one at that, which might mean a more liberal progressive climate on the island.

General Miles reinforced this sentiment in his first public speech:

> We have not come to make war upon the people of a country that for centuries has been oppressed but on the contrary to bring you protection . . . to promote your prosperity, and to bestow upon you the immunities and blessings of the liberal institutions of our government.

Many Puerto Ricans, particularly the autonomist leaders, felt perplexed. They did not, at the moment, feel "oppressed." Just seven months before, they had won home rule from Spain after years of struggle. Others, like Betances, were suspicious. Before the invasion, writing from New York to a friend, he said: "Surely, let the Americans help us gain liberty, but not push the country into annexation. If Puerto Rico doesn't act fast, it will be an American colony forever."

As joint U.S. and Spanish military delegations met to negotiate the peace, confusion reigned among the island's leaders, who were not consulted. The revolutionary junta in New York had, until now, favored the North Americans, believing they wished to liberate the island. In San Germán, some Puerto Ricans took the city, named a new mayor, and destroyed photos of the Spanish authorities. On October 18, Spain's flag was lowered at La Fortaleza, ending 405 years of Spanish domination. Five days later, in New York, Eugenio María de Hostos organized a League of Patriots, which argued for rapid transition from a military to a civil government and a plebiscite where Puerto Ricans could decide between annexation and independence; if the latter choice were favored, the island would spend a twenty-year transition period as a protectorate in order to prepare its government and economic structure. But de Hostos' demands were ignored, and he died five years later, disillusioned.

On December 19, 1898, the Treaty of Paris was signed, and Spain ceded the Philippines, Guam, and Puerto Rico to the United States. It also renounced its powers over Cuba, which became a U.S. protectorate. The U.S. also received $20 million in indemnization. No member of Puerto Rico's "autonomous" government was even consulted.

Puerto Rico was only a minor factor in the Treaty of Paris. The acquisition of the Philippines and the island of Guam would help turn the Pacific Ocean into "America's lake," as one U.S. official put it; coaling stations on these islands would stimulate America's shipbuilding industry and open up Asia for U.S. trade and influence.

In his instructions to the U.S. negotiators in Paris, President McKinley said:

> The abandonment of the Western Hemisphere was an imperative necessity. It involves no ungenerous reference to our recent foe, but simply a recognition of the plain teachings of history, to say that it was not compatible with the assurance of permanent peace on and near our own territory that the Spanish flag should remain on this side of the sea. This lesson of events and of reason left no alternative as to Cuba, Porto Rico, and the other islands belonging to Spain in this hemisphere.

Some American leaders called for the annexation of Cuba, but it would be costly to put the nation on its feet, and, also, there was a large Cuban revolutionary army to deal with.

Puerto Rico was different. The island was smaller and had no organized native army fighting for independence. The United States declared that "the cession of Puerto Rico is on account of ...

compensation for the losses and expenses occasioned . . . by the war."

It was hard, at the time, however, to imagine that the Americans could do worse to Puerto Rico than had the Spaniards. While the loss of its short-lived autonomy was a severe blow, historian Gordon Lewis believes that "nothing in Spanish national history during the twentieth century justifies [the] expectation" that Spain would have honored the autonomy of its ex-colony. After four centuries of Spanish rule, Puerto Rico had a tiny educated upper class, a tiny middle class, and a huge mass of peons. In an island of nearly 1 million people, almost all of the 300,000 blacks and mulattos were at the bottom level. Only 13 per cent of the populace was literate. Of 300,000 school-age children, only 21,000 were studying. Many families still lived in crude wood and thatch huts, subsisting on one meager meal a day. Jobs, when available, paid a few cents a day. Land distribution was lopsided: 2 per cent of the island's 39,000 farms contained 70 per cent of the cultivated land. There were only 175 miles of hard-surfaced roads; many of the rest were impassable when it rained. Puerto Rico's total property value was calculated at $29 million, with $18 million of this mortgaged at rates of up to 24 per cent interest.

America's first military governor, General John R. Brooke, who remained only until the end of 1898, made few changes. He left the cabinet and municipal assemblies intact, but did declare the authority of the U.S. Supreme Court. He was succeeded by General Guy V. Henry, who chose a new cabinet, lowered tariffs, and oversaw the change to American currency. Henry suspended the lottery and prohibited the cockfights (favorite targets of military governors, it seems) but, in his favor, he also suspended the collection of defaulted mortgages due to the island's financial crisis.

In late 1898, President McKinley had appointed a Protestant clergyman, Dr. H. K. Carroll, to head an investigation. After lengthy hearings, he reported that Puerto Ricans were "moral, industrious, intellectually able, obedient and respectful of law," and recommended that Washington grant full territorial status and allow islanders to elect their own legislature. But the U.S. military governor, General George W. Davis, urged the War Department to overrule the clergyman's view. "The people," Davis said, "generally have no conception of political rights combined with political responsibilities." The powerful Senator J. B. Foraker of Ohio (who was later unseated for taking bribes from large U.S. corporations) claimed the Puerto Ricans had "no experience that would qualify them" for self-government. In the meantime, autonomist leader Luis Muñoz Rivera tried once more to work within the established order; he founded the new Federal Party, which advocated identity with the United States, a civil government, full civil rights, and free commerce with the American mainland. Another new party, the Republicans, supported a similar platform.

During his brief term, General Davis tried to improve public health, tax laws, municipal government, and the judicial system but also committed a series of blunders. Typical was the naming of an American, Victor S. Clark, to head the Department of Education, in a country where barely a soul knew a word of English. Much of the friction in the early years of American rule stemmed from cultural and language barriers. Puerto Rico's leaders had at least been able to communicate with the Spaniards. Now, on their own island, they were forced to work through translators or stumble about in a strange tongue.

In municipal elections, held in July, 1899, Muñoz Rivera's Federals won forty-four towns and the Republicans twenty-two. During this period, in what appeared to be a symbolic last gasp of the nineteenth century, a terrible hurricane, San Ciriaco, swept up through the south coast, killing 3,000 persons, leaving a quarter of the population homeless, and wiping out the coffee and sugar crops, the mainstays of the fragile economy. General Davis asked Congress to let the island float a $10-million bond and establish a tax structure to repay it. Many months later, after ignoring his plea, and with a lassitude that characterized subsequent decades of U.S. rule in Puerto Rico, Congress granted $200,000 for the hurricane victims, about 80 cents apiece.

As the twentieth century approached, the United States was faced with a dilemma: what to do with its newly acquired territory of Puerto Rico, where a foreign language prevailed and which was far poorer than any part of the American mainland.

Although America had for years sought control of the West Indies, it had given little thought to the specifics of that control. The future of Puerto Rico, and its near-million population, was largely improvised. A military government seemed adequate as a stopgap measure in the first year, but what about later on?

U.S. Secretary of War Elihu Root knew that the military could not continue to rule; he recommended a civil government in which the key roles would be given to Americans appointed by the President. Puerto Ricans would be given a gradually increasing voice when this proved "safe." President McKinley's announcement a few days later closely paralleled Root's views.

The Foraker Act

A few months after the American landing in Puerto Rico, General Wilson enunciated what appeared to be the U.S. master plan:

> Puerto Rico will at first be governed by a military regime; then it will be declared an American territory, and later it will achieve the category of sovereign state within the Union. The duration of these periods will depend more or less upon the merits of the country.

The Foraker Act, in effect from 1900 to 1916, was the logical follow-up to the military regime.

With the Foraker Act, the U.S. Congress created a body politic called "the People of Puerto Rico," who were neither American citizens nor citizens of an independent nation. There would be a President-appointed Governor, an eleven-man Executive Council (with a majority of Americans), thirty-five elected Puerto Ricans in the House of Delegates (whose laws were subject to Congressional veto), and an elected Resident Commissioner, who spoke for Puerto Rico in the U.S. House, but had no vote there. The law, which also regulated commerce with the United States, stated that in judicial matters Puerto Rico fell under the jurisdiction of the Circuit Court of Boston. Puerto Rican leaders, hoping for a plebiscite that would result in either statehood, independence, or home rule, were stunned.

The broadly based Union Party, which took power in 1904 (and held it for twenty years), made continuous demands for a plebiscite. Independence sentiment grew as Congress ignored its demands, and island leaders chafed under control by a foreign governor. Hatred of the Foraker Act was so virulent by 1909 that the Puerto

Rico House of Delegates refused to approve any legislation, including the next year's government budget. It sent a memorial to Congress and to President Taft, complaining of "the unjust law which makes it impossible for the people's representatives to pass the laws they desire." Some Americans regarded the delegates' action as bordering on anarchy. "We have gone somewhat too fast in the extension of political power to them for their own good," President Taft said. The Union Party's paper, *La Democracia,* called Taft "openly and frankly imperialistic" and circulated a pamphlet in Congress, saying that "one million souls are living in Puerto Rico in an unbearable state of tyranny under the folds of the American flag." Congress answered by passing a bill that automatically carried over the previous year's budget for the Puerto Rican Government, thus crippling the impact of the delegates' protest.

As a result of this incident, President Taft sent Secretary of War J. M. Dickinson and General Clarence R. Edwards to inquire. Dickinson wrote to Taft, "It is clear that there is a general and almost universal desire and demand of all classes, interests and political parties for American citizenship." But, he added, such concessions could be disastrous to the island, jeopardize investments, and retard development. By 1912, Taft concluded, "I believe the aim to be striven for is the fullest possible allowance of legal and fiscal self-government, with American citizenship as the bond between us."

But Congress granted Puerto Rico no additional civil powers, and, by 1916, talk of independence was widespread. Even the pro-American daily *La Correspondencia* now clamored for independence. A new word, *pitiyanqui*—which literally means "tiny yankee" —came into vogue, to describe in contemptuous terms the Puerto Rican who casts aside his own culture and becomes a 200 per cent American. But the next year, before America entered World War I, as German ships prowled Caribbean waters, President Wilson signed a bill that would be transcendental in the island's history.

The Jones Act

The Jones-Shafroth Act, which Wilson signed on March 2, 1917 (popularly called the Jones Act), proclaimed American citizenship for Puerto Ricans. In previous hearings, the majority Unionist Party pressed for "Puerto Rican citizenship." They claimed that a sub-stantial number of islanders would reject U.S. citizenship if they were given a choice. Muñoz Rivera, who was now Puerto Rico's Resident Commissioner in Washington, asked for a plebiscite to test public opinion. As the leader of the island's major party and the sole elected spokesman in Congress, Muñoz Rivera declared at Senate hearings in Washington that, "according to the understand-ing of the Puerto Rican people, the concession of citizenship would interfere with their ambitions for independence." But Congressman John F. Shafroth of Colorado, the co-author of the bill, replied, "This talk of independence is an idle dream . . . it would be better to resolve the affair right now."

Muñoz Rivera's pleas were ignored. In September, 1916, after the House of Representatives had passed the citizenship bill, Muñoz Rivera sailed to San Juan, where he was met by a large crowd. A few days later he fell ill, and on November 15 he was dead. In dictating his "political testament" to Antonio R. Barceló, his young successor, Muñoz said, "The final end to the problem is the in-dependence of our homeland."

Before President Wilson signed the bill in March of 1917, a woman's suffrage group in New York protested against "self-government" for Puerto Rico "so long as it is denied the women of the United States." Granting citizenship to Puerto Rico, said the women, was "a war measure; the imminence of war makes it wise, the President thinks, to insure the loyalty of the Porto Ricans."

The people of the island were faced with a single option. They automatically became citizens *unless* they signed a document re-fusing it. José de Diego, leader of the insular House of Repre-sentatives, said, "Never before in the realm of international law has such a thing been seen in the democratic nations of the world: 1,200,000 human beings, who by the law of the Congress of a Re-public . . . are stripped of their natural citizenship, but under the menace and coercion of losing their right to vote or be eligible for public office . . . in the country of their birth and life." Only a handful refused.

The Jones Act allowed for greater participation by Puerto Ricans in domestic affairs but also made them subject to being drafted in a war to make the world safe for democracy; meanwhile, at home, an English-speaking governor, born in Kentucky, was ruling the roost, and since he was appointed by the U.S. President, he answered to no one but the man in the White House.

The Struggle for Home Rule Continues

Two years after the passage of the Jones Act, Puerto Rico's legislature asked Congress to permit a plebiscite, which would finally allow islanders to make a democratic choice. But this request died in a Congressional committee.

When, in 1920, Republican President Harding went on record as being against Puerto Rican independence, a flood of bitter anti- American cables and letters reached the House Insular Affairs Committee chairman, Horace M. Towner, who sent a note to the island legislature:

> I assure you that there is not now and there is not likely to be any considerable sentiment in this country for the independence of Puerto Rico. There is a legitimate ground for a larger measure of self-government, but that has been greatly injured by independence propaganda.

The next year, Harding appointed as governor E. Montgomery Reilly, a Kansas City businessman to whom he owed a political debt. In his inaugural address to the legislature, Reilly alienated the majority party, saying: "My friends, there is no room on this island for any flag other than the Stars and Stripes. So long as Old Glory waves over us, it will continue to wave over Puerto Rico."

He later wrote a letter to Union Party leader Antonio Barceló, which touched off two years of bitter relations:

> I want you to fully understand that I shall never appoint any man to any office who is an advocate of independence. When you publicly renounce independence and break loose from your pernicious and anti-American associates, then I will be glad to have your recommendations.

Barceló tried another approach in 1922. He suggested a type of autonomy, called the *Estado Libre Asociado* ("Associated Free State"), modeled after the Irish Free State, which would include a "permanent indestructible bond" between Puerto Rico and the United States. But a bill introduced in Congress died in committee.

Puerto Ricans grew more desperate. When, in 1928, the famous aviator Charles Lindbergh flew in on a goodwill tour and received a tumultuous welcome, local leaders persuaded him to deliver a note to President Coolidge, which said, "Grant us the freedom that you enjoy, for which you struggled, which you worship, which we deserve, and you have promised us." Coolidge, apparently irked, replied: "Certainly giving . . . greater liberty than it has ever enjoyed and powers of government for the exercise of which its people are barely prepared cannot . . . be said to be establishing herein a mere subjugated colony."

Despite the political problem, during the first three decades of American rule, the Puerto Rican economy was humming with activity. But a great part of the riches were being pocketed by large U.S. corporations, which had bought most of the good sugarcane land and exercised strong lobby power in Washington.

Then two hurricanes and the Great Depression brought a virtual collapse. The 1930's were terrible years; there was virtually starvation, mass unemployment, and political anarchy. In many ways, times were harder than during the Spanish colonial period. In reaction to Congressional aloofness, a militant Nationalist Party was formed. It was soon headed by a hypnotic orator named Pedro Albizu Campos, a Harvard Law School graduate who had served as an officer in the American Army. Since Puerto Rico had been autonomous from Spain in 1898, Albizu argued, the American acquisition of the island from Spain had been illegal in the first place. "Nationalism," he said, "is the only salvation, because it causes to be reborn in each of us the conscience of a free man, for whom human dignity is priceless, and who cannot conceive why he should not have the right to direct the destinies of his children or his homeland."

Albizu declared a republic and organized a group of militant, black-shirted followers who, convinced they could not progress by the ballot, next chose invective and later, in desperation, the bullet.

On Sunday morning, February 23, 1936, island police chief E. Francis Riggs was walking from church toward his office in San Juan. Suddenly a young Nationalist named Hiram Rosado approached and fired, hitting Riggs in the chest. As Riggs' chauffeur helped the stricken police chief to his feet, another Nationalist, Elías Beauchamp, came over, pulled a pistol and fired twice more, instantly killing Riggs. Rosado and Beauchamp were hustled to the police station. Soon, two shots were heard inside the station. The two Nationalists were dead. Police claimed they had run toward the gun rack inside the station. Even more moderate men were losing their tempers in Puerto Rico. When Ernest Gruening, then a Federal Government official, asked a rising young Puerto Rican politician, Luis Muñoz Marín (the son of Muñoz Rivera) to write an article condemning the Riggs murder, Muñoz replied that he would if Gruening would publicly condemn the murder of the two Nationalist youths. Shootings in the streets continued, and Albizu Campos and seven of his followers were sent to the Federal Prison in Atlanta, Georgia.

The next year, the Nationalists obtained permission to hold a parade in the city of Ponce on Palm Sunday, March 21. Governor Blanton Winship in San Juan called it "a defiance of all authority on this island," and revoked the permit. But the Nationalists ignored the countermand, and a group of young black-shirted cadets assembled to walk down Ponce's Marina Street. The police, heavily armed, blocked all side streets; a large crowd was on hand. The Nationalist band played Puerto Rico's gentle anthem, *La Borinqueña,* and the "forward march" order was given. Suddenly, a shot was fired. By whom, no one to this day has determined. There were soon twenty dead (including two policemen) and over 100 wounded, most of them peaceful bystanders, as the police panicked and triggered a withering crossfire. "A Nationalist riot," said Governor Winship. "A massacre," said the U.S. Civil Liberties Union, which later investigated. To this day, March 21 in Puerto Rico is remembered as the anniversary of *La Masacre de Ponce*.

Angered by this growing unrest, Senator Millard Tydings (a close friend of the slain Riggs) submitted a bill for independence "in four years," with tariffs rising in 25 per cent chunks yearly.

Muñoz Marín, who favored independence, argued that such immediate rupture would "ruin" Puerto Rico. The island's economy, he said, was geared to its long-standing colonial status, and it was America's moral duty to provide a more adequate transition.

Although many of the abysmal conditions of 1898 were still around as 1940 approached, great gains had been made in public health. Most notable among them was the work of Dr. Bailey K. Ashford, who had landed with the U.S. occupation forces in 1898, and later discovered that so-called tropical anemia was caused by hookworm, a parasite that fastened itself to the intestines and sucked the victim's blood. Ashford's discovery helped to reduce the number of hookworm deaths in Puerto Rico by 90 per cent and saved millions of lives worldwide. But such gains in health were not accompanied by economic progress; population nearly doubled and put more strain on the depressed economy. Per capita income was a mere $118 a year; farm workers, who formed the bulk of the labor force, were earning six cents an hour. The "elite" labor class—construction workers—earned $.22 an hour. The masses survived on "filling" starchy vegetables. Meat was almost unheard of for the poor. Seven out of ten persons were still illiterate (after four decades of U.S. control) and only half the children were in school. Life expectancy was only forty-six years, as thousands of infants still died of diarrhea, gastroenteritis, pneumonia, and influenza, and hundreds of thousands of adults were weakened by intestinal parasites.

The Muñoz Era

The year 1940 marked the rise to power of the Popular Democratic Party, led by Luis Muñoz Marín, who is the dominant figure in modern (perhaps all of) Puerto Rico's history.

During Muñoz's twenty-four years in power (the first eight as Senate majority leader under an American governor), Puerto Rico would experience more change than in four previous centuries. The Muñoz administration would preside over and give impulse to a new form of government, the building of an industrial economy, and great leaps forward in health and education.

Several propitious conditions converged to make this possible.

First, Muñoz was "destined" for the job; the son of Muñoz Rivera, the island's *líder máximo* at the turn of the century, he was well equipped, with a talent (in two languages) for writing, speaking, and inspiring others to work with him. His rise to power also coincided with the arrival of American Governor Tugwell (discussed later), who encouraged Muñoz' reformist zeal and matched it with his own. Very important, too, was the post-World War II economic boom, which produced the abundance of U.S. investment capital that Puerto Rico attracted for its industrial development program.

Muñoz Marín was born in San Juan on February 18, 1898, just ten days after Puerto Rico won autonomy from Spain. Before his first birthday, the Spanish-American War broke out. He was reared on politics. His father's father had been a town mayor. His maternal grandfather, Ramón Marín, a playwright and abolitionist, was jailed by the Spanish authorities for his anticolonial efforts. Muñoz's father, who led Puerto Rico's autonomist movement, later became the island's Resident Commissioner in the United States, where young Luis spent his formative years.

In 1916, when Muñoz Rivera returned to Puerto Rico and died of a liver ailment, his son busied himself as secretary to his father's successor in Washington. He also wrote articles for *La Democracia,* the San Juan newspaper his father had founded in 1890. His articles on America ranged far in subject and mood; he told Puerto Ricans of "spooning," he poked fun at Washington's high society, and he voiced his admiration for American literature. In 1918, when he started a bilingual magazine (*La Revista de las Indias/The Review of the Indies*) he met a young American translater, Muna Lee, who became his first wife.

In the following decade, he lived among writers and artists in New York and Washington. He befriended the famed poet Edward Markham, some of whose works he translated into Spanish. His by-line appeared regularly in the *Baltimore Sun,* the *New York Herald Tribune, Smart Set, The New Republic, The Nation,* and H. L. Mencken's *American Mercury.* In these journals, he wrote of Puerto Rico's colonial plight and, with disdain and wit, described some "Porto Ricans" (the American way of spelling the island's name at the time) who

. . . Americanize themselves out of a sense of their inadequacy as Porto Ricans. . . . They have Ethics and go in for Service. . . . Whether as a result of American tailoring or of psycho-biological imitation, their paunches no longer grow in the reticent Spanish fashion, but rather in the aggressive, genial American fashion. They are gregarious, and dull and oversimian. . . . The girls don't like them, and I maliciously suggest this fact as an issue to Porto Rican nationalists.

With influential friends in New York and Washington, and with his prolific pen, Muñoz was looked upon as the coming leader when, in 1931, he returned to Puerto Rico with his wife and growing family. The next year, he won his first public post, a seat in the Senate for the Liberal Party.

But Nationalist violence caused rifts in the Liberal Party, which lost the 1936 elections; Muñoz was expelled, and he returned to Washington. About that time, Muñoz's marriage ended in divorce. The woman who became Muñoz' second wife was Inés María Mendoza, a vivacious schoolteacher, who was outspoken about her proindependence views.

At the age of forty, Muñoz seemed to be finished as a politician. But together with a nucleus of young liberals (most of them proindependence), he inscribed the Popular Democratic Party on July 22, 1938, in Barranquitas, his father's birthplace. The Popular Party platform for the 1940 election made a surprising declaration: "The final political status of Puerto Rico is not an issue." This pledge united talented men of diverse political leanings, all willing to focus upon economic development. Their dramatic slogan was: "Bread, Land, and Liberty" (*Pan, Tierra, y Libertad*), and their emblem was the *pava,* the broad straw hat worn by the *jíbaro,* the rural peasant.

Muñoz proved to be a brilliant politician, with a great common touch. He enjoyed roaming the hills, kidding in earthy *jíbaro* Spanish with the country folk, and sharing their *cañita* (moonshine rum) or rich black coffee. Almost miraculously, and largely through Muñoz' uncanny rapport with the rural masses ("Lend me your vote, and take it back in the next election if I haven't deserved it"), the Popular Party slipped into power by winning only 38 per cent of the votes cast, against a long-entrenched Republican machine, which was backed by large U.S. sugar interests and which was notorious for buying votes for a few dollars or a new pair of shoes. The Populars won ten out of nineteen Senate seats and eighteen out of thirty-nine House seats.

Puerto Rico's economic crisis continued. When World War II began, the island sent men to fight in Europe and the Pacific. German subs in the Caribbean endangered shipping and caused food and supply shortages, which further depressed the economy. One Puerto Rican, now a successful salesman, recalls those days:

> I was raised in a horrible slum near Santurce. I didn't even have a pair of sl`oes to call my own. I joined up with the National Guard even before I was of legal age, but I was big and they took me. A lot of us joined so we could get a pair of decent boots and a good meal on Sundays, when we drilled. The sergeants kept complaining about how shoddy our boots looked, but man, we used to wear them all week to work in! As for the food, man, I was so hungry in those days, to get a meal I'd have killed Germans, Japs . . . even Puerto Ricans!

In 1941, President Roosevelt appointed Rexford Guy Tugwell (a member of his Brains Trust) to govern the island, where independence groups were gaining force as the economic crisis worsened. The United States was spending $30 million to build large air and naval bases on the island, to shield the Panama Canal from enemy attack. In his book *Puerto Rico: The Stricken Land,* Tugwell says:

> My duty as the representative of my country in Puerto Rico was to shape civil affairs . . . so that military bases which might soon, before they were ready, have to stand the shock of attack, were not isolated in a generally hostile environment. Two immediate tasks [confronted] us—that of meeting the shock of war and that of relieving distress. . . . Beyond that, if we could, we might do something even in those circumstances towards reconstruction.

Tugwell and Senate leader Muñoz worked together in reorganizing the government, with central planning and control of key industries, thus alleviating food shortages and smoothing the way for future economic development. In doing so, he also moved Puerto Rico closer to the United States, since the liberal reform program that he proposed showed that economic progress was possible, even under the island's colonial status. In March, 1943, Tugwell recommended that Congress "permit the people of Puerto Rico to elect their own governor." President Roosevelt supported the bill, adding that "the ultimate power of Congress" would not be diminished. That same year, a bill for independence was also submitted to Congress, with the support of Vicente Geigel-Polanco, floor leader of the Popular Democratic Party. Neither bill prospered. One U.S. senator, for example, said it was impossible to "reconcile complete independence . . . with the effective and necessary use of Puerto Rico for military control of the Caribbean."

As its reform program gathered steam, the Popular Party won a clear victory in 1944, with over 60 per cent of the votes and fifty-four out of fifty-eight legislative seats. Most of the Popular Party legislators at the time were proindependence. Impatient over Muñoz' reluctance to resolve the status issue, several resigned and formed the Puerto Rican Independence Party, led by lawyer Gilberto Concepción de Gracia. The *independentistas* felt that Muñoz and other Popular leaders were needlessly postponing the political status question. Prior to the split in 1945, U.S. Senator Tydings had introduced another independence bill, calling for a twenty-one-year transition period, in which Puerto Rico was to receive special economic treatment. Although the Popular Party's official policy was to refrain from political debate, twenty-two of its thirty-nine House members and eleven of its nineteen Senators endorsed the bill. This was somewhat of an embarrassment to Senate Majority Leader Muñoz, who asked Tydings to withdraw the bill and, instead, suggested a plebiscite, where all status alternatives could be voted upon. Tydings replied that there was no support for statehood in the United States at the time, which made a plebiscite senseless.

When Governor Tugwell resigned in 1946, President Truman appointed Puerto Rico's first native governor, Jesús Piñero, who had been the island's Resident Commissioner in Washington. The next year, while members of the Independence Party appealed to the United Nations for help in resolving "the colonial status in an era when the world is repudiating colonialism," the United States decided to allow Puerto Rico to elect its own governor.

For nearly half a century, from 1900 through 1946, Puerto Rico was governed by fifteen North American civilians, appointed by the U.S. President. With rare exceptions, they were an undistinguished lot. None mastered Spanish; few were familiar with the island's culture; few could have run their own home state.

In 1935, anger over the ineptness of one governor prompted Puerto Ricans to bomb his home and send letters to Washington petitioning his ouster. Another governor caused a drunken row at a White House concert and was shipped back to Puerto Rico to complete his term of office. Another, accused in the mainland press of improper action, forged a letter, using the name of a prominent Puerto Rican, and sent it to the press to defend himself. Another, asked by a U.S. Senate committee for his credentials as an administrator, replied that in his hometown he had once run a 5- and 10-cent store.

In 1948, islanders rejoiced as Senator Muñoz became Governor Muñoz, Puerto Rico's first elected native governor. The Popular Party finally took a stand on status, proposing an *Estado Libre Asociado,* an autonomous self-government, which would preserve relations with America. While such a stand was viewed as "traitorous" by those of Muñoz' ex-colleagues who were now in the Independence ranks, it was not altogether surprising. Muñoz' father had advocated similar autonomy from Spain, and, in the 1920's, the popular independence leader, Antonio Barceló, had even proposed an *Estado Libre Asociado.* Though Muñoz' economic views were socialistic, his politics were consistent with a long line of Puerto Rican reformers, who had flirted with independence and finally settled upon a middle road—autonomy—when confronted by what one might call the "realities" of dealing with a large colonial power.

In subsequent years, Muñoz has said that during the 1940's he was reluctantly convinced of the "economic impossibility" of independence by U.S. and Puerto Rican specialists who had reviewed the fiscal problems that the new Republic of the Philippines would be confronting and that Puerto Rico—with even less resources— would have to face.

On July 4, 1950, President Harry S. Truman signed Public Law 600, which allowed Puerto Ricans to draft their own constitution under the Commonwealth form of government.

It was a step forward in home rule, but those who believed in independence saw their hopes frustrated. On October 30, 1950, there were bloody Nationalist uprisings throughout the island. The first sign of trouble came when a green sedan parked at the entrance to La Fortaleza, the governor's mansion in Old San Juan, and six Nationalists—armed with pistols, rifles and a machine gun—sprinted from the car, yelling *"Viva Puerto Rico libre!"* They opened fire, but four of the six were killed by fire from the guards. The other two were captured alive. The violence spread. In Jayuya, seventy Nationalists seized the town, killing four policemen and setting fire to Federal buildings. In Ponce, Mayagüez, Utuado, and half a dozen towns, Nationalists attacked police stations with gunfire and Molotov cocktails. Governor Muñoz Marín called out the National Guard, which responded with bazookas, tanks, and planes. By week's end, thirty-one Puerto Ricans were dead, ninety were wounded, and hundreds were under arrest.

Three days later, in Washington, D.C., a pair of Nationalists—Oscar Collazo and Griselio Torresola—opened fire on the street outside Blair House, the residence of President Truman. Torresola was killed and Collazo wounded; one White House guard was also killed and two others were wounded.

In San Juan, police besieged Nationalist headquarters and filled it with tear gas. Albizu Campos surrendered and was subsequently sentenced to several years' imprisonment for armed insurrection. In New York, relatives and friends of the two Nationalists were rounded up for interrogation.

At his trial, Collazo denied nothing, explaining, "The American people don't know that Puerto Rico is a possession of the United States. . . . I think it would draw the attention of the whole world to Washington . . . if two Puerto Ricans were killed in front of his [Truman's] residence." Collazo was sentenced to death, but this was commuted to life imprisonment by President Truman.

Despite this violent interlude, Puerto Ricans approved the Commonwealth status in a referendum on June 4, 1951, by a vote of 387,000 to 119,000. Opponents called the vote unfair, since its only two choices were to adopt the new status or to remain a colonial territory; and many registered voters abstained. A strong controversy developed over the meaning of the new status. An exuberant Governor Muñoz said, ". . . we can proclaim to the world that the last juridical vestiges of colonialism have been abolished." But Joseph Mahoney of the House Committee on Interior and Insular Affairs said, "The U.S. Constitution gives Congress complete control and nothing in the Puerto Rican Constitution could affect or amend or alter that right." A Department of Interior lawyer, Irwin Silverman, put it more delicately, explaining that while Congress has "paramount power," it had "solemnly entered into a compact" with Puerto Rico, and, "it is our hope not to interfere" with the autonomy of the new island government. The independence bloc called the new status "colonial subservience," while the statehooders said it was a veiled move toward eventual separation. Muñoz, however, insisted: "We are not engaged in taking another step to self-government, this *is* self-government." He called commonwealth "a new alternative, equal in dignity, although different in nature, from independence or federated statehood."

The New Commonwealth Status

After a lengthy convention to draft the new Commonwealth Constitution, Puerto Ricans approved the document by a referendum vote of 374,000 to 82,000. On July 25, 1952 (the fifty-fourth anniversary of the American invasion of Guánica), a solemn ceremony was held in San Juan, as Governor Muñoz raised Puerto Rico's flag next to the Stars and Stripes to inaugurate the new form of government. In November, the Populars again won the gubernatorial elections with 61 per cent of the votes, but the Independence Party polled a surprising 19 per cent, and the Statehood Republicans were third with only 13 per cent.

Shortly after the elections, the United States advised the United Nations that Puerto Rico was "a self-governing territory." Until then, the United States was in the awkward position of having to issue annual reports to the U.N. Committee on Information from Non-Self-Governing Territories. After a bitter debate, the committee voted twenty-two to eighteen that the relation between the United States and Puerto Rico was embodied in a compact that

The flag of Puerto Rico: three red stripes separated by two white stripes, with a blue triangle containing a white star. The white star symbolizes Puerto Rico; the corners of the triangle, the legislative, executive, and judicial branches of government. The three red stripes symbolize the blood that feeds these three branches of government, and the two white stripes represent the rights of man and freedom of the individual.

An old engraving showing Taino Indians in the early sixteenth century drowning a young Spaniard to see whether the white man was mortal.

Institute of Puerto Rican Culture

San Juan, in a seventeenth-century Dutch print.

Institute of Puerto Rican Culture

Cabinet of Puerto Rico's brief autonomous government of 1897. Seated: Luis Muñoz Rivera, Francisco Quiñones, Manuel Fernandez Juncos. Standing: Juan Hernandez Lopez, José Sepero Quiñones, Manuel F. Rossy.

Institute of Puerto Rican Culture

Pedro Albizu Campos, the Harvard-educated lawyer who became an ardent champion of Puerto Rican independence and leader of the Nationalist party. This portrait of him by José Alicea includes his statement that "the fatherland is valor and sacrifice." Albizu Campos died in 1965 at the age of seventy-three.

The Ponce Massacre on Palm Sunday, 1937, a painting by Fran Cervoni.

Governor Luis Muñoz Marín raising the Puerto Rican flag on July 25, 1952, when the island's commonwealth status was inaugurated. This was the first time in history that the Puerto Rican flag was officially displayed. Governor Muñoz's wife, doña Ines, is at the left.

La Fortaleza in Old San Juan, the oldest executive mansion in continuous use in the Western Hemisphere, has housed Puerto Rico's governors since 1640.

Photos: Puerto Rico Information Service

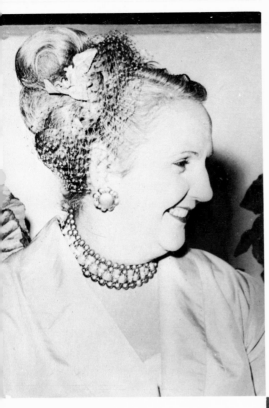

Felisa Rincon de Gautier, mayor of San Juan for many years, until her retirement in 1968.

Puerto Rico
Information Service

Teodoro Moscoso, the first director of "Operation Bootstrap," the island's industrial-development program.

Puerto Rico
Information Service

Rafael Hernández Colón, who became governor of Puerto Rico in January 1973.

Fort San Geronimo, now a military museum open to the public. In the background is a view of San Juan's Condado section.

*Puerto Rico
Department of Tourism*

Country scene in Puerto Rico.

Marvin Schwartz,
for Puerto Rico
Information Service

Aerial view of San Juan's Condado tourist strip, packed tightly with luxury hotels and apartments.

Puerto Rico
Information Service

could not be unilaterally amended, and by a twenty-seven to seventeen vote authorized the United States to stop submitting the reports. This was a bitter blow for independence backers, who accused the United States of having exerted strong pressure upon some Latin American countries to abstain from voting.

On March 2, 1954—exactly thirty-seven years after President Wilson signed into law the Puerto Rico citizenship bill—newspapers worldwide screamed out that a band of Nationalists had opened fire in the gallery of the U.S. House of Representatives. Lolita Lebrón, Rafael Cáncel Miranda, Andrés Figueroa, and Irving Flores Rodríguez had bought one-way tickets from New York to Washington, expecting never to return alive. Mrs. Lebrón rose first, waved a Puerto Rican flag and opened fire. The others followed, shouting *"Viva Puerto Rico libre!"* Five Congressmen were wounded by the fusillade before the terrorists were subdued. In Mrs. Lebrón's purse was a note: "Before God and the world, my blood claims for the independence of Puerto Rico. . . . This is a cry for victory in our struggle for independence." The four were jailed, together with thirteen others who were accused of involvement in the plot.

This violent act, as well as the Nationalist revolt of 1950, seemed "insane" and "suicidal" to most observers. But the Nationalists had their own rationale. In his book on Albizu Campos, poet Juan Antonio Corretjer tells of a revealing meeting with the Nationalist leader. When Corretjer asked whether Puerto Rico would be affected by the U.S. annexation of Hawaii and Alaska, Albizu replied: "I don't think they'll be brutish enough to annex Puerto Rico, but they'll have to be reminded that Puerto Rico is a nation and cannot be assimilated. And they'll have to be reminded, not with individual acts, but in a more general way." Thus, it seems that even Albizu's concept of "winning" the Nationalist revolt was to avoid statehood.

The Popular Party, however, swept the 1956 and 1960 elections by 60 per cent margins. The Independence Party dropped to 12.5 per cent in 1956 and plummeted to only 3 per cent of the vote in 1960, while the Statehood Republicans gained force, with 25 per cent and 32 percent in the two elections. To combat charges from both sides that commonwealth was "transitory, inferior and colonial," Muñoz moved to "perfect" the new status. He had tried in 1959, with a broad proposal (called the Fernós-Murray Bill), which would have eliminated all U.S. supervision and restrictions except those few common links, such as citizenship and defense, necessary to maintain permanent union. But Congress was apprehensive about the sweeping powers of the proposed new autonomy and never acted upon it. The Fernós-Murray Bill did, however, prompt lengthy Congressional hearings. A plebiscite was suggested to advise Congress of the mood of the public.

In July, 1962, Muñoz wrote to President Kennedy (the fourth U.S. President with whom he had dealt as an island leader): "It seems clear that the people . . . should be consulted again regarding the relationship . . . with the United States." Kennedy replied two weeks later, expressing "total sympathy." It was decided to name a joint U.S.–Puerto Rico Status Commission, composed of thirteen members (seven Americans and six Puerto Ricans), to conduct studies and hold public hearings.

Muñoz Steps Down. In the meantime, Governor Muñoz began to feel strong concern about the durability of the Popular Party, which was the main proponent of commonwealth status. As of 1964, he had been in power—either as Senate Majority Leader or Governor—for twenty-four years; he had become a virtual father-figure to the mass of the Puerto Rican public and enjoyed tremendous personal power and prestige. To enhance the continuity of the party he helped to found, he decided to step down. At a nominating convention in Mayagüez in August, 1964, he chose Roberto Sánchez Vilella, a long-time aide and Secretary of State of the Commonwealth, to be the party's candidate. In November, 1964, Roberto Sánchez Vilella became the second elected governor in the island's history.

By 1966, after two years of study, the Status Commission predictably announced that all three choices—commonwealth, statehood, and independence—were "worthy" and limply recommended that it be left up to Puerto Ricans to decide. It also proposed *ad hoc* committees to work out the knottier aspects of the U.S.–Puerto Rico relationship. Late in 1966, it was rumored that the United Nations would take a second look at whether Puerto Rico was truly self-governing. Soon afterward, the Popular Party majority pushed through a bill calling for a July 23, 1967, plebiscite.

The 1967 Status Plebiscite

There were strong protests. The Statehood Republicans declared a boycott, but their key leader, Luis A. Ferré, bolted to form "United Statehooders," in order to compete in the plebiscite. The Independence Party also abstained, but a university professor, Héctor Alvarez Silva, insisted that the independence status should be represented, and he formed a group.

Some feared dissension in the Popular ranks. When Sánchez Vilella became governor in 1964 he tried to rejuvenate the party, which had been in power for nearly one-quarter of a century; he promised a "new style" and surrounded himself with young liberal aides. This alienated some of the old party bosses, and shortly after Sánchez took office, a group emerged that favored Senator Luis Negrón López as the party candidate in the 1968 elections, nearly four years hence. Conditions soured between Sánchez and his old mentor Muñoz. The crisis grew to tragic proportions in early 1967 when Sánchez revealed that he planned to end his thirty-year marriage and marry an attractive young aide, Jeanette Ramos Buonomo, the daughter of a prominent legislator. When Sánchez became the butt of vicious public gossip, and seemed to control only a fraction of his party, Muñoz decided to lead the plebiscite campaign. He appeared at meetings of business, labor, and social organizations. He spoke on radio and television and visited all seventy-seven of the island municipalities, making as many as five speeches in five separate towns in a single afternoon. Over and over again, he stressed, "This campaign is the most important in our history. A wrong choice for a candidate in a regular election can be corrected every four years, but if Puerto Ricans make an error on July 23, they will be paying for it for generations."

"Fiscal autonomy," he said, "possible only through commonwealth, is the reason why Puerto Rico is fourth in the world in the rate of economic progress."

Since the independence cause appeared to stand no chance of winning, Muñoz aimed his heaviest guns against statehood. The statehooders were insinuating—in speeches and newspaper ads—

that commonwealth left the door open for independence, which
—according to them—was just one logical step away from a Castro
Communist-style dictatorship. To combat this fear campaign,
Muñoz emphasized the permanent union of the commonwealth
with the United States and insisted that independence was "impossible." On the other hand, he said, statehood meant the cultural
assimilation of Puerto Rico, and, "We are not just a bunch of
people, we are a people."

Thus, the combination of commonwealth's economic success in
the previous fifteen years, plus the immense weight of Muñoz'
personal prestige, accounted for a landslide vote. More than 60 per
cent of 702,000 voters in the plebiscite chose to maintain the commonwealth status. The statehooders won nearly 39 per cent, and
the *independentistas* won less than 0.6 per cent.

The 1968 Elections

It appeared, after the plebiscite, that commonwealth was on its
way to perfection, with gradually increasing autonomy via negotiations with the U.S. Congress. However, there was another hurdle
ahead in November, 1968: the next gubernatorial elections. And
there was concern over an imminent split in the Popular Party
due to what appeared to be ineradicable differences between in-
cumbent Governor Sánchez and the other party leaders.

In March, 1968, Governor Sánchez confirmed these fears when
he said that he would run for re-election in November. A year
before, when he admitted publicly to the break-up of his marriage,
he had said he would complete his term and not run again.

Even before the Populars' August, 1968, nominating convention,
it seemed clear that the party leadership would repudiate Sánchez.
The delegates chose Luis Negrón López by a solid majority and
strongly booed Sánchez when, in an unannounced speech, he
claimed that the convention was "undemocratic" and had been
manipulated by the party's old guard "machinery." Sánchez soon
formed his own political movement, the People's Party, with a
rising sun as its symbol, an appeal to youth as its strategy, and a
more militant autonomy as its politics.

In the meantime, a sixty-four-year-old industrialist, Luis A. Ferré, had formed the New Progressive Party. Ferré, a pro-statehood Republican born in the south coast city of Ponce, was the son of a Cuban immigrant who founded the Puerto Rico Iron Works, the forerunner of the big business complex known today as Ferré Enterprises. Ferré, a loser in three previous bids for the Statehood Republican Party, this time took advantage of the dissension among the Populars and general malaise among the fast-growing middle class, who blamed government for the poor state of roads and other essential services for suburbia. His party's symbol was a coconut palm tree, and its slogan was: "This has got to change!" He called for people of all political status persuasions to vote for him. The main purpose of his party, he said, was not statehood but better government, after twenty-eight years of "stagnation" and "dictatorship." The Popular candidate, Senator Negrón López, a rural lawyer and gentleman coffee farmer, was an astute man behind the scenes at the legislature, but lacked dynamism in his TV speeches and public appearances. Again, Muñoz tried to carry the banner, but for the first time his legend had lost some of its luster. He was loudly booed at some rallies, since many citizens sympathized with accusations that Muñoz had led the party's "machinery" in preventing Governor Sánchez' renomination. Muñoz and other long-entrenched Popular leaders were the subject of ridicule on a new, widely seen television satire show, which invariably depicted Muñoz as an aging *caudillo* and his lieutenants as fawning yesmen. Ferré, in the meantime, appeared often on paid television spots, presenting the image of a firm democratic leader who would raise the salaries of public servants, stamp out drug addiction and crime in the streets, save agriculture from ruin, and invigorate a government that had grown indifferent to the needs of the people.

On November 4, 1968, Ferré was elected governor of Puerto Rico. His New Progressive Party edged in with 44 per cent of the 875,000 votes cast, compared with 42 per cent for the Popular Democrats. The 81,000 votes won by Governor Sánchez and his People's Party had made the difference. As in the previous election, the Independence Party failed to win the necessary 5 per cent of the votes to automatically qualify for the 1972 ballot. They would have to register once more.

The Ferré Government. Ferré, however, did not win a clear mandate. The Popular Party retained the Senate by a slight margin, while the New Progressives held a thin edge in the House. Deploring a possible "tug of war," Ferré called for the Populars to "play fair," rather than exercise their legislative veto to torpedo his new government's program.

Ferré predicted a change in government "priorities" and called for more participation by the private sector, since "government can't do the whole job."

On political status, he said that "our party is committed to statehood, but status should not be decided in regular elections. There should be a status referendum whenever convenient, to test how people feel." Under statehood, he said, Puerto Rico must be allowed to "maintain its own Hispanic culture and language." He said that the island would be "ready to assume the financial responsibility of U.S. statehood by 1980," but cautioned that this depended upon "the desire of a majority of Puerto Ricans to request statehood and Congress' desire to grant it."

At year end, Muñoz announced that he was stepping aside as Popular Party leader and would merely retain his seat in the Senate.

"The New Life" Begins

During his campaign, Ferré promised *La Nueva Vida* (The New Life) for Puerto Rico after twenty-eight years of rule by the Popular Democratic Party. He tried to broaden his slim electoral base with salary raises for teachers and policemen and annual Christmas bonuses for all government employees. A new law required that private employers whose profits permitted were to do the same. A $1 hourly minimum wage was set for farmworkers. Ferré also began to sell, for $1, small government-owned *parcelas* (land parcels) to thousands of poor landless families living on them.

He also moved to fulfill other campaign promises. Trying to salvage a declining agriculture, he sought funds to mechanize sugarcane. He catalyzed police crackdowns on drug peddlers and announced plans for addict rehabilitation centers. He also gained grudging Roman Catholic Church acquiescence to the expansion of birth control information services to public health clinics all over the island (which could turn out to be the most significant achievement in his term in office). But Ferré's boundless zeal for state-hood also contributed to a growing polarization in Puerto Rican politics.

Merely by Ferré's victory at the polls, some *independentistas* and Populars grew pessimistic (even paranoiac), and grumbled that they would soon be railroaded into statehood against their wishes. Ferré did little to calm their fears. On July 25, at a parade to honor the 17th anniversary of the commonwealth status, he said in his speech that the Presidential vote would be "the most powerful weapon ever wielded by Puerto Rican hands."

Almost as if in reply, several thousand commonwealth sup-porters marched past him with Puerto Rican flags and banners that rejected "assimilation." The schizophrenic political mood was ac-centuated by a second parade a block away. A few hundred pro-independence marchers, dressed in black, were "mourning" the *other* July 25—in 1898—when "the American eagle seized Puerto Rico in its claws."

Ferré's actions in July came as no surprise. The die seems to have been cast in May, 1969, when Senate Minority Leader Justo Méndez of the New Progressive Party told the press that Ferré's election vic-tory proved commonwealth to be a "transitory" vehicle to statehood. The 1968 elections, he claimed, had nullified the 1967 plebiscite. He then announced his party's strategy for achieving statehood. First, an *ad hoc* committee would be named to try to gain the U.S. Presi-dential vote by the 1972 elections. If this were achieved, Puerto Rico would ask for two Resident Commissioners in Congress, with voting powers. Third, after the 1972 elections (presupposing a New Progressive victory), a plebiscite would be called, with the hope of a large statehood majority.

In mid-1969, Ferré adhered to this strategy. He announced that he would see President Nixon in Washington to ask that Puerto Rico be allowed to vote in U.S. elections. At the Conference of U.S. Governors in Denver, Colorado, that summer, he circulated a petition asking the governors to support statehood for Puerto Rico, provided that the electorate chose it in an "honest, clean referendum."

Opposition leaders censured the Governor for "ignoring the man-date of the people" who had favored commonwealth in the 1967 plebiscite. Ferré snapped back that "as a private citizen I have a right to express my views."

Muñoz Marín denounced Ferré's tactics of "assimilation" and called upon Puerto Ricans to defend their "cultural heritage."

As the criticism mounted from "respectable" (nonradical) quarters, Ferré became more conciliatory. He declared the coming September 23 a legal holiday, to mark the 1868 independence uprising in Lares. His speeches took on a soothing tone, assuring Puerto Ricans that statehood did not mean "the loss of our Hispanic culture," and that even *independentistas* should welcome the vote for America's President "as a way to democratically voice your views."

Politics was the gut issue of 1969. In the legislature, New Progressives and Populars tested each other's strength on bill after bill, voting along rigid party lines. Legislators vied for influence and key committee posts.

A major crisis was touched off on September 26, when the Federal District Court in San Juan meted out a one-year prison sentence for draft evasion to Edwin Feliciano Grafals, a young *independentista* who refused to enter the U.S. Army. After the court decision, youths from the Federation of University Students Pro-Independence charged the University of Puerto Rico Río Piedras campus ROTC building and set fire to it. Chancellor Abrahán Díaz González did not call the police ("a massacre would have occurred"), but he suspended seven students, prompting a march of 3,000 students "in solidarity" with the convicted draft objector and the suspended seven. A series of brawls erupted on campus between groups of ROTC cadets and proindependence students.

Leaders from the New Progressive Party and some sectors of the press began to call for the resignation of Chancellor Díaz, a forty-six-year-old Harvard Law School graduate, who had won a reputation over the years as an ardent civil rights defender.

The crisis intensified on November 5, when the University of Puerto Rico Academic Senate, at Díaz' initiative, voted to phase out the ROTC program over a two-year period

Then, the "backlash" occurred with surprising force. A protest march was organized to *favor* the retention of the ROTC program;

it was composed of ROTC cadets, their parents, and friends, who bristled at the "independence takeover of our university" and bore placards comparing Díaz with Fidel Castro.

The march soon degenerated into a rock- and Molotov cocktail–throwing match between the paraders and proindependence students on campus. When this was quelled, the marchers directed their fury against the headquarters of the Pro-Independence Movement, located above a storefront in Río Piedras Plaza, five blocks west. For two hours, ignoring feeble police attempts to disperse them, a mob heaved more rocks and firebombs at the charred façade of the Pro-Independence Movement building, which held forty members of the movement.

When a Lutheran minister told a policeman: "Please! There are human beings up there. You must stop this," he was told, "We've been ordered to keep out of it. Go up and defend them yourself if you like." When a lawyer arrived at the plaza and demanded that police restrain the mob, an officer's billy club opened a seven-stitch wound in his scalp. Later in the evening, when officers tried to clear the plaza, gently nudging people to the periphery, one middle-aged man shook his fist and yelled: "You tell *us* to go home! You let Mari Bras and his Communists burn down all the stores on the island, but you tell *us* to go home!"

Suddenly, a group of proindependence students arrived at the plaza and stood in front of the Pro-Independence Movement building, demanding police protection. Thirty helmeted officers charged them in a flying wedge, swinging billy clubs and sweeping them away from the site as though they were tenpins. In the confusion, a shot rang out, drawing a barrage of fire from the police. During the volley, one policeman on the street and two Pro-Independence Movement members inside the building were wounded. A subsequent search of the building uncovered no weapons, and the source of the first shot is still a mystery.

The attack against the building inflamed *independentista* tempers, and two weeks later, in a parade to protest the military draft, 10,000 marchers passed through the heart of the Condado tourist sector, waving flags and chanting: "*Yanqui* go home!"

Unable to prevent such demonstrations, the Ferré government focused upon the university. Changes were made in the nine-member Council on Higher Education, which appoints the chancellor. It now had five pro-statehood members, four of them appointed since Ferré took office in January. It became clear that they would vote in a majority bloc to remove "subversive" influences from the campus.

First, the Council overruled the Academic Senate's decision to remove the ROTC program. Later, in a long, stormy meeting, it fired Díaz and appointed University President Jaime Benítez as interim chancellor at Río Piedras.

At a news conference in his office, Díaz called his ouster "the culmination of a plan drawn up by the New Progressive Party to take the university by storm." His protest was supported by former Governor Sánchez, who called the dismissal ". . . a storm trooper assault against the university."

But Muñoz Marín and other Popular leaders reserved comment. One observer remarked:

> I know what Muñoz and the Populars are up to. They're going to let Ferré and his bunch polarize things so badly in the next few years, into irreconcilable left and right wings, that later they'll come along waving the olive branch, claiming that the middle-of-the-road commonwealth alternative is the only hope for peace in Puerto Rico.

Muñoz even went into self-imposed "exile" in Europe. Since the 1968 defeat of his party, he had tried to inject new blood into the aging Popular ranks. But no new leaders appeared, partly because of his own imposing, patriarchal presence. First he resigned from all positions of power in the party's ruling council, telling the press that he was "stepping aside for new faces." Then he resigned from the Senate, packed his bags, and sailed to Europe, hoping that the vacuum created by his absence would cause leaders to emerge.

During 1971 and 1972, the island's economy began to sag badly, in direct proportion to economic troubles on the mainland. Factories closed, businesses went bankrupt. Tourism faltered and the government assumed ownership of several hotels. The cost of living rose at three times the mainland rate, and the government (cringing at the political consequences) had to increase water and electric power rates.

Bombs exploded in several tourist hotels, and terrorists held a local radio station long enough to broadcast a tape that exhorted listeners to "revolt against *yanqui* imperialism." Puerto Ricans stayed glued to their radios, but such incidents warned that violence might escalate, and it did.

In March, 1971, three persons (including a police major) were shot dead on the UPR campus during a clash between pro-independence students and ROTC cadets. In apparent retaliation, the homes and businesses of prominent *independentistas* were burned down. "Violence and repression became a way of life for weeks," recalls one newsman.

Turmoil continued on several fronts. Hundreds of poor families built squatters' shacks on private or government land, often with the help of proindependence activists; in some cases, angry landowners had the shacks cleared with bulldozers.

There was a much-publicized confrontation with the U.S. Navy over Culebra, the tiny offshore island that for decades had been a target for naval bombardment practice. Rubén Berríos, head of the Pro-Independence Party, led a group that paralyzed naval maneuvers by holding a prayer meeting on the beach. Berríos and others were arrested and spent three months in jail. When Puerto Ricans of all political affiliations joined in condemning the navy's use of the island (several hundred Puerto Ricans live on Culebra), Washington promised to "phase out" its maneuvers there.

When the U.S. governors came to San Juan for their annual conference, there was such concern about mass demonstrations that a special limited access road was built directly from the airport to the governors' hotel. Several persons were arrested for alleged attempts to bomb the San Juan Naval Station, Federal offices in San Juan, and a U.S.-owned shopping center.

In an effort to "defuse the climate of vilence," Ferré invited independence leaders to the Fortaleza mansion for talks, but few accepted. Soon afterward, the Pro-Independence Movement, led by Juan Marí Bras, formally embraced Marxism at its yearly convention and changed its name to the Puerto Rican Socialist Party (PSP).

Political differences were temporarily put aside in late May of 1972, when all islanders joined in mourning. A trio of Japanese terrorists, acting on behalf of Arab guerrillas, had opened fire with automatic weapons against passengers in Lod Airport, Tel Aviv. Sixteen persons were killed in the slaughter; all were Puerto Ricans who were on a group pilgrimage to the Holy Land.

The mood of conflict continued. When the pro-statehood mayor of San Juan, Carlos Romero Barceló, attended a high school graduation ceremony, a girl student brandishing a Puerto Rican flag slapped his face. Only 10 per cent of the seniors at the University of Puerto Rico attended their graduation ceremony. The student council president paid tribute in his speech to the "mute protest" of absent students and professors, and walked out himself. As the Vietnam War escalated, 3,000 UPR students marched through the streets of Ríos Piedras, smashing the windows of U.S. chain stores.

The government, trying to boost tourism, sponsored the "Miss U.S.A." beauty pageant at a Dorado resort hotel. Terrorist bombs destroyed two hotel rooms and a car in the parking lot.

Later that summer, the Miss Universe beauty contest, also sponsored by the government, would be televised worldwide from the island. Police security was so tight that columnist Ismaro Velázquez remarked: "A few dedicated revolutionaries have put the entire government and police force into the embarrassing situation of having to lay siege to a town and a resort hotel, in order to have sixty beauties parade in front of a roomful of people."

A 1972 poll of "new voters" (between the ages of eighteen and twenty) showed that 18 per cent favored independence. Even Governor Ferré's own daughter announced publicly that she favored independence.

There were a record-breaking 345 strikes in 1972, and some picket lines degenerated into violence. The narcotics traffic continued to grow, and 1930's-style gangland murders took place in the streets as drug merchants clashed in power struggles. Several government officials became enmeshed in scandals that involved illegal land sales and coddling of influential tax evaders.

Governor Ferré tried desperately to reverse the negative course of events, but to little avail. Even his good contacts with Republican leaders in Washington proved of little value in eliciting Federal aid, as the Nixon Administration became paralyzed by the Watergate scandal and the U.S. economy slid downhill to recession.

The mounting crisis was not without its lighter moments. One planner proposed importing herds of hippopotamuses as a "novel, cheap" way to clean up water reservoirs, which were clogged by fast-growing water lilies. He offered statistics showing how many cubic feet of plants could be eaten by each animal per day. The project was abandoned when someone else demonstrated that the hungry hippopotamuses would dump an equal amount of fecal wastes into the reservoirs.

The 1972 Elections

Ferré's main challenger in the 1972 elections was Rafael Hernández Colón, the PDP's young Senate majority leader. Born in Ponce in 1936, the son of a former Supreme Court associate justice, Hernández Colón ("Cuchín" to his friends) studied at Johns Hopkins and later graduated at the top of his class at the UPR School of Law, where he attracted attention with a scholarly analysis of the Commonwealth's political status.

In 1965, when he was only twenty-nine, he was named Secretary of Justice. Three years later he won a Senate seat and rose to its presidency, with the backing of former Governor Muñoz Marín. For so young a person, he was remarkably level-headed, an advocate of conciliation and compromise. Some critics, in fact—remarking upon his apparent lack of "charisma"—called him "the old young man." But his political outlook was both "practical" and "liberal" enough to embrace the broad spectrum of viewpoints within the Popular Democratic Party.

The People's Party, which won nearly 10 per cent of the vote in 1968, had dissipated its strength so much in four years that Roberto Sánchez Vilella, its gubernatorial candidate in 1968, decided to run for a seat in the legislature rather than risk sure defeat by competing for the governor's job.

The same tactic was adopted by the Pro-Independence Party, which expected to improve its showing at the polls but harbored no hope of winning the governorship. Rubén Berríos ran for the Senate, and other party members sought seats in the House. Two "splinter" parties for independence (the Puerto Rican Union Party and the Authentic Sovereignty Party) also registered.

Before the campaign, the PDP leaders engaged in a tense debate that threatened to split their ranks. The issue was whether or not Puerto Rico's right to vote in U.S. Presidential elections could be a "possible avenue of development" of the Commonwealth status. Many argued that such a move could drive the island inexorably toward statehood. But Hernández Colón, Jaime Benítez (candidate for resident commissioner) and others urged that "the Presidential vote" be part of the PDP platform, perhaps in order to blunt perennial Republican accusations that the Populars were *independentistas* in disguise." The measure passed by a voice vote, but many shouts of protest were heard.

The two major candidates were already linked to mainland politics. In July, Hernández Colón was one of fourteen delegates to the Democratic Party convention in Miami Beach. The next month, Governor Ferré was an observer at the Republican Party convention in the same city.

Both major parties geared up for a bitter (and expensive) campaign, even hiring prominent strategists from the mainland. The PDP's chief "imported consultant was Joe Napolitan, who had worked with Senator Edmund Muskie. Ferré's party hired a firm whose principals included Harry Treleaven, a key figure in Richard Nixon's 1968 media campaign. The consultants earned the "going rate" of about $500 per day, lived in luxury hotels, held extensive "strategy sessions" (sometimes at poolside) and generated a blizzard of memos (in English). One proposal to the NPP said:

The approach we recommend is based on a close proximity involvement that makes the consultants an integral part of the campaign, yet their role and contacts have definite parameters and they are not a highly visible part of the effort.

Such jargon so impressed one NPP official that he bragged to a reporter: "We have the best consultants, the other side's are no good."

Hernández Colón's campaign received a strong boost when Luis Muñoz Marín returned from two years of "exile" in Europe. The wily seventy-four-year-old Muñoz chose to arrive just a few weeks prior to the election.

It was 92 degrees in the midday sun, but more than 150,000 people gathered in the vast parking lot of the Plaza de las Americas shopping center to greet him. The crowd's hysterical cheers were deafening as Hernández Colón tried to introduce Muñoz and then, overcome by the sheer emotion of the moment, began to cry.

Muñoz walked up to the microphone, raised his arms, and, in his familiar deep voice, said:

"Compatriotas."

The place exploded. Men and women cried. A few collapsed. People waved PDP flags and parasols. Muñoz raised both arms again, hushing the crowd, and then said:

"Populares."

Another outburst of joy. Men could be seen drying their tears with the sleeves of their shirts.

"Puertorriqueños . . . amigos todos." With five well-chosen, well-timed words, the aging leader had the crowd in his hip pocket. Former light-heavyweight champion and columnist José Torres, who was there, recalls:

> I was one of the many who had thought that the presence of Muñoz in Puerto Rico was going to be irrelevant to the victory or defeat of the Popular Party. But I changed my mind. He still has the magic. When people cried, collapsed and went hysterical, this "objective" agent had goose bumps.

During the next few weeks, Muñoz made countless radio speeches, while Hernández Colón concentrated on public appearances and TV shows.

Election day resulted in a clean sweep for the Popular Democrats, who took 51 yer cent of the vote.

Hernández Colón would govern from La Fortaleza, and Jaime Benítez would be resident commisisoner in Washington. The PDP won control of both legislative houses and took 72 of 76 mayoralty elections. All over the island, the blue-and-white flag of the NPP was removed from roof tops and windows and replaced with the red-and-white banner of the Popular Democrats. Ferré's NPP managed to hold the same 44 per cent of the votes as in 1968, but this time the Commonwealth forces were not divided. The People's

Party of Sánchez Vilella drew less than 1 per cent of the vote, as did each of the two "splinter" independence groups.

While the PIP drew only 52,000 votes (less than 5 per cent) in the governor's race, Senate candidate Rubén Berríos won 94,000 votes. It appeared that many *independentistas* had voted for Hernández Colón to prevent a statehood victory. Also, thanks to the law that guarantees minority representation, two PIP members won seats in the House. For the first time in twelve years, independence had an official voice in the legislature.

The New Government

On the morning of January 2, 1973, Governor Rafael Hernández Colón delivered his inaugural address from the steps of the Capitol Building. Most inaugural festivities were canceled because, two nights before, the island had been shaken by tragedy. Baseball star Roberto Clemente had died in a plane crash while trying to fly medicine and other relief materials to earthquake victims in Managua, Nicaragua.

The new governor dwelt on the "critical problems" of poverty, housing, and health that still affect "thousands upon thousands of Puerto Ricans."

He also pledged to develop the Commonwealth status toward "a maximum of self-government" via negotiations with Washington.

But during his first two years in office, Hernández Colón was engulfed by other, more immediate crises.

Above all was the island's economy, which continued to suffer from its own endemic problems, compounded by a worldwide "stagflation" (a deadly blend of economic recession and price inflation).

Describing the island as "a ship at sea in a storm of gloom," Secretary of State Victor M. Pons said, "We are spectators and victims of larger forces we cannot control."

Bankruptcies doubled in 1974 over the previous year. New U.S. investment in factories diminished because of "tight money" on the mainland. The government—required by law to balance its budget each year—had to borrow $100 million to make ends meet, because tax revenue was much less than anticipated.

The worst of several large strikes was called by the 3,000 employees of the government-owned Aqueducts and Sewers Authority; the governor was forced to call out the National Guard to prevent the sabotage of water supply systems. Proindependence groups had been relatively dormant, because the PDP government did not provide such obvious protest targets as beauty pageants or a U.S. governors' conference. But now they offered strong support to the labor movement, taking part in strikes wherever possible.

Political terrorism continued. Bombs went off in four island cities, and targets included the San Juan offices of ITT and a U.S. Army Reserve motor pool in Ponce. A group known as FALN (Armed Forces of National Liberation) set off bombs in midtown Manhattan that damaged the buildings of such corporate giants as Exxon and Chase Manhattan. That same week, a proindependence rally in New York's Madison Square Garden attracted 20,000 supporters, who demanded "a U.S. Bicentennial without colonies."

When newly confirmed Vice President Nelson Rockefeller and Secretary of State Henry Kissinger· flew to Puerto Rico for a brief rest during the 1974 Christmas holidays, bombs damaged two San Juan branches of the Chase Manhattan Bank (of which Rockefeller's brother David is board chairman).

Up to that point, the terrorism had brought no fatalities. But on January 11, 1975, independence sympathizers gathered in a restaurant in Mayagüez, prior to a rally in the town plaza. A bomb killed two men and injured ten persons, including a six-year-old child. Independence groups blamed "right-wing extremists, backed by the CIA."

Two weeks later, in New York's financial district, a bomb burst inside the front door of a crowded restaurant, killing four persons and injuring fifty others. A note found in a phone booth near the blast, signed by the FALN, took credit for the bomb, claiming it was "in retaliation" for the "CIA-ordered bomb" in Mayagüez. Violence was engendering violence.

As unemployment soared to above 14 per cent and inflation continued at double the mainland rate, the government tried to control prices of basic commodities, but hoarding and the reaction of the business community drove prices still higher. The government opened a string of regional food warehouses, hoping to cut prices by reducing "middleman" handling. There was hope that the poor would be aided by expansion of the Federal food stamp program and that public works jobs could be created with Federal funding.

In the midst of these crises, Hernández Colón tried to fulfill party platform goals to make the island more self-sufficient or autonomous. The Puerto Rico Telephone Company was purchased for $346 million. Three major U.S. shipping lines were also purchased, to give the island its own maritime fleet and, it was hoped, reduce the costs of imported food, consumer goods, and industrial raw materials. But critics complained that the high prices paid for the phone company and the shipping lines constituted "highway robbery."

The financial doldrums continued. To boost tourism, slot machines were legalized in major hotels. To set an example, Commonwealth cabinet officers took voluntary pay cuts.

At the end of 1974, newspapers totted up a crime "box score" that was "unprecedented": a total of 83,000 crimes meant a 20 per cent increase over 1973, with robbery up 76 per cent and murders 37 per cent.

Columnist Juan M. García Passalacqua enumerated the island's hit parade songs of 1974, noting that they were an accurate index of popular sentiment. They dealt with "a woman who is sick of men governing the island, a party where there is only one chicken among too many guests, a complaint about the lack of rice and gasoline, the cry of a *jíbaro* talking about Puerto Rico as a bleeding people . . . a complaint of people who are sick of 'the same thing' year in and year out."

Some of Puerto Rico's "essential contradictions" were becoming "more visible," said a *San Juan Star* editorial. The governor, it said, "carried to Washington the traditional fight for more autonomy from Federal laws. But in the same briefcase, he carries pleas for more and more Federal dollars."

In many respects, Puerto Rico is back where it was nearly a century ago. There is far greater individual liberty and wealth, but the island—once a poor stepchild of Spain—is now in somewhat the same position under the United States. Puerto Rico's emissaries now hop jets to Washington, just as they once boarded ships for the arduous voyage to Madrid.

"Our relationship with Washington," says one middle-aged Puerto Rican, "reminds me of the old Spanish tune that goes *'No quiero que te vayas, ni quiero que te quedes.'* That means, I don't want you to leave, nor do I want you to stay.' "

To moral absolutists at both extremes of Puerto Rico's political spectrum, such a dilemma is outrageous. But not to the pragmatists who have tried to guide Puerto Rico's "placid little boat" for the greater part of the past century. What good is there, they might respond, in aiming for a distant port, if you can't keep the ship afloat in the first place?

Although he retired from an active role in politics a few years ago, Luis Muñoz Marín continues to be the most influential figure in the island's contemporary history. Once comfortably in the countryside, his Trujillo Alto home is now surrounded by the material progress that he helped to bring about. Where, a few years ago, one heard, after sundown, only the pleasant call of the *coquí,* its song is now sometimes drowned out by cars on a new superhighway that passes directly in front of his small estate. The government of the island is still run by Muñoz' colleagues or his protégés. To the extent that any man can shape his world, today's Puerto Rico— in all its complexity—*is* Muñoz. Its brash laissez-faire economy and humane government welfare statism, its hodgepodge of North and Latin American values, its midway political status—all reflect his brillance and ambivalence.

During his long career on the tightrope, statehooders called Muñoz everything from a Communist to an *independentista* in sheep's clothing. The *independentistas,* in the meantime, say he "betrayed" his early ideal. But men of all political shades concede that Muñoz is the type of political giant who occurs rarely in a nation's history. In a society of political mavericks, given to the bickering and rhetoric that spawns a galaxy of mini-factions, Muñoz held together a movement that ruled Puerto Rico for over a quarter of a century. With shrewd tactics and language, with wit and style, and, sometimes, with anger, he persuaded (by the ballot, not the bullet) his people to follow him along an uncharted course, to an undefined destination.

In retrospect, he turned out to be very much like his father, who once wrote:

> . . . if it were possible to open the heart of every Puerto Rican, and if it were possible to see the collective soul of the million beings who inhabit this forgotten rock, we would see there written, in indelible letters, the word "independence."

and who also wrote, "Let us limit our desire to the dictates of reason, rather than waste our energies in fruitless combat. . . . Today's world is not one of dreams and mirages. Platonism leads nowhere in our era."

In a recent interview, Muñoz defended the validity of the commonwealth status which he founded:

> Before the Popular Party, political status was conceived as an *a priori* condition in order to bring about change. If you were for independence, you were for independence because in the abstract it was a good thing. The same for statehood. Then you made your economic and social arguments as a rationalization to tally with your *a priori* conception on political status. But our approach was different. The people of Puerto Rico have no shoes for their feet, they haven't enough food, or schools; wages are miserable, working hours are long. *This* we must solve first. We made the political status the servant of what kind of civilization the people of Puerto Rico wanted for themselves, instead of making the civilization subservient to the political status conceived *a priori*.

In his view, commonwealth needs only perfection. He wishes that a moratorium would be declared on the status issue "for thirty to fifty years."

On the much discussed issue of Puerto Rican culture, Muñoz feels that:

> . . . the culture of a people, in the anthropological sense, is duly protected by the more self-government they have. I assume the people of Puerto Rico want permanent union with the United States, so they must have the maximum of self-government within

that permanent union, which commonwealth does, more than state-hood.

And, when asked what kind of culture will that produce, he replied: "I don't know. I may not like it, you may. But if the people have self-government, the culture they produce is the one they should have."

At the age of seventy-seven, Muñoz Marín knows there is little more he can do to radically change what he, more than any man in Puerto Rico, has wrought. Now it is up to younger men. Speaking at the grave of his father in July, 1973, Muñoz said that Puerto Rico was "on the verge of a new era." He noted that, while the island had achieved great economic growth, 13 per cent of Puerto Rico's families must subsist on less than $500 a year. "We are mired in an unjust and perplexing world," he said, asking, "is it fair that we legitimize the right of some to dispose of millions, with or without personal merit . . . while there are others who live in squalor and misery?" As for political status, he said: "I hear talk about tightening or loosening the ties between Puerto Rico and the United States. I say to all my countrymen that to tighten sometimes chokes and smothers, and that the only democratic way to strengthen bonds is to loosen and destroy chains."

Thus modern Puerto Rico, with all its problems and great promise, is the monument that Muñoz leaves behind. But with the political status yet undecided, critics and admirers can only be tentative in appraising the Muñoz era.

Proindependence writer César Andreu Iglesias, who has been one of Muñoz' most severe (and perceptive) critics, is too honest a man to make a final judgment now. Recently he wrote: "From every point of view, for better or worse, Muñoz is the key man of the times. What he is really worth as a man, and especially as a leader of his people, only the future can tell."

5 The Economy

The people of the Commonwealth need jobs and want work. . . .
Manufacturers are automatically exempt from federal taxes in Puerto
Rico. You pay no corporate or personal taxes. And by Commonwealth
law, you are exempt from Puerto Rican taxes. . . . In the chemical
industry, the profit-to-sales ratio averages 48.9 per cent in Puerto
Rico against 5.9 per cent on the mainland . . . one company in the
Fortune 1000 earns more than 30 per cent of its total corporate profits
from its plants in Puerto Rico.

—*Fomento* advertisement in
Time magazine, 1974

Since World War II, factories have replaced—and dwarfed—farms
as the dynamo of Puerto Rico's economy. Until the recession of
1974, the island's economic growth rate was about 10 per cent
yearly, a figure that outpaced the expansion of the European Common Market and was matched by few nations in the world.

Puerto Rico's gross national product was $6.4 billion in 1973, far
higher than any of its Caribbean neighbors.

Net income in 1973 was $5.3 billion, compared with only $1.9
billion a decade before, and a mere $225 million in 1940. Manu-
facturing generates about one-fourth of every net income dollar
and is largely responsible for a vigorous construction and commercial sector. Tourism and agriculture, in that order, are the next
largest growth areas of the economy.

TABLE 2. Employment in Puerto Rico

	1940	1950	1960	1970	1973
Labor force (in thousands)	602	686	625	827	921
Employed (in thousands)	536	596	542	738	810
Unemployed (in thousands)	66	88	83	89	111
Percentage of labor force unemployed	11	13	13	11	12
Employment by industry (in thousands):					
Agriculture, forestry and fishing	230	216	125	74	58
Manufacturing	56	55	81	141	163
Commerce	54	90	97	138	170
Government	19	45	62	113	154
Other	177	190	177	272	265

Source: "Socio-economic Statistics of Puerto Rico, Fiscal Years 1940, 1948, 1950, 1960 to 1973," Commonwealth of Puerto Rico, Puerto Rico Planning Board, Bureau of Statistics.

Despite these gains, Puerto Rico is very poor in comparison with the United States. Its 1973 per capita income of $1,834 a year (compared with $118 in 1940) was about one-third of the U.S. level. A large middle class has been created, but nearly two of every three families are below the Federal poverty line.

A growing population and the rapid decline of farm jobs have kept Puerto Rico's official unemployment rate at a chronically high level of 10 per cent, which soared to 18 per cent in early 1975. Between 1960 and 1973, the number of employed persons grew from 542,000 to 810,000, but the labor force increased so quickly that the number of unemployed also grew—from 83,000 to 111,000. The crisis would be more severe if more than 750,000 Puerto Ricans had not migrated to the United States since World War II.

The high official jobless rate does not tell the whole story. Unemployment hovers close to 30 per cent if one counts the *ociosos voluntarios* (voluntarily idle), who neither work nor seek a job since their lack of skills makes the task seem hopeless. The "voluntarily idle" do not figure in labor force statistics on unemployment.

Island economist Hubert Barton claims that "underutilization of human resources . . . is about six times greater than the U.S. average. It is about double the amount of unemployment experienced by the United States in the great depression of the 1930's."

Puerto Rico must run fast to keep the jobless rate in check because it imports about half the goods and services it consumes. Since half of any wage increase goes into higher demand for imports and does not stimulate local production, the multiplying power of new dollars is low (on the other hand, about 98 per cent of a U.S. wage increase goes into domestic consumption, creating many more new jobs).

The island's place within the U.S. tariff and monetary structure attracts American investors because stable politics, modest wage scales, adequate productivity, and long tax-exemption holidays equate to high profits. This would not be so if Puerto Rico were fully subject to the flat minimum wage required by the U.S. Fair Labor Standards Act. Because of Puerto Rico's still-impoverished living standard, Washington allows minimum wages to be fixed on an industry-by-industry basis. Review boards, comprising representatives from labor, management, and government (Federal and insular) examine each industry and raise minimum wages on a cautious basis. However, when Federal wages are raised on a percentage basis, these increases are effective in Puerto Rico. Thus, a combination of locally and federally induced actions have caused wages to increase at a faster rate than the U.S. average in recent years.

The possibility of vigorous economic growth has been due to the man-made conditions created by Puerto Rico's planners. The island's autonomy allows the flexibility needed to legislate a separate economic "climate."

With a limited land area and a large population with a high birth rate, as well as scant local investment capital, it was decided to bet heavily on manufacturing (which offers higher wages and more yield per acre than farming). If factory jobs were wanted, the key question asked by Puerto Rico's pragmatic leaders was: How can we attract investors, plenty of them, and fast? Their answer was to offer every conceivable incentive.

An economist who came to Puerto Rico after World War II

first viewed the idea of industrial tax exemption as "abhorrent," but a Puerto Rican colleague smiled and said, "You'll learn." Today, the same economist says that "Puerto Rico's economic muscle was developed on the idea that our internal homogeneity (political, cultural, social) would enable us to play pragmatic games," such as the "Operation Bootstrap" industrial incentives program. "This has worked, and can continue to do so," he says.

There is an undercurrent (sometimes a public outcry) of concern over the *"americano* invasion" of the island's economy, but few complaints are heard from the wage-earning class, many of whom for the first time have a job, an automobile, and a decent home. They seem to care little whether their company's profits flow to San Juan, New York, or Copenhagen, so long as they get a share. Critics of the present development program—there are many—will receive little broad-based support unless they offer some viable alternative. In fact, many Puerto Rican wage-earners claim they prefer to work in *americano*-owned firms because they say they enjoy better wages, fringe benefits, and working conditions than those offered by traditional local entrepreneurs. "The old *latino* businessmen," said one factory hand recently, "think they're back in the 1940's. They want you to work for next to nothing." On the other hand, there is little awareness here of the struggles endured by the American labor movement earlier in the twentieth century to win worker rights that U.S. corporations now concede as "a cost of doing business."

Manufacturing

More than 100,000 of Puerto Rico's 163,000 manufacturing workers are employed in the 1,700 factories "promoted" by the Economic Development Administration (*Fomento,* in Spanish), the government agency responsible for industrial growth. Return on investment in *Fomento* plants averages better than 20 per cent a year and, in the new chemical industry, has gone as high as 48 per cent.

Close to one-third of the *Fomento* plants produce wearing apparel. The next largest areas are food products, electrical products, footwear, textiles, metal products and machinery, and chemicals. Four stages trace the rise of industrialization in Puerto Rico:

(1) before 1940, "manufacturing" meant a sugar mill, a cigar-wrapping shop, or a home in the hills where a housewife sewed gloves (precut in the U.S.) on a piecework basis; (2) in the 1940's the government tried to build an industrial infrastructure by opening its own plants to make key products from scrap or native raw materials; (3) in the 1950's, an influx of U.S.-owned subsidiary plants imported raw materials and used labor-intensive methods to make textiles, apparel, and electronic parts; and (4) in the 1960's, there was growing emphasis upon heavy equipment and high capital investment industries, especially the processing of imported petroleum into chemicals that serve as new raw materials for other island-based plants. Armed with charts that show the impressive profits made by U.S. investors in light industry, *Fomento* began to aggressively seek heavy industry. It had a convincing argument: new factories enjoy a minimum of ten tax-free years and up to twenty-five years if they locate near rural "poverty pockets"; the labor cost differential between Puerto Rico and the U.S. is considerable; the government leases or sells new factory buildings at modest rates; it also offers marketing data, trains personnel, and, sometimes, gives loans to new ventures.

Those who criticize the industrial incentives system on a "moral" basis claim that it unfairly permits companies to reap high profits, without leaving a share in the island treasury. But those who support the program insist that, without such incentives, U.S. investment would not be attracted to the island. They add that the 1,700 plants in the tax-free program employ thousands of workers who *do* pay taxes, and those workers' incomes generate nearly twice as many indirect jobs, which also produce tax revenue. Furthermore, they say, a study made in 1966 showed that of 265 companies whose tax exemption had expired, 218 of them found it profitable enough to remain open, as taxpayers (Puerto Rico's corporate tax rate is lower than that in the United States, and Commonwealth law allows flexible depreciation allowances after the tax holiday; also, expanding companies can build a factory next door, which qualifies as a brand-new, tax-exempt business).

A brief historical review is helpful in understanding how manufacturing growth occurred and how the island's small, sensitive economy has been hurt and helped by external conditions.

Early 1900's

Of 1 million population in 1909, Puerto Rico had only 15,000 factory workers. During the next decade, nearly one-third of the island's few factories were bankrupted by import competition.

But World War I brought about a large home needlework industry, because America could no longer import European embroidery across the submarine-infested Atlantic. Thousands of women worked at home while tending to their children, and their husbands labored in seasonal cane cutting.

The Depression

The Depression hit Puerto Rico with the force of a hurricane. Sugar prices fell, and two real hurricanes (1928 and 1932) nearly crushed the limping economy.

In addition to the sugar crisis, the needlework industry (which employed 40,000 women, mostly at home) was hit in 1935, when a Federal law set $.25 as the minimum hourly wage. Employers, paying one-sixth that amount, deserted and needlework exports fell from $20 million (1937) to $5 million (1940). During that terrible decade, almost all the cigar and cigarette plants also vanished.

The outlook was bleak. Sugarcane provided one-sixth of Puerto Rico's total income, one-fourth of its jobs, and two-thirds of its export dollars. One out of three factories was cane-related, with sugar mills, refineries, rum distilleries, and molasses plants.

In the mid-1930's, America's "New Deal" Government transferred jurisdiction over Puerto Rico from the War Department to the Department of Interior. A new Puerto Rico Emergency Relief Administration gave direct or indirect help to almost one-third of the population via public works projects. By 1935, the Puerto Rico Reconstruction Administration began to operate under large Federal subsidies.

The 1940's

The dovetailing of three circumstances spurred change: (1) World War II had stimulated the U.S. economy; (2) a new reformist government took power in Puerto Rico; and (3) when Federal taxes on Puerto Rican rum sold in the United States were remitted to the local treasury, the island had a development "stake" of $160 million.

In the first attempt to develop a modern economy, the Popular Democrats put raw materials to use in a cluster of government-owned plants. A cement factory used local limestone and other materials; a glass bottle plant used silica sand; plants were opened to make paper cartons for shipping rum bottles to the mainland, shoes, clay products, and to process local fruit.

This drive was organized by Puerto Rico Industrial Development Company, created in 1942 by the government, which also organized a central Planning Board and a Government Development Bank. By 1947, the cement plant was returning healthy profits and the other plants were not far from doing so, but there were problems. It was difficult for government to negotiate wages with its 2,000 factory employees. Expansion capital, which might have enabled the plants to weather the storm, was scarce. Unemployment remained very high. And some U.S. Congressmen and investors were grumbling about "the crazy socialistic experiment going on down in Puerto Rico."

The next year, it was decided to sell the plants to local industrialists and to seek outside private investment for new enterprise. By 1950, the "socialist experiment" was over.

The 1950's

"Operation Bootstrap" was born under the aegis of *Fomento,* which sent emissaries to visit corporations on the mainland and launch an advertising campaign in the United States to promote industry, tourism, and rum. Another positive step was the government's decision to build the island's first modern luxury hotel, the Caribe Hilton, which it leased to the Hilton chain on a profit-sharing basis. The hotel, which has long since paid back the initial investment, now gives the government a profit of $2 million a year, and—more important—primed the pump for private hotel ventures. (The Hilton was also a pleasant place for U.S. businessmen to stay as they contemplated opening an island factory; the prospect of making periodic inspection visits to the new subsidiary and enjoying the sun and casinos on an expense account cannot be underestimated as a plus-factor in the final decision.)

In the early 1950's, when the Korean War caused a tight U.S. labor market, investment money was deflected to the island. Between 1950 and 1954, new factory jobs quadrupled to 22,000, and over 100,000 Puerto Ricans migrated to America, where unskilled jobs were plentiful.

In 1953–54, the U.S. business recession after the end of hostilities in Korea slowed both investment and migration. Several island apparel and footwear plants closed, victims of this slump.

The crisis abated in 1955 when, for the first time in Puerto Rico's history, manufacturing passed agriculture as an income generator. Tourism also grew, and *Fomento* opened a Puerto Rico Industries Department to encourage local venture capital.

By the end of the decade, Puerto Rico had over 500 new factories, employing 45,000 workers. Plant managers (almost half of them native) found that island workers—despite a low level of formal education—were readily trained and productive. The main problem was a high turnover rate, since the most skilled often migrated to higher mainland salaries or were bid away by other local companies.

The 1960's and 1970's

Average factory wages rose, from $.89 an hour in 1960 to $1.68 in 1969, and to $2.38 in 1974, but the differential remained large; U.S. plant workers still averaged over $1 more per hour than those in island plants.

New plants were larger and more highly automated, and the capital-intensive petrochemical industry began to come "on stream," while some apparel and other labor-intensive factories migrated to countries with lower wage scales. Management was (and is) plagued by a shortage of skilled workers (electricians, tool and die makers, mechanics). It is hard to find them in a society where most middle-aged adults were born on a farm; the government offers college scholarships for studies in engineering and the sciences, but it is not deluged by applicants in a society that prizes traditional professions, such as law or medicine, or white-collar work.

Since the mid-1960's, Puerto Rico has been fairly successful in attracting heavy industry. On the south coast, several petrochemical plants have sprung up in fields that once nourished sugarcane. These factories pay higher wages than do the apparel plants, and they hire more men (about 60 per cent of the *Fomento* factory workers today are women). The new petrochemical plants need relatively few people (the multimillion dollar Phillips Petroleum "core" plant, for example, employs only 350), but government planners hope for an eventual "seedbed" return, since the petrochemical operations produce many synthetic raw materials, which may attract more labor-intensive plants.

Agriculture

The expansion of manufacturing has been accompanied by a sharp decline in agriculture. In 1950, Puerto Rico's farm products earned $186 million. By 1973, farm production was worth $321 million, but agriculture now represents a much smaller share of the economy, in both jobs and income.

Sugar, coffee, and tobacco—the traditional export "cash crops"— are still important, but they have been crippled by labor shortages, the pressure of new housing upon farmland, and the lack of investment in modern methods. Thirty years ago, one of every four workers earned his living from the land. Today, the ratio is one in fourteen; factory jobs are not only easier but they pay much more.

A modern agriculture is slowly emerging. Livestock and dairy products, such as beef cattle, pigs, chickens, eggs, and milk, now constitute over half the dollar volume of local farms. Sugar, vegetables and fruits, coffee, tobacco, and molasses represent the remainder. Experiments in the cultivation of home-grown rice are also being conducted.

Farming is moving toward the intensive cultivation of reduced land areas, higher wages, and machines to do the work of several men. The painful by-product is the social problem caused by the phasing out of traditional life styles among thousands of rural families, few of whom have the know-how or capital needed for "modern" farming.

The plight of fifty-year-old Ramón Méndez is shared by many men his age. He owns six acres of jagged hilltops and deep ravines in the northwest mountains. For years, he supported his wife and six children by working half the year in nearby canefields belonging to the mill. His wages of $.60 an hour, together with the $300 yearly he earned from two acres of his own cane, plus a few hundred from selling fruits and vegetables during the "dead season," gave him $1,200 a year. On his own farm he produced enough staples, such as eggs, chickens, plantains, bananas, peas and yams—and on special occasions, he slaughtered a hog—to survive. Three years ago, "When costs went up and sugar prices went down, I wound up owing the mill money!" The next year, the mill closed.

Too old to adapt to factory work, he now plants a few crops on what was once cane land, gets an occasional day's work when a contractor builds a home nearby. He looks to the city, where he has never lived. He also thinks about migration to the United States (he has never been there and speaks no English) where he could earn $2.30 an hour picking tomatoes. But he hesitates to leave his wife and young children alone. He is too proud to go on relief. "The young fellows don't want to sweat the way I have," he says. His twenty-one-year-old son left the island three years ago, before finishing high school, and now drives a truck in New Jersey. His two younger sons, now in grade school, will also probably head for the city when their time comes.

Thus, the countryside is filled with women, young children, and old men (half of the farmers are forty-five years old or more, and 14 per cent are past retirement age).

Sugar Cane

Sugar, the perennial "king" of Puerto Rico's economy, is in serious trouble.

Before 1900, cane was only moderately important, but large U.S. interests built mills and bought vast tracts of land. In 1952, production reached a peak of 1.3 million tons; there were 19,000 farms planted in cane and thirty-six sugar mills. Since then, 7,000 farms and sixteen mills have disappeared; others are in precarious states. The 1973 crop yielded only 249,000 tons.

Twenty-five years ago, there were 148,000 men to cut the cane. Today there are only 14,000. Farmers Association President Orestes

Ramos has said that immigrant workers from Jamaica. Haiti, and Barbados should be called in, but the idea is strongly opposed. Over 100 cane-cutting machines have been purchased, but they are useless on hilly terrain. Occasional storms and severe south-coast droughts have also hurt the sugar crop.

The sugar industry is regulated by Federal and local laws, which limit the amount of cane that may be processed and refined. This also guarantees Puerto Rico about 7 per cent of the U.S. sugar quota, at prices far higher than those on the world market. In recent years, production has fallen far short of the annual quota of 1.3 million tons of sugar. Washington will inevitably cut this quota to a level closer to actual output and dole out the rest to other sugar producers, such as the Dominican Republic, which must often sell its surplus at low world prices.

Sugar, now going through a period of downward readjustment, will probably level off when cultivation is limited to flat land where machines can do the work. It now takes eighty-five man-hours of field labor to plant, grow, harvest, and deliver enough Puerto Rican cane to grind a ton of sugar. In Hawaii, machines and high-paid operators take only twelve man-hours to do this job. Government planners see the drop in cane production as inevitable, but its total disappearance would also cause raw material crises in the rum, molasses, and bagasse industries.

Other Crops

Puerto Rico's rich, dark-roast coffee, whose bushes grow under the protective shade of larger plants, once graced the dining tables of Europe's most elegant homes. For many years, the Vatican's coffee came from a small farm in Puerto Rico. But at the turn of the century a hurricane and U.S. tariff barriers dealt telling blows to the industry.

Coffee is still an important crop, and it receives government price support and export subsidies to help it compete with production from abroad.

Tobacco was cultivated before Columbus arrived. In 1822, an American visitor wrote that Puerto Rico's tobacco is "more highly esteemed by the Dutch and Germans than that of Cuba, and always commands the highest prices." Today, many of the cigars sold in the United States are manufactured in Puerto Rico, from a combination of local and imported tobacco. The largest plant is Consolidated Cigar in Cayey, which makes many well-known brands (Muriel, Dutch Masters, El Producto). Small amounts of chewing tobacco are also home-grown and retailed in the country by men on horseback.

Puerto Rico's main starchy vegetables are plantains (the most important by far), sweet potatoes, taniers, yams, and dasheens. Some of these are exported to Puerto Rican communities on the mainland. On the south coast some cane land now produces tomatoes, sold fresh locally and to neighboring islands and, also, processed into canned sauce, juice, and catsup. Similar agroindustries are under way with pineapple and guava.

The major fruits are pineapples, oranges, avocadoes, mangoes, lemons, papaya, acerola, guava, and tamarind, some of which are exported. But due to irregular production and haphazard marketing, many fresh fruits are also imported from the U.S. mainland.

Dairy and Livestock

Dairy, livestock, and poultry production, which has a high per-acre yield and also enjoys a ready local market, has flourished in the past two decades. The adoption of modern methods and the availability of locally produced animal feed have been key factors.

Milk output (now 27 per cent of agroproduction) exceeds the per capita level on the U.S. mainland. Gains have also been made in beef, pork, chicken, and eggs, but these meet strong competition from U.S. producers who fly in their refrigerated products at, sometimes, lower prices.

Agriculture's Future

Despite Puerto Rico's limited land area (it has only about one-fourth of an arable acre per person, one of the lowest ratios in the world), its good climate, growing local market, and potential for air-shipping certain products to the mainland make its future promising. The family farm, however, is fast becoming an anomaly and serves more of a social than an economic need. Tomorrow's successful farms will have to follow the pattern of industrialized states, such as New Jersey, with efficient production and marketing techniques, coordinated with nearby canning, processing, and packing plants.

In the meantime, the government tried to ease the farm labor shortage by lifting wages (via subsidies to employers) to $1 an hour by 1971.

Tourism

Puerto Rico has converted its most plentiful natural resource—year-round summer weather—into a profitable industry. When Cuba and the United States severed relations in 1962, Puerto Rico's already growing tourism industry took on speed. Good climate, attractive beaches, and low-cost air connections to the U.S. eastern seaboard have helped the island become the most-visited area in the Caribbean.

Between 1963, and 1973, tourism income grew from $85 million to $317 million per year.

The island had only 600 guest rooms in 1940. Today, nearly eighty hotels (more than half in San Juan) have about 8,500 rooms. The 40,000 visitors of 1940 have since multiplied to over 1.3 million a year; about half of these are Puerto Ricans who live in the United States and come to visit friends or relatives.

Most tourist attractions—shops, restaurants, and supper clubs that feature famous U.S. entertainers—are in the "Miami-ish" Condado and Isla Verde sections of San Juan, facing the Atlantic coast. Also popular is nearby Old San Juan, with restored Spanish colonial homes, museums, historic fortresses, and even discotheques and hippies, who congregate about a block from El Convento Hotel, a restored sixteenth-century convent, which highlights flamenco dancing.

Other types of hotels are also available, such as the informal Hotel Barranquitas in the mountains (which is operated by the government as a training school for hotel employees) and the luxurious Dorado Beach estate, several minutes from San Juan, with hundreds of acres of palm-treed golf links. All of this in a "foreign" atmosphere, which is not too "foreign," since the drinking water is safe and many Puerto Ricans, fellow American citizens, speak English.

Cultural events, such as the annual Casals Festival, the Puerto Rican Theater Festival, concerts, art exhibits, and first-run films in English (with Spanish titles) also make the island attractive for the visitor.

About 90 per cent of Puerto Rico's tourists come from the United States, and most are from eastern states, such as New York, New Jersey, Pennsylvania, and Florida. Many tourists also hop over to nearby St. Thomas (half an hour on a local carrier) to buy duty-free cigarettes or liquor. They also frequent the government-supervised casinos in the larger hotels.

As hotel (and casino) revenue climbs, there has been increased concern over possible Mafia infiltration. Government officials claim that some persons "with interests in hotels here maintain close friendships" with members of the Mafia and professional gamblers who "stay in the hotels, but are not registered." They have also criticized the practice of some large hotels, which fly in junkets of heavy gamblers from the United States, offering them free room and board if they buy $500 worth of chips in advance.

Major hotels derive from one-fourth to one-half of their income from gambling casinos. Loopholes in local tax laws permit hotels to charge sizeable parts of their total overhead deduction against their casino operations. For example, a hotel with a gross income of $8.9 million a year, including $2.2 million from its casino, was allowed to deduct over $900,000 in overhead against its casino (whereas overhead was really $100,000). This gives the hotel $800,000 in tax-free income.

There is also concern over the conversion of some parts of San Juan, particularly the once sedate Condado section, into ugly, over-commercialized zones.

But tourism is an efficient dollar-producer. It employs over 9,000 Puerto Ricans at fairly good salaries. The multiplier of the tourism dollar is 3.7, higher than dollars from manufacturing, which depend upon imported raw materials.

But hotel occupancy rates dropped from 81 per cent in 1960 to 67 per cent in 1973, largely due to soaring costs in luxury hotels, where rooms run as high as $100 per day.

In order to lure more visitors, the government recently allowed the installation of "one-armed bandits" in gambling casinos. Also, to appeal to families with more modest income, it has created a chain of small, quaint Spanish-style *paradores* in more remote areas of the island.

Mining

Puerto Ricans have been told so often—even in their grade school texts—that the island lacks mineral resources, that no one really believed the news headlines in early 1965. They said that copper ore deposits worth $3 billion had been found in the rugged mountain country of the northwest, near Utuado, Lares, and Adjuntas. Even today, after a decade of controversy over royalties, possible contamination, and other details, with the signing of the copper mining contracts still imminent, many islanders still express doubt.

In the early sixteenth century, Puerto Rico's economy was based on gold mining, but the small deposits soon ran out. Since then, the most productive aspect of mining has been nonmetals, such as cement, sand, gravel, stone, marble, clays, lime, and salt, which earn about $40 million a year.

Until the copper was found, the mining of metal ore seemed improbable. There are also large known deposits of iron (mixed with nickel and cobalt) near Mayagüez, but the housing there may be worth more than the ore beneath it. Geological studies on the north and south coasts also hint at possible petroleum deposits, but four probes have been fruitless.

It came as somewhat of a shock, then, in early 1965, when it was announced that two U.S. companies (Bear Creek Mining, a subsidiary of Kennecott Copper, and Ponce Mining, a subsidiary of American Metals Climax) planned to exploit copper deposits here. Land speculation in the area began. Conservationists warned of contamination hazards. *Independentistas* claimed the companies would be "stealing" the copper because they would pay low royalties to the government and enjoy tax exemption. Some radical groups opposed the mines under any circumstances, mainly, it seems, because American companies were involved.

Since then, numerous studies have been made and extensive bargaining has been carried out between the government and the companies; contracts are still unsigned but it appears that they plan a joint venture with two mines and a smelter operating for twenty-five to thirty years, with an investment of $100 million. The gutted open-pit mine area "could" be converted into lakes, the companies say.

During the negotiations, the government seems to have extracted better financial terms than those originally agreed upon. An Ecuadorian engineer said in 1970, however, that these terms were "not nearly as good" as those arranged in his country, where Kennecott offered Ecuador 50 per cent of the profits in a new mining venture (much more than it had offered in Puerto Rico), only to be outbid by a Japanese firm that offered 85 per cent.

Fishing

Puerto Ricans consume more fish per capita than do North Americans, but much of it is in the form of *bacalao,* dried salted codfish imported from the north.

The island's surrounding waters are too deep to attract large, commercially exploitable schools of fish. But four large plants in Mayagüez and Ponce process and can tuna caught in modern ships, which roam as far east as Africa's coast and, also, cross the Panama Canal to "farm" the coastal waters of Peru. These plants provide a major portion of the tuna for America's east coast markets.

Salt water sports fishing has grown in popularity. Several world record catches have been made off Puerto Rico, which is described as "the outstanding blue marlin fishing spot in the world" by Esteban Bird in his book *Fishing off Puerto Rico.* Other abundant sports fish, he says, are Allison tuna, dolphin, arctic bonito, sailfish, pargo, snook, sabalo, and wahoo.

Forestry

During the nineteenth century, as population grew from 155,000 to nearly 1 million, the forests shrank from 75 to 25 per cent of the island's surface, as trees were felled for home building and kitchen fuel. By 1950, only 9 per cent of Puerto Rico was forested.

But strict conservation measures by Federal and insular agencies have permitted a comeback, and trees now cover 19 per cent of the land. The first major step was the takeover, in 1903, of the 28,000-acre Luquillo Forest Reserve by the government, which has also distributed millions of young trees to private farm owners. The increase of cement homes and gas or electric cooking ovens has also relieved much of the demand for timber. To combat erosion, a number of grasses (including the imported pangola and kudzu) have been widely planted, spurred by government cash incentives. The pangola is also excellent for cattle grazing. The government forest reserves have become popular weekend retreats for tourists as well as locals, seeking respite from the new suburbia, where most trees are felled to make way for homes and highways.

Currency

Puerto Rico's currency system is, today, the same as in the United States, except that Spanish words are used to describe American money. A dollar, sometimes called a *dólar,* is also called a *peso.* A half-dollar is a *medio peso* and a quarter a *peseta.* The English word "dime" is often used to describe the ten-cent piece, although *vellón de diez* is also employed. A nickel is called *un vellón de cinco,* and a penny is called a *centavo,* a *chavo,* or, more colloquially, *"una perra,"* meaning a female dog, something virtually worthless. In the countryside, some oldtimers still refer to Spanish coinage, such as when they say *dos reales* for a quarter, or *seis reales* for 75 cents.

Until the early nineteenth century, Puerto Rico used the coins of many nations. The most important was the Spanish milled dollar (*peso de cordoncillo*) and its fractions, according to Edward H. Roehrs, a specialist in Puerto Rican currency. These eight *real* pieces were minted in Mexico, Lima, or Guatemala and circulated in Puerto Rico, together with coins from France, England, Mexico, and the United States. Even after Spain's colonies went independent in the mid-1820's, Spanish-American coins continued to circulate in Puerto Rico.

In 1857, a Spanish Royal Decree ordered all crudely made cob silver coinage withdrawn from circulation. By the 1870's, coins were so scarce that they were punched with holes, making them worthless elsewhere, to prevent their removal from the island. In 1895, when orders came to prepare Puerto Rico's own currency, all silver coins were withdrawn and temporary *billetes de canje* ("notes of exchange") were circulated, bearing the inscription *Isla de Puerto Rico*. In 1896, coins with the same inscription, similar in design to those used in Spain, were introduced in Puerto Rico. When the United States took the island in 1898, local money was withdrawn and replaced by U.S. currency, at the rate of 60 American cents per *peso*.

In the countryside, in the late nineteenth century, plantation owners and merchants improvised their own local money because of coin shortages. These tokens were known as *riles* (a corruption of the Spanish *real*), *fichas,* or *chapas*.

Plantation owners stamped over old currency of other countries with the symbol of their farms or, sometimes, minted their own crude copper or brass coins. The denominations were often rooted in agricultural terms. For example, an *almud* token stood for about five gallons of freshly picked coffee, since rural Puerto Ricans call such a dry measure an *almud*. Another denomination was the *"jornaldiario,"* which means, literally, a day's work. Since the farms were often in isolated areas, many tokens were only redeemable in the owner's "company store," where he sold the peons food and clothing.

Another form of currency was the *vale,* a crude type of check, upon which the employer wrote out varying amounts of payment, such as: *"Vale* in favor of Sinforiano Camacho, for a day's work with the bees, which is worth forty cents."

Some *vales* could be spent only at the plantation owner's company store, and since many of his workers were seasonal and depended upon his credit throughout the year, they were in perpetual debt. This later led to a law in Puerto Rico that all workers had to be paid in cash.

During the nineteenth century, myriad forms of currency were invented for local use. There were gambling casinos, such as the one in Yauco, whose chips were equivalent to money. Thus, a man who won at the tables the night before could present his chips at a store the next morning when he went shopping.

The oldest known coin which mentions Puerto Rico is a two-*real* piece, dated 1747. Worth about $.25 at the time, it was recently auctioned in New York for $400. The coin, issued to commemorate Fernando VI's ascent to the Spanish throne, shows the traditional kneeling lamb symbol of the island and is inscribed with the Latin *"Portus Dives,"* meaning Rich Port, or Puerto Rico.

Trade and Commerce

After Mexico, Puerto Rico is the largest customer for exports of U.S. goods in all of Latin America. At the same time, the United States is by far the major buyer of Puerto Rican goods. The only other countries in the world that bought more from, or sold more to, the United States were Canada, Japan, the United Kingdom, and West Germany.

Puerto Rico has a large and growing balance of payments deficit. In 1973, its exports were $2.4 billion, compared with $3.4 billion of imports, for an unfavorable balance of $1 billion (it was about $650 million in 1969). The deficit is partly alleviated by funds from Federal agencies and money sent by Puerto Ricans on the mainland to their families. But the plain fact remains that Puerto Rico consumes much more than it produces.

Exports

"New" products—those made in plants established since World War II—now represent the bulk of the island's total exports. These "new" exports are clothing and textiles, chemical products, petroleum and derivatives, machinery, tobacco products, shoes, processed foods, toys, costume jewelry, and metal and paper products, in that order. "Old" exports, such as sugarcane, are declining steadily, with the exception of rum, an important revenue source, which has held steady.

Nearly 87 per cent of Puerto Rico's exports go to the United States, and about 7 per cent go to the Virgin Islands (much of this consists of goods first imported to Puerto Rico), while the remainder goes to foreign countries, mainly Holland, the Dominican Republic, Venezuela, Colombia, Guyana, Surinam, and Haiti.

Imports

Nearly 80 per cent of the $3.4 billion that Puerto Rico imported in 1973 came from the United States.

The nature of imports has changed; in 1950, about 48 per cent were family consumer goods, 40 per cent were raw materials and intermediate products, and 11 per cent were capital goods and equipment. Today, first place is occupied by raw materials and intermediate products (47 per cent), followed by consumer goods (36 per cent) and capital goods and equipment (17 per cent). There has been rapid growth in durable consumer goods, such as electrical appliances and cars (138,086 new cars were registered in 1973, compared with 25,806 in 1960).

Local Commerce

About one-fifth of Puerto Rico's work force is engaged in some branch of commerce, which includes wholesale-retail product sales and service establishments. There are over 40,000 different businesses in Puerto Rico, ranging from tiny owner-operated *colmados* ("grocery stores") to huge chain stores, such as Sears, Woolworth's, Walgreens, J.C. Penney, Franklin's, Grand Union supermarkets, and so on.

Chain stores, grouped into air-conditioned shopping centers, have revolutionized retail marketing on the island. It is now far more efficient, and savings have been passed along to the consumer, although prices are still high. The large chain store is usually American-owned (but Puerto Rican–managed). This, naturally, has brought charges of a "takeover" by foreign interests." However true this may be, it is hard to foresee a short-term change in this trend, since shoppers flock to these stores, which "showcase" their goods more attractively, have convenient parking, and are more liberal with credit. A few "native" entrepreneurs with the capital and expertise to adopt these practices are flourishing, too. Small commerce, particularly that which offers services—restaurants, beauty salons, TV shops, bars, flower shops, auto repair shops—is predominantly in the hands of Puerto Ricans.

Banking and Finance

Puerto Ricans asked Spain to open a bank on the island in 1812, but it was not until 1850 that the London Colonial Bank opened its doors—and closed them three years later—when local merchants exerted pressure in order to maintain their monopoly on granting loans. After two more bank failures, the Caja de Economía y Préstamos opened in 1881, and it endures today as the oldest (and perhaps smallest) island bank. Of today's large banks, two were founded during the Spanish colonial era: the Banco Popular in 1893, and the Banco Crédito y Ahorro Ponceño in 1894.

Today, Puerto Rico has twelve commercial and two government banks, with nearly 200 branch offices, including mobile units that serve rural clientele. Branches of local banks are also located in New York City and compete with American institutions for the financial patronage of the Hispanic community.

Between 1960 and 1973, total bank desposits in Puerto Rico's banks have risen from $562 million to $3.6 billion.

Local banks are now as attractive and efficient as those found on the U.S. mainland and offer identical services. Modern electronic equipment is now widely used, and checking account customers receive computerized monthly statements.

Among the specialized institutions are the Government Development Bank (founded in 1948), which audits the Puerto Rican government, provides credit to private enterprise, and assists the government in floating long-term bonds on the Wall Street market; the Housing Bank (founded in 1961), which provides credit for low-income families to acquire homes on mortgages of up to forty years; and the Cooperative Development Administration, which promotes the growth of local co-ops and has over 100,000 members, most of whom use the organization for low-interest loans.

Several U.S. financial agencies are also active in Puerto Rico and provide over $100 million a year in credit for agriculture, housing, public works, and commerce. These include the Production Credit Association, the Baltimore Bank for Cooperatives, the Federal Intermediate Credit Bank, the FHA, and the Small Business Association.

Debt

Years ago, country people kept their savings in earthen vessels known as *tinajas*, which they buried in the ground. But the age of the *tinaja* is long past, and Puerto Rico's "now-oriented" society has adopted the philosophy of "buy now, pay later" with a vengeance.

Faced by a scarcity of local investment capital, government and private industry borrow abroad to finance roads, schools, hospitals, factories, and hotels. The new middle class, with rising incomes and even faster rising expectations, has responded to liberal consumer credit policies.

Many families spend in excess of their incomes. Credit cards, revolving charge accounts, and loans for vacation trips are now common in Puerto Rico. Banks mail customers blank checks (good for up to $300) with which they can pay their income tax. Although private savings have increased from $152 million in 1960 to $838 million in 1973, the loans outstanding have gone through the roof—from $450 million in 1960 to $3.1 billion in 1973.

Puerto Rico's public debt is growing in real and proportional terms: from 9.2 per cent of total personal income in 1960 to 15 per cent today (this is still modest, however, compared with the 51 per cent in the United States, which is saddled with huge Federal defense expenditures).

From one viewpoint, Puerto Rico is "in hock" to outside creditors for many years to come. But Commonwealth officials contend that the public debt "is not necessarily a burden for future generations" if imported resources are used for "permanent improvements," the benefits of which will be enjoyed by tomorrow's adults. A recent "Report to the Governor" warns, though, that "if these resources are used for current government expenditures [such as salaries] the public debt *will* constitute a future burden." Since much of the government's personnel structure depends for its continued operation upon imported capital, the line between "current expenses" and "permanent improvements" is, at best, thin, if not blurred.

With such extensive debt at all levels of the society, Puerto Rico's economy rests on fragile underpinnings, but it has been held aloft, for now, by a buoyant optimism about the future.

Taxes and Tariffs

In 1970, about 230,000 Puerto Ricans (representing less than half of the island's family units) prepared tax forms, and only 170,000 paid some amount of tax. This reflects the extent of poverty on the island, and also suggests considerable tax evasion by persons at both extremes of the income ladder, whose earnings are not subject to withholding taxes.

Because of this low participation, and the fact that many new factories enjoy ten- to twenty-five-year tax exemption, the government derives much of its income from excise taxes on various items (household furniture, clothing, footwear, medicines, and food are exempt). The heaviest excise tax is on cars, new and used, which can run from $200 for a small foreign vehicle up to thousands of dollars for a luxury model.

To help reduce its large negative trade balance, the government offers tax exemption on island-made products exported to foreign countries. Maritime companies that ship freight to foreign countries also receive ten years of tax exemption.

Despite haphazard collections, government revenue from income tax increased from $62 million in 1960 to $205 million in 1969. The government has launched a publicity plea to "keep Puerto Rico in your heart; your taxes pay for more schools and hospitals." But violations—or legal evasion—are the norm, even in "respectable" circles. Not one of Puerto Rico's seven major banks paid a cent of income tax in 1969.

Transportation

Ships are the lifeline for over 90 per cent of Puerto Rico's off-island commerce, most of which is with the U.S. mainland.

There is a disadvantage in Puerto Rico's being subject to the U.S. Coastal Shipping Law, which requires the use of American vessels between domestic ports. Even though Puerto Rico is over 1,000 miles from America's mainland, it is considered "domestic," and its manufacturers may not use less expensive foreign freighters.

The disadvantage has been reduced somewhat by the use of modern containers, which are lowered or rolled off on tractors and connected to waiting trucks, thus cutting handling costs and eliminating jobs. Now, according to the government, it costs only 4.3 cents to ship a pair of shoes from San Juan to New York, while it costs 8.5 cents via truck from New York to Chicago (which does not explain why consumer goods cost more in San Juan than they do in Chicago).

Because of the growth of crude petroleum imports and refined product exports, the south coast port of Guayanilla (owned by private manufacturing firms) has become Puerto Rico's key industrial port. The government-owned San Juan port is by far the most important for tourism and dry cargo, including consumer goods. Other ports (government and private) are at Aguadilla, Ponce, Mayagüez, Jobos Bay, Fajardo, and Arecibo. Puerto Rico has little internal sea traffic, except for a commuter ferry system between San Juan and Cataño (across San Juan Bay) and another ferry that connects Fajardo and the islands of Vieques and Culebra.

Puerto Rico's commerce and industry have been hard hit by mainland shipping strikes, which require the island to keep its warehouses full of essential products. During one strike in 1968, air cargo was needed to transport vital materials in order to avoid factory shutdowns. In 1974, the government purchased three major shipping lines that serve Puerto Rico in a move to reduce shipping costs.

Air Travel

Puerto Ricans are among the most "flying happy" people in the world, since jobs, relatives, and friends are often located on the U.S. mainland.

Total in-out air traffic has multiplied by sixty in three decades. To handle the increased flow and larger jets, San Juan International Airport was built in 1955 above a mosquito-infested Isla Verde marshland six miles east of San Juan; it replaced Isla Grande Airport, right in town, which is still used for light planes. The large airport now handles 5 million passengers and 200 million pounds of cargo a year; this makes it one of the busiest airports in the world, with more traffic than Berlin, Dallas, Zurich, Madrid, and Athens.

Puerto Rico's airport has a distinctly local flavor. It has been the scene of colossal traffic jams, since huge delegations of friends and relatives often congregate to welcome or see off a traveler. In the terminal, next to sun-baked tourists carrying Rolleis, one still sees the old *abulea* (grandmother) fingering her rosary beads or the solemn young man from the country, in a dark suit, carrying a shiny new suitcase, off to seek work in the truck gardens of New Jersey or the factories of New York or Chicago.

The main air destinations from San Juan are New York–Newark, Miami, Hartford, Washington–Baltimore, Philadelphia, and Chicago. Late in 1970, direct jet service was announced from the south coast city of Ponce to New York.

San Juan is also a jumping off point for South America and the Caribbean, while small "taxi" lines provide commuter service between San Juan, Mayagüez, Ponce, Vieques, and Culebra.

Land Travel

With one car for every five persons, Puerto Rico ranks sixth in the world in auto ownership. On weekdays San Juan's grinding traffic jams prompt some suburbanites to leave home at sunrise to beat the crush. By 1985, if the present growth of motor traffic continues, the only solution, according to one local columnist, is to "add a second floor to the island."

Puerto Rico has 6,100 miles of cement or blacktop roads that link all its cities. The number of registered vehicles has risen from 27,000 in 1940, to 179,000 in 1960, to 675,000 in 1973.

The government-owned Metropolitan Authority has a fleet of buses for San Juan, but service is spotty in the suburbs and countryside. There is also an intercity bus service, including a westward express to Mayagüez. New air-conditioned buses are called *pingüinos* because they have large cartoon-style penguin figures attached to the front to suggest their cool comfort.

Taxis are most common in tourist and business centers. But the *público*—faster than the bus, cheaper than a taxi—is still the favorite mode of intercity travel. These are large U.S. model cars, or "mini-buses," which accept passengers along established routes and charge fixed rates by distance. People flag them down in the same fashion as private taxis. San Juan has several *público* pick-up areas where drivers wait near their cars, which have signs denoting the city to which they travel. As people walk by, the drivers shout "Mayagüez!" or "Ponce!" or "Toa Alta!" until they have filled their cars, whereupon they speed off. Some *público* drivers have been traveling the same route for years and are well-known to passengers. (For example, there is *El Ciego,* the Blind Man, an elderly gentleman with thick glasses, who claims to have never had an accident in his many years on the road.) The island's several thousand *público* drivers have a strong union and represent a potent political force. A *público* strike on election day, for example, could cripple the vote total in many rural areas, where private cars or buses are rare.

Increased auto traffic has caused a high accident rate in Puerto Rico, twice the U.S. average, due to inexperienced drivers and faulty roads. There were 603 traffic fatalities in 1973, compared with 273 in 1960.

In 1970, Puerto Rico became the fifth place in the world to adopt a novel compulsory auto accident compensation plan that covers the entire population. Once the police certify that an accident has taken place, victims are paid by administrative procedures; no fault must be proved through court action. Every person who registers a motor vehicle pays $35 a year to finance the plan. Compulsory motor vehicle inspection was also begun.

Trains. Puerto Rico's first train service, La Compañía de los Ferrocarriles de Porto Rico, was begun in 1891 by a Spanish engineer and taken over by the American Railroad Company in 1902. It followed the coastal plain, connecting San Juan with Mayagüez and Ponce. Helen Tooker, a long-time resident, recalls the train system in the *San Juan Review* magazine:

> At night, the haunting, oddly exciting, faraway sound of the train's whistle could be heard through the tropical night . . . the company . . . operated freight trains after sundown [and] provided sleeping car service between Ponce and San Juan. . . . As late as 1950, the first-class ticket between San Juan and Mayagüez cost only $1.50 and the second-class, 95 cents. Speed was never a characteristic of these trains. They ambled from station to station . . . with frequent halts at whistlestops . . . Train No. 1 departed from San Juan station at 7 A.M. and reached Ponce about 5 P.M.

Aboard the trains, she recalls:

> Venders would invade the coaches at every station . . . at Vega
> Baja and Manatí venders would sell, in season, *pajuíles*, the cashew
> fruit and nut. At Arecibo, there would be a stop for coffee and the
> local specialty was the *empanadilla de ceti*, a fish sandwich. Isabela
> was famous for its *queso de hoja*, small "leaves" of native white
> cheese. At Aquadilla *pecesitos de colores*—gold fish caught in pools
> thereabout—could be bought in a jar of water for twenty-five cents.

In 1929, the first locomotive used on the island was sent to Henry
Ford's transportation museum, but Ford's own automobiles helped
to push the train into extinction. *Públicos* would often lure passengers from the train platform by offering faster, cheaper service.
The train crossings were dangerous; about fourteen persons each
year died in accidents. Other lawsuits arose when sparks from trains
caused canefield fires. The company filed bankruptcy in 1947, but
train employees ran the line for several years more. Finally, the
government took much of the land for roads and public works,
ending a colorful chapter in island history. The only remnant of
a railroad is a few miles of private track along coastal areas for
sugarcane transport.

A rapid rail transit system for metropolitan San Juan has been
in the blueprint stage for years. It would consist of twenty-seven
miles of track from a central terminal, fanning out in four directions to the suburbs.

Energy and Power

Puerto Rico has a modern electrical power system, which serves
over 96 per cent of its population, compared with 80 per cent
in 1960. The system meets a present demand that is triple the
amount used a decade before, and over thirty times the 1940 demand, when only one home in four had electricity.

Electricity is provided by the government-owned Water Resources Authority. Per capita power consumption (a good yardstick
for development) is now about one-fifth of that in the United
States; but demand grows by 15 per cent yearly (twice the U.S.

rate) as more people buy appliances, new communities are built, and new factories open. By the ominous-sounding year 1984, Puerto Rico should quintuple its power use, matching today's U.S. figure.

The island has no known coal or petroleum deposits and, until the 1950's, depended mostly upon a series of artificial dams to generate hydroelectric power. But these limited water resources now supply only 10 per cent of the power; the rest is generated by thermal plants, using imported oil.

Three private companies were the first to produce and distribute electric power in Puerto Rico, but they were bought out by the government in the 1930's and 1940's.

In 1964, the first nuclear power reactor in Latin America, an experimental BONUS design, was established near the south coast at Rincón. It was shut down after three years because of unsatisfactory performance. But a nuclear power reactor—large enough to provide electricity for a community of 200,000 persons —was planned for the south coast by the mid-1970's. The shift to reactor power was favored for several reasons: (1) hydro power is limited and subject to droughts; (2) fossil fuels, such as petroleum, are subject to shipping strikes and have already seriously contaminated San Juan's air; (3) nuclear power is viewed as "clean," although studies must still be made on disposal of wastes and the effect of overheated sea water (used as a coolant) upon the marine environment. In 1972, however, plans to build a nuclear energy plant at Jobos Bay on the south coast were rejected, because the site was close to a potential earthquake zone. For now, the issue of nuclear energy is dormant, but not dead.

Labor Unions

The "father" of Puerto Rico's labor movement is Santiago Iglesias Pantín, a Spanish-born socialist who came to the island in 1896, after being deported from Cuba where he had spent nine years of proworker agitation. The first Monday in September is Labor Day in Puerto Rico, but it is also called Santiago Iglesias Day, in his honor. In 1898, when the Americans invaded, Iglesias was in a jail cell. A year later, despite hounding by the police, he led strikes and protests, which won an eight-hour workday. He also won the reinstitution of the *lector* ("reader") in the tobacco and cigar factories. The *lector* read aloud from books and newspapers while the workers, many of them illiterate, performed their monotonous tasks.

When Iglesias was sentenced to three years in jail on a murder charge, he had to go to the U.S. Supreme Court for a reversal. While in the U.S., he joined the American Socialist Party and gained Samuel Gompers' support.

Iglesias' union, the Federación Libre de Trabajadores (FLT), consisted mainly of seasonally employed, low-paid canecutters. He could not win collective bargaining for the sugar industry until 1933. Instead, he formed the Socialist Party (a branch of the mainland movement) and tried to gain prolabor legislation. His union and his party alienated many local liberals who favored independence. Iglesias was pro-American and advocated U.S. citizenship and eventual statehood, since local industry, dominated by the Spanish colonial heritage, · was violently antilabor, and his strongest support came from labor groups in America. His union, affiliated with the American Federation of Labor, lasted for forty years. The Socialist Party achieved some gains for the workers during 1915–24, when it was at its peak, but it never gained legislative control. In 1924, the Socialists were forced into an uneasy coalition with the conservative Republicans in order to gain a piece of the power. Iglesias later went to Washington as Puerto Rico's Resident Commissioner. The FLT lost its AFL affiliation in 1950 and now has only a few thousand members.

The Confederación General de Trabajadores (CGT) was formed in 1940 by forty-two independent unions, led by the strong Unión de Choferes. Coinciding with the rise to power of the Popular Democrats, the CGT was a volatile alliance of far leftists, liberals, *independentistas,* and autonomists. It organized most of the sugar workers with the help of the Popular Party. The first break in the CGT came in 1945 when the Pro-Independence Party was formed, and some members split away. By 1949, the CGT, cleared of its large independence factions, affiliated with the CIO.

As U.S. industry grew in the 1950's, international unions flocked to Puerto Rico. The first to come, attracted by the new apparel and textile plants, were the ILGWU and the Amalgamated Clothing Workers. They have since been joined by the Seafarers, Teamsters, and others, who, together with the Packinghouse, have been raiding each other and shuffling for position.

By the mid-1960's, the Popular Democratic Party's "prolabor" image had lost much of its luster. Years before, the PDP absorbed most labor leaders into its ranks, and these men were instrumental in passing legislation on minimum wages, vacations, disability insurance, and myriad measures that favored workers. But, as the ruling PDP sought to maintain a "healthful climate" that would lure new industry, its labor leaders were torn by conflicting loyalties. Many of them lost touch with their working class constituencies. A few years later, new leaders emerged from within the ranks of labor, unfettered by demands for party loyalty.

Perhaps the most important recent development in Puerto Rico's economy (and the society as a whole) has been the growth in size and militancy of the labor unions.

The island's work force is still not as unionized as those on the U.S. mainland or in Europe. Most factories are small, and—thanks to existing laws—conditions are often decent enough to blunt the desire to unionize. Many workers are more concerned about job security than wages; in some small towns, for example, there are only a few factories, and job options are scarce.

Nevertheless, despite high levels of unemployment on the island, the labor unions have grown more demanding. This is prompted to a great degree by the cost of living, which has risen at three times the rate on the U.S. mainland. In late 1974, factory workers were earning an average of $2.38 per hour, well below the mainland rate. Also, "real" take-home pay (adjusted for inflation) was only $57.62 per week, while groceries in Puerto Rico cost 20 per cent more than in the U.S. northeast. At the same time, labor leaders are not unaware of the fact that most factories in Puerto Rico are highly profitable. The average ratio of profits to sales in the textile field, for example, is 15 per cent for *Fomento*-promoted plants on the island, compared with only 1.9 per cent for plants in the U.S. In machinery manufacturing, *Fomento* plants yielded a 32 per cent profit, compared with only 4.6 per cent on the mainland.

In 1964, there were only fifty-four strikes island-wide, involving a mere 7,886 workers. In 1974, ninety-five strikes involved 22,109 workers. In the space of one year, the number of man-days lost from strikes doubled to 289,397.

Both government and management have expressed concern over the apparent leftward and proindependence shift of many labor unions. But, if one examines the facts, proindependence groups have merely occupied a vacuum created by the indifference of the major parties.

During recent strikes by the Puerto Rico Telephone Company and a major newspaper (*El Mundo*), proindependence forces joined picket lines, offered legal services, raised bail for jailed strikers, and even served coffee. At the conclusion of three strikes, workers (most of whom are not independence sympathizers) approved an official vote of thanks to the proindependence groups for their help.

Some of the island's most effective union leaders are *independentistas*. One example is Pedro Grant, head of the Boilermakers Union of the AFL-CIO, who also coordinates the United Labor Movement, a group of thirty unions that include workers from private industry and government. Librado Saez, president of the Petrochemical Workers Union, is also a member of the central committee of the Puerto Rican Socialist Party. Others include Luis Pagán, head of the local Teamsters Union, and Juan B. Emmanuelli, who heads the Insular Workers Syndicate.

But, according to Pedro Grant, most labor leaders vote for the PDP; however, "they are young people whom the PDP can't control."

"People are becoming aware that a pat on the back doesn't put bread in the mouth," says one labor leader. "Government paternalism," he adds, "has played a role in Puerto Rico, going back to the old Spaniard who sweated the life's blood of the *jíbaro* and then paid for his burial. Big deal."

Some observers predict that labor union growth augurs the emergence of a class struggle in Puerto Rico. One thing is sure:

As membership drives continue, as strikes proliferate, the labor movement will play an important role in the island's destiny.

The Future of the Economy

The fact that Puerto Rico's economy has grown by about 10 per cent a year for the past two decades has trapped the government in a "success syndrome."

The dread of failure has prompted a yawning "credibility gap" in government reports, especially those that deal with the industrial promotion program. *Fomento* press releases glow with an optimism that rarely fails to be reflected in the gullible insular press.

A classic example is that of Phillips Petroleum, which opened an oil refinery on the south coast in the mid-1960's. Jubilant townspeople composed a *plena* folktune, whose lyrics assured that prosperity was just around the corner. This seemed justifiable since *Fomento* claimed that Phillips and other "satellite" plants using petroleum by-products would create 60,000 new jobs. Phillips today employs 1,100 workers in two plants and may expand for another 800 jobs; it has confirmed no further growth plans.

"If you went back through the daily newspapers over the past ten years," says one observer, "and added up all the new plants that *Fomento* has announced, together with the new jobs that were to be created, it would appear that we were one of the wealthiest industrial centers in the world."

After one strips away the tinsel, however, *Fomento* has been an efficient promoter of jobs. In 1972, for example, more than $1.3 billion of the island's $1.8 billion in exports were produced in *Fomento*-promoted factories.

But the economic recession of the 1970's has bared the fragility of the island's development program. Of the 3,000 factories promoted by *Fomento* in the past two decades, more than 1,000 have folded. One year, while 159 plants opened, 100 shut their doors. In 1974, *Fomento* administrator Teodoro Moscoso said that 155 plants had recently closed (a loss of 4,000 jobs) and "moved elsewhere in the Caribbean." The nearby Dominican Republic has lured away many U.S. manufacturers with its own *Fomento* program, long-term tax exemption, and wage levels that are only one-fourth of Puerto Rico's. Puerto Rican officials now grumble about factories "running away" to such cheap labor areas as Haiti and the Dominican Republic, in much the same way that years before U.S. labor leaders complained that mainland factories were "running away to Puerto Rico."

Difficulty in luring new investment was just part of Puerto Rico's problem in a dismal 1974. Because of rampant inflation, a 10 per cent rise in GNP was totally wiped out and the island's economy had its first "negative increase" in memory. For the first time in its history, the Commonwealth government had to borrow money (over $100 million) to balance its budget, and an even worse deficit (about $200 million) was predicted for the next fiscal year. The crisis was so severe that the island hoped to use Federal "manpower" funds (whose purpose is to give jobs to the unemployed) in order to avoid government job layoffs. Business failures doubled, and the construction industry was at a standstill. The only area of the economy that seemed to prosper was agriculture, where inflation contributed to record food prices and profits.

Things were so bad that one business specialist described 1974 as marking "the close of a nearly unchecked surge of island growth that ran for more than two decades."

Until the recent recession, says one economist, "there has been a naive attitude that things will continue to climb." However, he claims, fast-rising wages and fringe benefits without a corresponding increase in productivity have made Puerto Rico "less attractive to outside investment." He also blames Federal minimum wage increases for "raising the cost of doing business" and says that the island needs "a larger measure of autonomy in setting its own wage levels."

In the countryside, he claims, most people, rather than remain jobless, would be more than willing to work for under the established minimum. He adds:

You know how many factories are *really* brought to Puerto Rico? You find a guy in New York with a brassiere or dress factory. He's planning to open a second plant somewhere. "Whaddya want to go to Mississippi for? It's miserable there. Take a jet to Puerto Rico.

Just three hours. Take a swim. Bring your mistress!" Once the guy's here, he makes a bundle, tax-free, in the first ten years. Wages go up gradually, but he won't leave, because he's content, so long as he's making a profit. But you've got to get him here in the first place, with attractive bait.

Some argue that Puerto Rico's wooing of investment capital and tourism from abroad is "unhealthy" and keeps the island in a perpetual state of dependence.

After hearing this, a technician who has spent years with the industrial development program said, "You're absolutely right. And the minute someone comes up with some alternative that works better, I'll be the first to join him. In the meantime, I'm too busy looking for jobs for our people to worry about it myself."

It appears that few people, however, are searching for alternatives to the present program, which is the product of innovation and willingness to break with old patterns in the 1940's.

In the past two decades, few original economic development ideas have been born in Puerto Rico. The government has been "locked in" to a rigid scheme, where absentee corporations are viewed as the panacea. The creation of a Puerto Rican Industries Department, to encourage local capital, has been little more than a sop to critics, who warn of the "takeover" of the economy by absentee interests. The creation of Puerto Rican–owned cooperatives remains an unfinished task. Impressive statistics on membership in local co-ops reveal that—except for a few supermarkets—most are merely employee credit unions, which facilitate not local production but consumption of imported goods. The creation of government-owned industries and businesses to meet crucial raw material needs or alleviate specific poverty pockets goes strongly "against the grain" of ideological beliefs among today's leaders (many of whom approved of such ideas two decades ago).

In the mid-1960's, for example, the government decided to seek shares in some new ventures opening in Puerto Rico. The idea was to make the people of Puerto Rico "shareholders" in these profitable new firms, and also—via seats on the board of directors—to have at least a minor voice on such policies as marketing, environmental pollution, and others. A major step was the purchase of 25 per cent of the new Phillips Petroleum Refinery, which yielded nearly $3 million in profits for the government by the second year of operation. But, yielding to pressure from Phillips, the government sold back its shares in early 1970. This move was defended by some officials, who claimed that "government has no place in private industry," despite the fact that two government-owned hotels (leased to private firms) have returned substantial profits over the years.

In 1951, economist Harvey Perloff, who has studied the island's development, praised the "realistic" approach of the Scandinavian countries in solving their economic and social problems:

> They have learned that labels are relatively unimportant . . . they have developed a system in which private enterprise, cooperative groups and government enterprises all have their own place and are blended together in a balanced and effective manner. This . . . is a desirable model for Puerto Rico, rather than any doctrinaire notions about socialism, private enterprise, and so on.

However, it appears that today such a "realistic" approach to Puerto Rico's socio-economic problems is, if not dead, certainly dormant.

Teodoro Moscoso was the administrator of the *Fomento* program for its first twenty years and, after a decade's hiatus, recently returned to the job. He agrees that the island's approach to development "has not altered much" since the 1950's.

"With the entire Third World undergoing an upheaval through development efforts of many kinds," Moscoso believes that Puerto Rico's approach needs "a thorough look . . . some innovative ideas . . . preferably by someone not much over thirty." Thus far, that someone hasn't come along, or hasn't been listened to.

6 Government

The Constitution

Puerto Rico's Constitution, in force since 1952, calls for a republican form of government, with executive, legislative, and judicial branches, all "equally subordinate to the sovereignty of the people."

The Constitution is modeled after that of the United States but has some extra features to strengthen civil rights. Printing presses may not be confiscated. The death penalty is prohibited, as is wire-tapping (although Federal and insular security agents are in frequent violation). It outlaws discrimination "on account of race, color, sex, birth, social origin, or condition, or political or religious ideas." This made women eligible for the first time to serve on juries and guaranteed that illegitimate children born after the Constitution took effect would enjoy the same rights as legitimate offspring, including that of inheritance. Workers have a "right" to a "reasonable" minimum wage, an eight-hour day, and time-and-a-half for extra hours. Labor may bargain collectively, strike, and picket. While there have been serious lapses, the Constitution is observed with a diligence matched by few nations. An under-educated citizenry, often unaware of its own rights and those of others, is the major reason for violations of this liberal document. (Tests of public attitudes, in fact, show that the Constitution is considerably more liberal than the people. Of a cross-section of the population interviewed: 64 per cent said they would deny free speech to persons with antireligious attitudes; 33 per cent would be willing to imprison members of Communist groups; and 37 per cent said that, for fear of reprisals, they would stay silent if they knew a town mayor was rifling funds.)

Taxes and Tariffs

A government's power to levy taxes provides some measure of the extent of its sovereign powers. The tax situation in Puerto Rico perhaps best illustrates the island's complex midway position between statehood and nationhood.

Come April 15 of every year, Puerto Ricans send their income tax returns to the Commonwealth Treasury Department in San Juan, not to Washington. With some minor exceptions, Federal taxes are not in force. Because Puerto Ricans do not pay Federal taxes, they do not take part in Federal elections.

The insular tax is a bit stiffer than the Federal tax bite (for example, a married couple with two children and gross income of $15,000 pays $2,163 in Puerto Rico, compared with $1,820 in the United States). However, real estate taxes are far lower than prevailing mainland rates. On the first $15,000 of assessed value of a house—provided the person lives in the house—there is no tax at all, and most homes, old and new, are assessed far below market value. For example, the owner of a modern $40,000 home in San Juan paid only $120 in property taxes last year.

Puerto Rico also exercises its discretion *not* to levy taxes, by granting long exemptions to new industries (see Chapter 5, "The Economy").

Since so many companies are tax exempt, and since so many individuals are either too poor to pay taxes or avoid paying them, the government derives an important share of its income from excise taxes on various items (household furniture, clothing, footwear, medicines, and food are exempt). The heaviest excise tax is on cars, new and used, when they are brought to the island. This tax can run from $200 for a small vehicle up to thousands of dollars for a luxury model.

For the purpose of Federal customs taxes, a person in Puerto Rico is in the United States. He can move goods to the mainland without declaring duty, except on alcoholic beverages, tobacco, and plants. The first two are taxed by the Federal government because they do not carry U.S. internal revenue stamps. Plants sent on flights to the United States are inspected to control the spread of crop diseases.

Federal internal revenue taxes are not paid, except for Social Security taxes and—under some circumstances—income, gift, and estate taxes by U.S. citizens born on the mainland who reside in Puerto Rico. U.S. Customs' proceeds on goods imported to Puerto Rico from foreign countries, as well as Federal excises on goods made in Puerto Rico for sale on the mainland, are returned to the Commonwealth treasury.

The Official Anthem

Since 1952, Puerto Rico's anthem, *La Borinqueña*, has been sung together with the U.S. national anthem at all official occasions. The music of *La Borinqueña* is gentle and lovely, and the official lyrics speak with nostalgia of Puerto Rico's discovery and the island's natural beauty. More recently, however, advocates of independence have stood with fists raised and sung the original lyrics, composed in 1868 by poetess Lola Rodriguez de Tió. These lyrics, written at the time of Puerto Rico's abortive attempt to free itself from Spain, exhort the island's people to "awaken from your dreams . . . to the patriot's call" and assure them that "our machete will give us the freedom that awaits us anxiously."

The Executive Branch

The governor of Puerto Rico is elected by popular vote every fourth November. There is no limit on re-election; Governor Muñoz served four terms. Candidates for governor must be thirty-five years old and, during five preceding years, be a U.S. citizen as well as "a citizen and bona fide resident of Puerto Rico." The salary of the governor was raised from $25,000 to $35,000 per year in 1972. (Until 1964, it was $10,600 because former Governor Muñoz refused a raise until he left office; legislation approved during his final term became effective for his successor.) The governor is also nominal commander-in-chief of the state militia (which is actually the Federally funded National Guard). In his absence, he is succeeded by the Secretary of State, whose appointment requires the approval of both houses. The Cabinet, consisting of the various department secretaries, is appointed by the governor with the advice and consent of the Commonwealth Senate.

Puerto Rico's government is highly centralized. The executive branch encompasses the governor's office and a vast bureaucracy of agencies, departments, and public corporations. Such key services as education, health, police, fire protection, electricity and water are under the executive branch, which has more than 100,000 employees. If we add these to Federal, legislative, and municipal employees, about one of every five workers in Puerto Rico holds a government job (compared with one of every seven in 1968).

Answering directly to the governor's office, which is housed in La Fortaleza Mansion in Old San Juan, are several organizations that range in size from the 600-employee Planning Board to a few small advisory committees. Also in the executive branch are the departments run by the secretaries of agriculture, commerce, education, finance, health, justice, labor, public works, state, consumer affairs, natural resources, and social services. Nearly half the sixty thousand employees of these departments are in education, and half of the remainder are in health, which maintains public clinics throughout the island.

Next are twenty-four executive agencies, the largest being the 7,000-man police department. Thirty public corporations include those concerned with electric power, the University of Puerto Rico, aqueducts and sewers, communications, ports, urban renewal and housing, the Medical Center, the Metropolitan Bus Authority, and the Agricultural Experimental Station. In 1974, the government purchased the Puerto Rico Telephone Company from ITT and was negotiating to buy a shipping line and create its own merchant marine. With this centralized system, the governor is very influential. He appoints more than six hundred executive and judicial branch officials.

Puerto Rico's government structure has been called "a model of public administration." Strong central powers were inherent in the Spanish colonial government that ruled the island for four centuries. When the U.S. military took over in 1898, central powers were also viewed as an efficacious means of keeping control over the populace. Also, in the 1940's, when the island suffered the extra burden of World War II rationing, a centralized government was able to take emergency measures that would ensure adequate flows of food and key raw materials for the economy. While planning is no longer as "central," it is ideally geared for economic development. If, for example, such basic commodities as power and water were left to municipal control, the attraction of outside industry would be greatly hindered, as would improvements for the citizenry. (At times, centralization and the recent acquisition of computers in several agencies have had surprising consequences. Both the police force and the motor vehicle bureau of the public works department are under the executive branch; thus, an unpaid traffic ticket in the tiniest hamlet, at the farthest end of the island, may show up as an extra charge when it comes time to pay for one's license plates in San Juan.)

Structural changes have been accompanied by improvements in the quality of government. The 1947 Personnel Law did away with much of the "spoils" system and created a merit basis for about half the government's jobs. The merit system also blunted prejudices, which once made it difficult for dark-skinned Puerto Ricans to gain jobs in certain government offices. Public employees today are, on the whole, darker-complexioned than those in private banks or offices.

There is still strong political prejudice. When the pro-statehood New Progressive Party took power in 1969, many procommonwealth Popular Party members complained they were unjustly removed from their posts. Over the years, *independentistas* have suffered most. During the 1950's, McCarthyist witchhunts removed many from their jobs. Even today, some agencies will not hire them, while some refuse to "collaborate" with a pro-American government.

The New Progressives are not the only offenders. The Popular Democrats, in power for twenty-eight years, used public resources for political ends. In many large agencies, employees were asked for "voluntary" cash gifts to the party. At election time, some agency heads abandoned their offices and took to the campaign trail, using government vehicles and equipment, either at no cost or for low, "symbolic" fees. Also, mayors who belong to the party in power enjoy uncanny success in having their petitions for favors answered. After the Popular Democrats regained power in 1972, dozens of University of Puerto Rico professors were dismissed "for economy measures," but by some coincidence the majority of those who lost their jobs were *independentistas*.

The Federal Government

The U.S. Government employs several thousand people in Puerto Rico, including a large contingent of military. From Washington, it manages all of the island's external affairs and regulates many of its internal activities. Consulates of several foreign nations are located in San Juan, but the island has no diplomatic relations with any country. (It once had an industrial incentives office in Paris and now has an office in Santo Domingo to stimulate trade). The island also invites Latin American, African, and European government officials to attend such occasions as its Commonwealth Day on July 25. In 1972, Washington named Commonwealth Labor Secretary Julia Rivera de Vicenti as U.S. "alternate delegate" to the United Nations, mainly to counter embarrassing charges by the Cuban delegate that Puerto Rico is still a U.S. colony.

Sometimes, in athletics, Puerto Rico acts as a nation, e.g., when it competes in Caribbean or Central American olympiads. It has even opposed the United States in some international sports tournaments. But, other than in sports, Puerto Rico is viewed as part of the United States, particularly by Latin Americans, who voice little sympathy for the island's middle-of-the-road status. (Quite a row ensued in April, 1967, for example, when a Venezuelan professor, speaking at the University of Puerto Rico, said that South Americans do not consider Puerto Rico part of Latin America. When he added that "the phrase man does not live by bread alone is just the contrary here," the students became so incensed that the forum was hastily suspended. The Venezuelan, shaken by the students' emotional reaction, later said, "You know, for a moment there, I felt we were really in Latin America.")

There are U.S. Army, Navy, Air Force, and Coast Guard bases

in Puerto Rico. The FBI and Secret Service have agents on the island, mainly to keep an eye on radical *independentistas* (it seems that the radicals keep an eye on them, too, because a Socialist League newsletter once published what it described as a list of names of sixty-two locally based FBI agents).

The Post Office and the Customs and Quarantine services are operated by the Federal Government. Flight procedures are ruled by the Federal Aviation Agency. Radio and TV stations are licensed by the Federal Communications Commission. Almost every Federal agency or department, from the Weather Bureau or the Soil Conservation Division to the Peace Corps and the Selective Service System, is represented. In 1967 it was also revealed that the Central Intelligence Agency had set up a "listening post" on the secluded southwest tip of Puerto Rico to monitor radio broadcasts from the Caribbean and South America.

A substantial amount of Federal money is also spent on the island. In 1973, for example, the Puerto Rican government received $507 million for programs in education, health, surplus food for the poor, unemployment insurance, public housing, highway construction, and other projects. An additional total of $177 million was spent to operate Federal agencies on the island ($104 of which was in the area of national defense). Another $482 million was paid by Washington to island residents in veterans' benefits, Medicare payments, and Social Security pensions. But most of this latter amount is matched by the contributions of Puerto Rican workers, who have Social Security and unemployment insurance deducted from their paychecks.

Federal benefits include low-interest loans to government for electrification and public housing and to farmers, veterans, and small businessmen. The Federal Housing Administration and the Veterans Administration also guarantee private housing loans ($81 million worth in 1974).

Federal outlays in Puerto Rico now approach one-fifth of the island's income per capita. This permits many essential services to be rendered, but there is also concern over the growing dependence upon Federal funds by those who seek autonomy or independence.

On the other hand, the United States also derives considerable benefits from Puerto Rico, including rent-free land for military bases. About 13 per cent of the island's tillable surface is said to be in Federal hands. Much of this is forest reserve, but substantial tracts have been used for bases. The U.S. Navy base at Roosevelt Roads (near Fajardo on the east coast) is one of the largest in the world. The Navy appears to be well entrenched in Puerto Rico, but technological changes in waging war have diminished the strategic value of Puerto Rico for the first time in its history. In this era of intercontinental missiles and submarines that fire nuclear weapons, the United States has reduced its holdings of military camps on the island. Ramey Field, the huge Strategic Air Command base near Aguadilla on the northwest coast, has virtually been closed down, and much of the land will be purchased by the Commonweath government. Because of such changes in technology, former Governor Roberto Sánchez Vilella said recently that Puerto Rico's strategic location had diminished in importance. "Military is through," he said, adding that the primary interest of the United States in Puerto Rico was now "economic."

There is little friction among the general populace since a good deal of the Federal presence is relatively "invisible." Most military bases are in enclaves that affect only the periphery of the population. Most Federal employees are Puerto Rican, and their salaries are higher than local government levels. Many of the agencies have a "benevolent" image because they dispense Federal welfare checks or loans, or matching funds for public housing, schools, and highways.

While few government leaders challenge the Federal presence, they often seek greater participation in decisions. Former Governor Muñoz, in trying to illustrate how the Commonwealth status might be improved, has said that he agrees with the "substance" of Federal laws that affect the island, but wants more power for Puerto Rico in their application. He also feels that Puerto Rico should grant its own radio and TV licenses.

Puerto Rico has no military. The local National Guard is part of the U.S. military system, which keeps several bases on the island and manages defense affairs. The U.S. military uses Puerto Rico as a training center and defense outpost for the southern sector of the mainland. A substantial portion of the military force is composed of Puerto Ricans (in 1970, more than 145,000 of the 787,000 adult males on the island were veterans of the U.S. Armed Forces, and 7,000 men were serving in the military).

The main influence of the military is its presence, which stabilizes the political scene and makes any attempt at violent overthrow of the government appear suicidal. The military is also irksome, to varying degrees, to some sectors of the populace. Independence advocates, naturally, feel that U.S. soldiers are foreign "intruders." But even government officials sometimes express anger over military maneuvers on Puerto Rico's offshore islands of Vieques and Culebra. Vieques is used for massive amphibian maneuvers that stunt the island's potential in agriculture or tourism. The Navy uses parts of Culebra and its offshore cays for ship and aerial bombardment practice, which harasses its 700 residents and limits their use of coastal water on certain days of the week. Over the years, one Culebran child has been killed and two others injured when they picked up live explosive charges found on the island's farms. The Navy insists that it exercises utmost care in its target maneuvers, but Culebrans warn that tragedy is inevitable. They point to an incident several years ago, when a Navy bomber mistook an observation post on the island for the target and blew its nine occupants to bits. In the early 1970's the Culebra issue was aired in the world press. In Puerto Rico, it became the only issue that has united autonomists, statehooders, and *independentistas*. Several times activists have camped out on the target beaches, forcing the Navy to cancel scheduled ship-to-shore bombardments. Finally, the Navy agreed to seek unpopulated alternate target sites in the nearby sea, but the issue has not been fully resolved.

The Legislature

Puerto Rico's bicameral legislature convenes in the three-story white, marble-domed Capitolio, atop a bluff that faces the Atlantic Ocean, near the entrance to Old San Juan. The *Senado* has 27 senators and the *Cámara de Representantes* has 51 representatives. Two senators are elected from each of eight senatorial districts and 11 others compete for "at large" seats, which have no constituency. There are also 40 representative districts, with one house member from each, and 11 "at large" house seats. The legislature meets each year from January through April, but one-month extensions to complete last-minute business are usually required.

Legislators must read and write Spanish *or* English, be citizens of the United States, and have resided in Puerto Rico for two years prior to election. The minimum age is thirty for senators and twenty-five for representatives. In theory, an English-speaking American qualifies for a legislative seat. But since the working language of both houses is Spanish, he would be severely hampered in his functions, and his campaign speeches would not be understood by most of his constituents. Three North Americans have been legislators since 1900, but all were long-time residents. One of these was the late New England–born Elmer Ellsworth, a farmer and founding member of the Popular Democratic Party, who was so firmly rooted in Puerto Rico's land and culture that, when he died, some of the warmest eulogies came from *independentistas*.

The Constitution safeguards a minority voice in the legislature. If two-thirds or more of the seats in either house are won by a single party, the number of seats is increased (by a maximum of nine in the Senate and seventeen in the House), and these are reserved for minority party legislators who hold "at large" seats. With more than one minority party, extra seats are apportioned according to the electoral strength of each group.

This law was passed because local politics was ruled for many years by one party, or by a coalition of parties. In 1948, for example, the Populars won 95 per cent of the legislative seats, while their candidate for governor won 61 per cent of the votes; the law assures that a party's legislative strength more closely corresponds to the showing of its gubernatorial candidate. The Populars proposed this minority safeguard law while they were in power.

Legislative Power

Bills approved by both houses become law when the governor signs them or if he fails to act within ten working days. The legislature may overrule the governor's veto if it passes the bill for a second time by a two-thirds majority.

Legislative salaries are low (they have recently been raised to

$9,500 per year, plus per diem, and $22,500 yearly for the leader of each house). Most lawmakers serve part-time and devote themselves to private business (many are lawyers, merchants, labor union leaders, and farm entrepreneurs). Few of them have the expertise to create or evaluate new laws, nor do they have funds to hire consultants. Thus, many laws are born at the Planning Board, or within some agency of the executive branch, and voted upon without substantial challenge or scrutiny.

Since Puerto Rico is small, there is little regional factionalism in the legislature. The society is too homogeneous, for example, for there to be a Southern Democrat bloc holding fast for special geographic interests. Most lobbies and power blocs are organized along industry lines (banking, petrochemicals, agriculture, tourism, organized crime, etc.).

The New Legislature

From the late 1940's until the middle 1960's, the Popular Democratic Party enjoyed such a legislative majority that virtually any law desired by the PDP "establishment" was assured of passage. (During one six-year period, for example, the Senate rejected only one of Governor Muñoz' 761 appointees.)

All that ended in January, 1969, when Governor Ferré and the New Progressive Party won a narrow election victory. The NPP had only a twenty-six to twenty-five advantage in the House, and the Popular Democrats kept control of the Senate by a fifteen to twelve margin, thus giving them veto power over new legislation.

The first sessions of the new legislature were marred by bitter debates and occasional fisticuffs. When one PDP senator questioned the "moral strength" of a colleague on the other side of the aisle, the aggrieved NPP senator shot back, "You insolent bastard!" and the fists began to fly. Soon, the merits of every issue were colored by the political affiliation of its proponents.

The Populars accused Ferré of weakening programs they had planned during the previous year, and the governor, in turn, complained that they were sabotaging his new program. When he proposed a raise for teachers, the Populars, in their zeal not to let Ferré take credit for it at re-election time in 1972, proposed an even more generous raise; so generous, in fact, that the governor nearly refused to sign the bill, and bands of teachers picketed La Fortaleza, while funds were sought to cover the increase.

In the 1972 elections, the PDP won control of both houses (and 72 of the 78 mayoralty jobs), but the NPP retained a strong opposition voice in the legislature.

No scandals have yet rocked the Puerto Rican government that match the scale of the Watergate affair or other related incidents of high-stakes influence peddling in the Federal government. Nor does one hear of the blatant thievery that goes on in Haiti or the Dominican Republic, or that characterized Cuba under Batista.

This does not suggest that the government is free of blemish. In fact, during the past few years each of the two major parties has taken delight in "exposing" the corruption of its rival, and a free press has made front page material of the mudslinging. A few examples:

The Treasury Secretary (formerly the auditor of a sugar mill) prodded the Government Development Bank into making multi-million-dollar loans to mills owned by relatives of Governor Ferré. The Land Administration sold a large tract of land for about one-third its market value to a real estate firm headed by two major contributors to PDP campaigns. Influential businessmen have had indictments for tax evasion quashed. One man, who earned $500,000 in a three-year period and filed no tax returns, was fined only $600 after pleading guilty in court.

In 1971, the Urban Renewal and Housing Authority sold a tract of prime suburban land for $24,000 (it was appraised at $100,000) to a relative of a top aide to the agency executive director. The same agency fed $86,000 in legal fees to a lawyer whose brother was the agency's board chairman.

A survey of the insular House of Representatives showed that eleven members had wives, in-laws, or other relatives on the Capitol payroll; the majority leader set the example, employing his wife, father-in-law and two brothers-in-law. He was outdone by the mayoress of Trujillo Alto, who had no fewer than sixteen of her husband's relatives on the town payroll. In fact, when the new mayor of Dorado submitted a motion to prohibit himself from employing or contracting his own relatives, one paper humorously called him "a renegade" and accused him of "heresy."

But, according to one Cuban who now works in the Puerto Rican government and who lived in Batista's Cuba, "the people here are innocent amateurs when it comes to graft. How often do you hear of a Puerto Rican policeman taking a bribe? Why, in Havana, even the head of the garbage collection took millions with him when he fled for Miami. Some garbage!"

However, Puerto Rico's surging economy has increased the stakes of the game. The real temptations have only just begun. Since most decisions flow from the executive branch, it is there, not the legislature, that the likelihood of malfeasance (now or in the future) exists. One hears steady rumors (but no proof) of under-the-table fees received by key technicians at the Planning Board, where new construction is approved, where routes of new highways are mapped, and where business and residential areas are zoned. There are also strong pressures upon *Fomento,* which recommends tax grants for incoming industries and regulates mining contracts and gambling casino permits.

Organized crime has apparently made some inroads. In 1974, a bill was proposed to allow slot machines in tourism hotels. One legislator, whose committee was to study the bill (and who later came out enthusiastically in favor of slot machines), allegedly received free food, rooms and trips from one hotel. This was nothing compared to the case of House Vice Speaker Severo Colberg, a prominent critic of slot machines. His wife was approached in a restaurant by a man who offered to bribe him generously if he kept silent. When this didn't work, Colberg received midnight phone calls threatening to bomb his home and kill his children. A Senate committee reported that it found "no evidence" of bribery or pressure for passage of the slot machine bill, which soon after became law.

More subtle forms of white-collar "proposal piracy" have been uncovered by the *San Juan Star.* Two large American bond management firms—L. F. Rothschild Co. and Lazard Frères—submitted ideas to the Government Development Bank. The first idea was for the government to buy pollution control equipment and rent it to private industries that might not be able to afford to own such equipment. The second idea was to float low-interest bonds to finance low-cost housing. Both ideas were turned down or unanswered. Some months later, the government said it would implement the ideas. However, the firm managing the concepts would be the First Boston Corporation, a competitor of Rothschild and Lazard Frères. (First Boston has had a long, intimate relationship with the Commonwealth government. Among other things, it made the financial feasability study of the government's purchase of the Puerto Rico Telephone Company and then managed the bond issue involved in the purchase.)

The Judicial Branch

Puerto Rico has its own Supreme Court, composed of a Chief Justice and eight Associate Justices. It also has nine superior courts, thirty-seven district courts, and forty-two justices of the peace in rural areas.

To be eligible for appointment, Supreme Court members must have been admitted to practice law in Puerto Rico ten years earlier and must have resided on the island for five years. Retirement is mandatory at age seventy.

The island's official courtroom language is Spanish, except in San Juan Federal District Court where (despite the fact that the U.S. Attorney, the Judge, and most of the clientele are Puerto Ricans) English is required. The courts are under the jurisdiction of the Circuit Court in Boston, but appeals may go as high as the U.S. Supreme Court.

The island's judicial system was unified in 1952 by reforms written into the new Constitution. U.S. legal authorities have described the change as "an almost revolutionary reorganization, which embodies reforms well in advance of those adopted by even the most progressive states."

The 1952 reform required the appointment, rather than the election, of judges. It forbade judges to engage in political activity and guaranteed them substantial independence from the executive and legislative branches. The unified court structure also solved jurisdictional problems by empowering all courts to hear any case.

The increased crime rate, however, has multiplied caseloads, causing long delays between arrest and trial. But to safeguard against these abuses, the Constitution provides that no person may

governorship. Most of the commerce, tourism, and industrial development is centered in San Juan; however, the mayor has less effective power than his counterparts in the United States. For example, his firemen and policemen are not "his"; they respond to the government's executive branch.

Perhaps no politician was more "political" than the former lady Mayor of San Juan, Felisa Rincón de Gautier. Doña Fela, as she is known, retired after the 1968 election. During her long period at City Hall, she was an elegant figure, with her turbans, Spanish fans, and gregarious manner. One winter, she flew a planeload of snow down from New York for San Juan's slum waifs to enjoy. She often used public funds to make personal-seeming gifts to long-waiting lines of the poor: toys and candy for the children, sedate parties for the old ladies on relief. She responded well to the personalistic culture of her time. When a slum dweller from La Perla needed roofing materials for his seaside shack, he saw Doñ Fela, who gave him a *papelito* ("little slip of paper") to help him get the materials from some government warehouse. This problem-solving apparatus was politically prudent and humane, but, in the later years, hardly up to the scale of San Juan, a city that could no longer be fixed with *papelitos*.

The aging Doña Fela gave way to a young lawyer, Carlos Romero Barceló, a member of the NPP, who won the 1968 election by a good margin, partially because of the Barceló name (which is revered in local politics) and also due to his youthful, sleeves-rolled-up image. Romero, who is Yale-educated and married to a North American woman, wants statehood. But he has focused on more mundane issues, such as prompt garbage collection. Despite the NPP's loss of the governorship and many legislative seats in the 1972 elections, Romero easily won a second term as San Juan's mayor. He is regarded as the NPP's strongest gubernatorial candidate in 1976.

Elections

Puerto Rico has more than 1.5 million eligible voters, and 84 per cent of them voted in the 1972 elections. This rate of participation is among the highest in the world. (In 1972, only 55 per cent of American voters took part in the Presidential elections. Other countries with high rates of participation are Germany, 91 per cent; France, 81 per cent; Japan, 72 per cent; and Britain, 88 per cent.) Puerto Ricans and other U.S. citizens who are permanent residents of the island for a year or more may register to vote when they are eighteen years old. A referendum in 1970 lowered the voting age from twenty-one to eighteen, adding about 200,000 persons to the list of eligible voters.

Election procedures in Puerto Rico have their unique aspects. Citizens vote in a previously assigned place, usually a school in their neighborhood. Their identification is checked against a registry book. At a specific hour, the doors are closed and voting begins; ballots are checked off in privacy, folded, and deposited in a large box. Only when all people have voted does the policeman outside open the door, which makes it virtually impossible for anyone to vote in more than one precinct.

Widespread illiteracy until two decades ago (it is still about 11 per cent) prompted parties to develop symbols that attract the voter's eye. These symbols are used on posters, flags, car decals, lapel pins, and TV commercials. The Popular Democrats since 1940 have used the *pava,* the broad-brimmed straw hat of the rural peasant. The New Progressives use *la palma* ("coconut palm"); the People's Party uses *el sol* ("the sun"). Even literate citizens commonly remark, "I voted with the *pava*" or "with *la palma,*" because it is catchier and more colorful than the party's name.

Recently, a Puerto Rican who moved to the United States decided to register as a voter in New York City. When confronted by the names of the four major parties (Democrat, Republican, Conservative, and Liberal) he asked in Spanish of the bilingual election official: "Which is the party of *la pava?*"

Since *coco* ("coconut") is also a slang word for "dollar," the New Progressive Party effectively used this imagery in its campaign, announcing that "the *cocos* will rain down upon Puerto Rico when the party of *la palma* achieves statehood." Music is also a favorite weapon; all parties strive to compose a hit jingle. Here again, music lends itself to the use of *la pava, la palma,* or *el sol,* in a bouncy *merengue* or a *plena,* rather than the tongue-twisting, lusterless official name of the party.

TABLE 3. ELECTIONS IN PUERTO RICO
(in thousands of votes)

Party	1948	1952	1956	1960	1964	1968	1972
Popular Democratic Party	392.0	429.0	433.0	457.8	487.2	367.3	609.6
Statehood Republican Party	88.1	85.1	172.8	252.3	284.6	4.3	—
New Progressive Party	—	—	—	—	—	390.9	524.0
Independence Party	66.1	125.7	86.3	24.1	22.1	25.3	52.1
Christian Action Party	—	—	—	52.1	26.8	—	—
Socialist Party	64.1	21.6	—	—	—	—	—
Reformist Party	28.2	—	—	—	—	—	—
People's Party	—	—	—	—	—	84.1	2.9
Authentic Sovereignty Party	—	—	—	—	—	—	.4
Puerto Rican Union Party	—	—	—	—	—	—	1.6
TOTAL	638.6	661.6	692.2	786.4	820.9	871.9	1,190.7

To register, a new party, or one that fails to earn 5 per cent of the votes in an election, must gather notarized signatures in at least three-fourths of the voting precincts, and their total must exceed 5 per cent of the total votes cast for governor in the previous election (to qualify for 1972, new parties needed 46,000 signatures). In Puerto Rico, many people sign for a new party, not always because they intend to vote for it, but "to give them a chance." The usual technique is to staff a table at a town plaza, or shopping center, with a party official and notary public, and ask passers-by to sign up.

An electoral subsidy law, passed in 1957, provides public funds for party campaigns. Main parties receive $75,000 per year and $150,000 in an election year. Newly registered parties, also, receive public funds, in accord with the number of votes they poll. The law prohibits personal gifts to parties in excess of $600 a year; to get around this, in an era of rising costs, wealthy persons sometimes cosign bank loans for political parties.

The Federal Relations Act

The source of the controversy over the island's political status is the Federal Relations Act, which spells out Puerto Rico's linkage with the U.S. Government. Public Law 600, issued in 1950, which permits the framing of a Puerto Rican constitution, did not completely repeal the previous colonial relationship outlined in the 1917 Organic Act. It erased those parts of the Organic Act dealing with local government, but left intact what is known as the Statute of Federal Relations. A part of the Puerto Rican Constitution (which the U.S. Congress insisted upon as an amendment) says the following:

> Any amendment or revision of this constitution shall be consistent with the resolution enacted by the Congress of the United States approving this constitution, with the applicable provisions of the Constitution of the United States, with the Puerto Rico Federal Relations Act, and with Public Law 600.

Thus, Congress inserted a few words that contradict the principle of self-government. For example, it defines the Puerto Rico Constitution as extending to "the island of Puerto Rico and to the adjacent islands *belonging to the United States*."

How, one asks, can Puerto Rico be "freely associated" if it belongs to the United States?

Pedro Muñoz Amato, a noted educator, says, "If the Federal Relations Statute can be amended unilaterally by Congress, then there is no compact with the Puerto Rican people on these matters. Either it never existed or it is destroyed by unilateral action."

The Constitution is a step forward, he says, but "the passive consent of the governed is not equivalent to their democratic participation in the framing of the laws and the selection of the representatives that are to rule over them." Since Puerto Rico cannot vote in Congress, he says, the only way to make its Constitution valid is to guarantee island participation if future amendments are made to the Federal Relations Statute.

Congress has not yet accepted the idea of real association, which —in the judicial sense—could be achieved by changing a few short, but crucial, paragraphs.

Puerto Rico tried to clarify the relationship, in 1959, in a bill submitted to Congress to amend the U.S.–Puerto Rico compact. Known as the Fernos-Murray Bill, it sought to eliminate the part about "adjacent islands belonging to the United States," on the grounds that it made Puerto Rico appear to be a possession, rather than a self-governing commonwealth. The failure of this bill in Congress was a bitter disappointment to Luis Muñoz Marín, the architect of the commonwealth status.

The farthest Washington would go was, in 1964, to consent to a study of the U.S.–Puerto Rican political relationship. The Status Commission study analyzes the question in rich detail, but offers no solution. A referendum after the study (in 1967) reaffirmed the strength of the commonwealth status among Puerto Rico's electorate, but Congress has not responded to island attempts to "perfect" the status.

Although the United States permits the local government to exercise considerable autonomy, Puerto Rico still legally "belongs" to the United States. It is questionable—except in some extreme emergency—whether the United States would risk world censure by exercising its "ownership" of the island to intervene in commonwealth government affairs. But the Federal Relations Act continues to be a thorn in the side of those who hope to legitimate commonwealth as a permanent, dignified form of government.

7 The People and Society

Saturday nights are special. The nickelodeons play late into the night, and . . . Old Tomás Famanía, who has all his teeth and walks straight . . . and glories in his more than sixty years, comes up from his thatched shack at the beach to dance. He usually picks rumbas, and his partners will be Ceferino Hernández' daughters and granddaughters, none of them more than eight years old. The bachelors stand at the bar drinking their rum neat—each drink downed in a swallow from a tiny paper cup. The more affluent buy half pints of rum (called "Shirleys" after Shirley Temple) and finish them sitting at the tables. The teen-age males play pool on the much-ripped table in Cheo's bar and watch the girls walk by.

—From *Workers in the Cane,* by
SIDNEY MINTZ

Despite their vague political status, Puerto Ricans are as ethnically distinct as Mexicans, Frenchmen, or Norwegians. They share a unique Hispano-Caribbean heritage that stretches back nearly half a millenium in time; their language is Spanish, spoken with a Puerto Rican accent and spiced with local idioms. Puerto Ricans share many common traits with their Spanish-speaking neighbors in Cuba and the Dominican Republic, but differences between these three island societies are apparent to all but the most casual of tourists. One might even argue that the long history of colonial dependence has become an integral part of the Puerto Rican "identity," or has, at least, created a curious void in it. Certainly, the last seven decades of association with the United States have caused substantial change in the nature of Puerto Rico's society.

Unlike the new American states of Alaska and Hawaii, which are sparsely populated or lack large "native" populations, Puerto Rico is densely peopled; and of every 100 residents, ninety-one are native-born. Half of the remainder are the U.S.-born offspring of return migrants.

The greatest catalyst for changing the Puerto Rican "identity" is the fact that about *one-third* of all its native sons and daughters live in the United States. And it is not always the same third, due to constant in-out migration. Even on the mainland, Puerto Ricans cluster together, resisting efforts to divide them into the black and white racial categories that prevail in the eastern United States. In New York City, the darkest-skinned Puerto Rican will bristle at being called a Negro. "No," he will reply, "I am a Puerto Rican." It is noteworthy that most racial surveys in New York classify Puerto Ricans in a category apart from whites and blacks despite the fact that, in terms of physical characteristics, there is no such thing as a Puerto Rican race.

Puerto Rico's apparently undefinable but unquestionably singular identity has impelled even those who favor political assimilation with the United States to assure everyone, as former Governor Ferré did, that "while the United States is our *nación* ['nation'], Puerto Riso is our *patria* ['homeland']." This view is, of course, disputed by autonomists and independence supporters, who insist that Puerto Rico is both the *nación* and *patria* of its native sons, but the mere fact that Ferré—a steadfast opponent of independence—should be concerned with the defense of Puerto Rico's ethnic identity is significant. Even he, as does every other Puerto Rican, refers to the island as *el país* ("country" or "nation"), which only proves that semantics is a lively sport on this Caribbean island.

Ethnic Roots

Puerto Rico's earliest citizens—some 30,000 copper-skinned Taíno Indians—were killed, frightened off, or absorbed by Spanish colonizers in the sixteenth century. Next came an influx of African slaves. Since the Spaniards brought few women with them, the white, black, and red races were mixed in a stew that has bubbled quietly during five centuries. Today, sizable minorities of *blancos* ("whites") and *prietos* ("dark-skinned") or *negros* ("blacks") occupy the poles of the skin-color spectrum, and they blend gradually into the dominant middle (perhaps half the population) of the Puerto Rican people, who are either almost-white, or almost-black, or often remarkably Indian, and who fall into a catch-all category known as the *trigueño* ("tan," "swarthy," "olive-skinned," "darkish").

There have been other ingredients in this genetic bouillabaisse. In the late eighteenth and early nineteenth centuries, Frenchmen came from Louisiana when it was bought by the United States, and from Haiti when the slaves revolted. The Latin American wars for independence brought loyalist Spaniards and Venezuelans. As the slave-sugar economy flourished, Scottish and Irish farmers came. When slavery waned, many farmers and laborers came from the province of Galicia and the Canary Island. In the 1840's, a labor shortage brought Chinese coolies to Cuba and Puerto Rico where, in the latter, they helped build the Central Highway. Italians, Corsicans, and Lebanese also spiced the melting pot.

North American immigration grew after 1898, but as early as 1873 a small community of *americanos* founded an Episcopal church in Ponce. The North American community numbers more than 40,000 today (including many transients); a growing minorits of *continentales,* as they are called here, have intermarried with Puerto Ricans, creating such exotic names as William Smith González, or Roberto Ruiz MacDonald.

The Cuban colony has swelled from 1,000 to 20,000 since the 1959 Castro Revolution. Following the Cubans, in mid-1965 nearly 10,000 Dominicans fled the chaos of Santo Domingo's civil war. There are also 7,000 persons of Spanish birth or parentage and small alien communities from South America, Europe, Asia, and Africa.

In the United States, the "wretched, teeming masses" of immigrants usually begin at the lower rung of the socio-economic ladder. But most newcomers to Puerto Rico possess the skill and capital that enable them to climb quickly to the upper or upper-middle strata. North Americans are often employed as managers or high-salaried technicians with local subsidiaries of U.S. corporations, or start their own businesses. Many Cuban immigrants have their own firms, mainly in the field of commerce, or are employed as well-paid technocrats. Only the Dominicans, who come from a society poorer than Puerto Rico's, have, in general, begun at the bottom, in factory or service jobs, including domestic work, which many Puerto Ricans no longer seek.

Race Relations

Fuzzy lines between racial groups discourage color prejudice. Slavery's small role (compared with some Caribbean areas), and its peaceful abolition, also contributed to lessen race tension.

A hint of racial harmony came as early as 1770, when Puerto Rico's Governor declared that all free children—white, mulatto, or black—should be educated. Marriage, though, especially in the upper classes, was another matter. Some families endured ludicrous trials, known as *limpieza de sangre* ("blood purification"), to prove that no African blood flowed in their veins, thus entitling their members to marry into another "good" family. Folk tunes and idiomatic expressions treated blacks in a pejorative or comic manner. Friendly whites were often, and still are, paternalistic. But there was no government-instituted discrimination. Once slavery was abolished, the law opened public places to all. There were no separate rest rooms, or water fountains, or rear sections of public vehicles for blacks. It was the numbing heritage of slavery that deprived blacks of the tools needed to compete in the "free" society. But even in the nineteenth century, a few black and mulatto Puerto Ricans achieved distinguished places in their community. Outstanding among them was José Celso Barbosa (1857–1921), a doctor who served in the cabinet of the autonomous government (in 1897) as Undersecretary of Education and, later, formed the Statehood Republican Party. Before him was Rafael Cordero Molina (1790–1868), whom one local historian describes as "the Puerto Rican who has come closest to sainthood." A shoemaker, Cordero also had a small school where, for more than half a century, he offered free instruction to poor children.

The U.S. presence has enhanced the awareness of racial differences among Puerto Ricans. Since most American immigrants are white, and wealthier than the average islander, success is equated with whiteness. The Spaniards, too, were white, and, generally, wealthier, but they tolerated—and often engaged in—interracial marriage. Most Americans continue their life style in Puerto Rico, staying to themselves or gravitating toward white Puerto Ricans.

A Civil Liberties Commission in 1958 reported that while racial tension in Puerto Rico is not "critical," intolerance in the United States has negatively influenced the island. It quoted many blacks and whites as saying they would feel "uncomfortable" in a nightclub full of people of another race. Some whites complained of colored families moving in next door. When white families were asked the old question, "Would you like your daughter to marry one?" half said no, but only a few said they would forcibly prohibit the marriage.

Prejudice is strongest, says the study, in some private schools, in university clubs, in some private businesses and in some residential sectors. Not a single black employee was visible in any bank office in the entire San Juan metropolitan area when the study was made. Only four black faces were counted in eighty-five San Juan business establishments. Pressure from legislative committees and from the press has now relaxed color prejudice in the business world, although some firms have only "token" Negroes working for them.

But it is ludicrous to suggest that the racial situation resembles that of the United States. The Senate Majority Leader for many years (who nearly became governor in November, 1968) was the "Indian-ish" *trigueño* Luis Negrón López, who is a wealthy lawyer and gentleman farmer. A dark-skinned mulatto, the late Ernesto Ramos Antonini, occupied the powerful Speaker's post in the House of Representatives. A black economist was the head of the island's Manufacturer's Association. The poor comprise people of all colors. While few white Puerto Ricans marry blacks, those in the larger "tan" population mix freely with either extreme. Puerto Rico's police force is probably darker than the populace as a whole. Thus, many factors required for racial tension are absent. When "Black Power" advocate Stokeley Carmichael visited Puerto Rico in 1967, he soft-pedaled the racial issue and spoke out against

United States "colonialism." On the other hand, Roy Innis was able to found a small CORE chapter in the nearby Virgin Islands, where black-white racial divisions are more marked.

Religion

In the year 1928, when the crops thirsted for rain in a certain rural *barrio* of southeast Puerto Rico, the citizens resorted to an old ritual known as the *rogativa,* or group supplication. They marched up and down the dusty road, praying for rain. Two weeks later, Hurricane San Felipe devastated the *barrio*. One oldtimer who recalls the catastrophe says, "They haven't celebrated a *rogativa* there since."

Many Puerto Ricans regard spiritual affairs in the same eclectic manner.

At the turn of the century, when the U.S. Army invaded Puerto Rico, an Army chaplain remarked, "Puerto Rico is a Catholic country without religion." More recently, island writer Pedro Juan Soto refined the thought somewhat when he observed, "Puerto Ricans are a religious people in search of a religion."

Well over 99 per cent of the population is Christian, with about 80 per cent Roman Catholic. The remainder are Protestants: Baptists, Methodists, Lutherans, Episcopalians, and Pentecostals. The Jewish Community Center in San Juan has a few hundred member families, most of them nonnative residents. There are also small groups of Mennonites and Mormons, and San Juan has a Salvation Army and a Watchtower Bible and Tract Society.

But the prevailing mood is a kind of "womb to tomb" Roman Catholicism, with little practice in between. The average Puerto Rican has been baptized, confirmed, and—when the time comes—will receive the last rites of the Catholic Church.

Christianity permeates even daily conversation. It is common in the countryside for a child, when entering or leaving the home, to request a *bendición* ("blessing") from the father, who will respond, "May God and the Virgin bless you." In planning a matter as casual as meeting for lunch the next day, many Puerto Ricans will add, *"Si Dios quiere"* ("God willing"). Common expressions of surprise are *"Ay virgen!"* and *"Ave María!"* both of which refer to the Virgin Mary. Even more frequent, to express or plead for compassion, is *"Ay bendito!"* which is short for *"Bendito sea El Señor"* ("Blessed be the Lord").

Almost all homes in Puerto Rico, from mansions to shacks, are adorned with pictures of Christ, crucifixes, or figurines of saints. Children are taught to fear *el diablo* and to respect *Papa Dios* ("Father God"). People often cross themselves when passing in front of a church. Each year, towns and villages celebrate festivals honoring their patron saint. Periods such as Holy Week, or between Christmas and Three King's Day (Epiphany), feature many masses and processions. When a new business opens, be it a mammoth bank building or a humble laundromat, the ubiquitous priest appears, with holy water and a blessing.

But Puerto Rico's Catholicism is hardly orthodox; it is often mixed with personalistic saint worship, spiritism, and superstition. Protestantism, especially the "swinging" revivalist variety, is a growing force.

Catholic church attendance (and participation in confession) is low, with prayers at home to a favorite saint often substituting for going to mass. Consensual marriage—ignoring both church and civil authority—is common among the poor. It is mainly among the rich and in the growing new middle class that one finds frequent church attendance and confession. Even here, a study of 200 wealthy Catholic families showed that while 142 wives and 91 husbands attend church often, only half the women and one-seventh of the men confess regularly.

While Holy Week is generally solemn, the annual patron saint festivals are times for merrymaking, with gambling and dancing in the plazas, which are full of ferris wheels, merry-go-rounds, and penny-pitching booths. Christmas is also a time of party-going and fun. In San Juan, during the annual festival to honor St. John the Baptist, the traditional midnight dip in the ocean (in which even the mayor participates) is a mere punctuation mark in a long night of partying.

To illustrate the mixed attitude toward the church, though many poor couples live in consensual union, they will usually have their children baptized.

Religiosity is more common outside the church. In rural villages, a person near death will be visited by friends and relatives, who maintain a night-long *velada* ("vigil"); the women pray inside the home; the men, after paying their respects, will often sit outside chatting, where they are served black coffee, soda crackers, and cheese. The night after death, a *velorio* is held, and much the same ritual is celebrated, although the men outside may down a nip of *cañita* (clandestine cane rum) to combat the cool night air. Drunkenness or loud talk on such occasions is deplored, and imbibing rarely, if ever, evokes the bonhomie of the proverbial Irish wake. In some regions of the island, rosaries are recited for nine nights after the funeral.

The Catholic Church has had a long, checkered history since its establishment on the island in the early sixteenth century. On the positive side, it was a pioneer in opening new territories. Many pueblos were founded by priests, whose small, thatched-roof missions in remote zones served scattered rural settlers. In a few years, a town plaza was marked off, with a permanent church building at one end and the municipal hall at the other forming the nucleus for a new community.

The church also maintains medical services and schools, including Catholic University in Ponce and a number of good primary and secondary schools. Its religious festivals and activities, often the only recreational outlets in isolated communities, help foster a sense of community cooperation.

On the other hand, the church preached loyalty to Spain, even under the tyranny of military rule. Despite early church resistance to enslavement of the pre-Colombian Indians, the church opposed the abolition of slavery in the nineteenth century.

In 1969, Padre Salvador Freixedo, a Jesuit priest who wrote a book (*My Church Sleeps*) criticizing church dogma and voicing compassion for divorcees who wished to remarry, was banned from exercising his priestly functions. The crisis was headlined in daily papers for two weeks, as pickets for and against the priest marched in front of the archbishop's home in Old San Juan. Many felt that Padre Freixedo, a Spanish-born liberal who for years has supported working class causes, may have been rash in some of his statements, but they also felt that the church was far too harsh in its reaction.

His book sold about 10,000 copies in Puerto Rico, making it one of the island's all-time bestsellers.

The Catholic Church's distance—spiritual and geographical—from the rural masses has led to the evolution of an unorthodox creole Catholicism; as well as a flowering of Protestant sects and various spiritualist groups. Many members of the growing middle class do not relate to the deterministic image of Catholicism, which prizes humility and promises paradise in the after-life. They are more drawn to the Protestant ethic of hard work and material achievement, of man's ability to change his fate. Many poor people, on the other hand, find solace in the catharsis of the revivalist wing of the Protestant religion.

Protestantism was long considered heresy in Puerto Rico. Not until the 1800's did the Spanish Crown permit Protestant churches to be built in Ponce and Vieques, after Queen Victoria transmitted the plea of several English families who had settled there.

After 1898, American religious groups looked southward to the Caribbean and saw over a million potential converts. To avoid needless rivalry, the U.S. Methodists, Baptists, and Episcopalians "divided up the cake" beforehand and created exclusive territories for proselytizing. By 1919, a Protestant Evangelical Council was formed, and some Puerto Rican ministers were trained. But little impact was made on the rural, poverty-stricken island. By 1942, the American Protestant hierarchy reported with some chagrin that its ministry was "middle class . . . alien to Puerto Rican society and to the economic structure and life of the community." Sunday collections were so scanty that the American parent body was obliged to pay large subsidies.

The creation of a Puerto Rican middle class, more than a change in the nature of the Protestant Church, has attracted new adherents. There were enough on Easter Sunday, 1967, for Billy Graham to pack a baseball stadium in San Juan, where he addressed the throng with the help of a Spanish interpreter standing at his side.

But of an estimated 300,000 Protestants on the island, only about 70,000 belong to the major sects.

The rest belong to the revivalist movements such as the Pentecostals, the Seventh Day Adventists, or to the home-grown church opened in 1940 by a near-legendary woman named Mita, who died in 1970. She also opened Mita churches in the Spanish-speaking sections of Chicago and New York and in Santo Domingo. At one of her packed revival meetings, held the same week Billy Graham came to town, she referred to him as "the gringo with the big white teeth, who has come to steal away my parishioners."

The poor found it easy to identify with Mita, a woman whose thoughts may have been in the heavens, but whose words and methods were down-to-earth. The Mita sect has its own business and provides needed services to its followers; membership sometimes results in upward social mobility. After Mita's death, members of the sect continued its operation. The poor also identify with Pentecostal lay pastors, who have usually emerged from their own ranks and who offer living proof by their example of one's ability to advance by faith and hard work. Churches are usually storefronts in working-class districts or converted small suburban homes.

The Pentecostal faith, which offers group singing and emotional public testimony, also demands the discipline of exemplary dress and behavior, including abstinence from tobacco and alcohol; this helps the poor withstand the apparent hopelessness of their existence.

The sometimes traumatic migration to New York's hostile environment is ameliorated, too, by joining a revivalist group. A 1948 survey showed that 5 per cent of New York's 300,000 Puerto Ricans were Pentecostals. Today, with some 1 million islanders in New York, about one family in ten belongs to, and helps support, a small church, which receives no subsidy. Led by pastors from their own *barrio*, singing the old biblical hymns, in Spanish translation, to the rhythm of caracas and tambourines, the Puerto Rican poor have, in effect, created a church of their own.

Espiritismo ("spiritism") is frowned upon by the church, but attracts many Puerto Ricans, who feel that it does not conflict with more orthodox religious practices.

There are different types of spiritist beliefs. Some practices, such as the use of certain herbs to remedy real or imagined ills, rest on the fringe between superstition and common sense folk medicine. Some of the herbs have no real therapeutic value; others are dangerously toxic; but some are used as active ingredients in "store bought" medicines. These herbs are found growing wild in the countryside or bought in urban stores known as *botánicas,* which feature a bizarre variety of merchandise. Herbs, such as mint and rue, are prepared as teas for intestinal disorders. Others are mixed with alcohol into *alcoholado* and rubbed on for aches and pains. The *botánicas* also sell incense, candles, and powders of different colors, which have alleged magical properties, and figurines of Christian, African, and Oriental symbols. Numerous *botánicas* flourish in Hispanic *barrios* on the mainland, where they attract a mixed clientele of Puerto Ricans, Cubans, Dominicans, Haitians, other West Indians, and some North Americans.

The spiritualist medium, who contacts the dead or analyzes a visiting stranger's troubles and offers advice, is another popular branch of the occult in Puerto Rico. Nathan Leopold, who researched this field on the island, writes that spiritualism had its roots among uneducated country people but the remarkable thing has been "the rapid spread, both geographic and social . . . [it] flourishes in the big cities as well . . . it has spread to the learned professions . . . many doctors, lawyers, and professors are firm believers." He tells of a small town near San Juan where one medium, a garbage truck driver who is also a brilliant conversationalist, holds *consultas* on Saturdays and general services on Sundays. People line up at 5 A.M., to be attended two hours later.

In some remote villages, peasants cultivate ancient beliefs in witches and spirits; there are occasional touches of African witchcraft culture in coastal areas inhabited by descendants of slaves. Expanded medical services in the countryside have reduced the use of folk cures, but superstitions associated with love and hate prevail. These are gradually waning, however. People who swear to the existence of spirits will often say that "they existed years ago, but not nowadays."

There is still considerable fear among the uneducated of *el mal del ojo* ("the evil eye"). The greatest concern is for attractive infants, who are the object of stares from covetous strangers. To ward off this threat, some parents adorn the child with a bracelet known as the *"asabache,"* which is usually a jet-black bead or piece of plastic. It is said that this practice dates back to ancient Egypt.

Perhaps the most powerful religious-mystical tie in Puerto Rico and in other Latin American cultures is the *"compadrazgo,"* which, literally, means coparentage. It resembles the concept of god-parentage among Christian North Americans, but is far more solemn. Parents will select *compadres* ("godfathers") and *co-madres* ("godmothers"), generally, when a child is baptized. This has strong practical reasons; in times of crisis, which are frequent among poor families, *compadres* can be counted upon to lend a helping hand. In some cases, a poor family may seek out a rich *compadre*, whose wealth or influence may at some time in the future provide crucial aid to the godchild. The wealthy *compadre* will usually accept, often out of friendship, sometimes to tap the labor of his poorer *compadre*, who may be a worker on his farm.

But the *compadrazgo* is more than a system of improvised social security. It has a definite mystical quality. Two unrelated men who cultivate a deep friendship may wish to "seal" it by becoming each other's *compadre*, without any baptism being necessary. This is tantamount to adopting a new brother. In some cases, even, a man fearing that a neighbor friend is covetous of his wife will try to neutralize his rival's lust by making the potential rival his *com-padre*. Cuckoldry in such a case would be considered doubly treacherous and evil. (This recalls the case of a promiscuous woman, a prostitute, in one of Oscar Lewis' studies, who remarked that she could not bring herself to make love to a man who was her *compadre*.)

Casual acquaintances will sometimes call each other *compadre*, or *compai*, to express friendship, but the formal *compadre* relationship implies deep respect.

Language

One afternoon, an American resident of San Juan drove up to a gas station to have the spark plugs of his car changed. Having consulted a Spanish-English dictionary beforehand, he asked the attendant to put in new *bujías* and, in return, received a puzzled gaze. Finally, after the car owner lifted the hood and pointed, the attendant smiled and said, *"Ah! Los espares!,"* which is an Hispanicized version of "the sparks."

After seven decades under United States stewardship, Puerto Rico's Spanish is liberally sprinkled with English "loan words." English is a required second language in the schools. There are English-language publications and radio and television stations. Since the United States is the hemisphere's main producer of new technology and also dominates commerce, the island's Spanish vocabulary has had to stretch to accommodate words that describe new tools, processes, and products.

The degree of impact of the English language depends upon geography and economics. One hears less English in the countryside than in San Juan—and less among the poor, who have limited contact with schools and white collar jobs, two sources of English usage. One encounters more English (and often better Spanish) among the wealthier classes, who are involved in commerce or the professions and who may have studied at U.S. universities. Return migrants who have spent their formative years in the United States may speak a tangle of both tongues, known as "Spanglish."

Spanish was the only language of any prominence used in Puerto Rico during the 400-year Spanish colonial period. But when the United States took over in 1898, it tried to use English instruction as a political tool to absorb Puerto Rico into the American governmental system. English was established as the official language in the schools, when neither the teachers nor the students understood a word of it. This was called the Clark Policy, after Education Commissioner Victor Clark. Two years later, a new commissioner, Martin Brumbaugh, made Spanish the medium of instruction in the first eight grades and English, from the ninth through the twelfth. In 1905, Commissioner Roland Falkner went back to the Clark Policy; but in 1916, Commissioner Paul Miller compromised and made Spanish the teaching language in grades one through four, Spanish and English in the fifth grade, and English in grades six through twelve.

In 1934, José Padín, a Puerto Rican, returned to the Brumbaugh policy of 1900; and in 1937, José Gallardo began a series of changes that, by 1942, made Spanish the teaching medium in grades one through six. English was emphasized in junior high school, and both English and Spanish were used in the senior high schools.

In 1948, Puerto Rico's first native elected Governor appointed

Commissioner Mariano Villaronga, who made Spanish the medium of instruction in all grades, with English as a required second language, to be taught in special daily classes.

Adrian Hull, an English-language specialist in Puerto Rico, notes that "practically every type of language policy for the teaching of English in the public schools of Puerto Rico has been tried with the exception of having English and Spanish as the language of instruction on alternate days." And, he adds, this possibility was suggested.

Although Spanish now prevails, English enjoys prestige because of its monetary value. "Improve your personality, learn English," was the sign of one adult night school in Hato Rey. "Secretary: must be bilingual" is frequently seen in newspaper want ads. An occasional ad will say that "Only English is essential."

International teen culture also peppers local Spanish with anglicisms. Urban youngsters talk about *jipis* ("hippies") and memorize the song lyrics of the Supremes, the Beatles, Tom Jones, and other pop music stars. The second most popular radio station in San Juan features American pop music for *tineyers* ("teenagers").

But, except for Spanish-speaking islanders who lived in the United States, one senses that Spanish in Puerto Rico has great resilient strength. External currents may add new words, and even alter syntax, but it is highly unlikely that Puerto Rico's "new Spanish" will be English.

Most educators agree that if Puerto Rican children were better trained in Spanish they would more readily learn English, too, without any loss in the richness of the vernacular. But language instruction continues to be viewed as a political tool by all sides. Late in 1969, Governor Ferré flew back from Washington and announced that he was seeking Federal funds to expand English language instruction—to speed Puerto Rico on the way to statehood. The critical reaction of the *independentistas,* following the Governor's nonpedagogical statement, was as inevitable as sundown following sunrise. Thus, Puerto Rico's language problem is much more than one of mere communication.

University of Puerto Rico philologist Rubén del Rosario does not think that the Spanish language here is in grave danger of disappearing, " . . . unless we should become a state of the Union, whereupon English would most certainly prevail within one hundred years."

He believes that the Spanish spoken in Puerto Rico, Cuba, and Santo Domingo is "basically alike, and the same as the rest of Latin America." As for frequent word mixing, there are many words such as *bar, coctel, record, standard,* and *ticket* which are used in almost all Hispanic nations. In Puerto Rico, "only a few hundred English words are used; these in no way affect the basic structure of our language. Most of these foreign words refer to new ideas and new objects for which there was no traditional equivalent."

He notes that the common Spanish word for "rum"—*ron*— was imported from the British Antilles some hundred years ago. The word "*fohtró*," based on the American dance (foxtrot) of the 1920's, has evolved here into an idiom for "fight" or "tussle." The word "*plei*" (from the English "play") describes a party among friends or a romantic episode. "This type of word," he says, "is absorbed into our language and enriches it."

Puerto Rico's Spanish has also been enriched by at least 500 Indian words, most of which relate to flora and fauna. Some are used throughout Latin America, but others are 100 per cent Puerto Rican, such as "*guajana*," referring to the silvery tassels of the sugarcane stalk. Puerto Rico has twenty-nine cities, including Arecibo, Guayama, Mayagüez, and Yauco, with Indian names. Some African words—*bembe* ("big lip"), *quimbombó* ("okra"), and *guineo* ("banana")—hark back to the epoch of slavery.

Puerto Rico has many other words, such as *agallarse* ("become ruffled and angry"), *chévere* ("great," "well-done"), and *pon* ("hitchhike"), which are local inventions, resulting from the addition of prefixes or suffixes to existing words.

Population and Birth Control

A few years ago, it was announced that Hormigueros, a small town in southeast Puerto Rico, had no space left to bury its dead. The few empty gravesites were reserved, and urban sprawl prevented expansion of the cemetery. Until new land was found, the dead of Hormigueros were taken to nearby Cabo Rojo, San Germán, or Mayagüez.

Hormigueros is a microcosm of the island's spiraling population problem. It took over 400 years after Columbus discovered Puerto Rico for the population to reach 1 million. Only forty years later, a second million was added. Today, there are 2.9 million people and a population density of 871 per square mile.

Public health measures have cut infant mortality and stretched average life expectancy from forty-six (1940) to seventy-two (1972), a figure higher than the U.S. average. In 1940, 198 children were born each day, while 94 persons died, for a yearly natural increase of 37,911. By 1972, births were down to 189 per day, but deaths plummeted to 52 daily, leaving an annual population gain of 49,903. At the present growth rate, Puerto Rico's population will reach 4.3 million by the year 2000.

Were it not for the mass migration of Puerto Ricans to the mainland in the past two decades, the island would already have 4.5 million people.

What looks like a population explosion is really, says one local writer, a "poverty explosion." The family whose parents graduated from high school has an average of 2.2 children. But parents who have not attended school bear an average of 6.3 children. Some poor families have as many as 15 or 20 children. Today, more than four persons in ten are under eighteen years of age. With relatively few wives working, this means that the male breadwinner must feed a large household.

Until 1936 it was a felony to offer birth prevention information. In 1948, the privately run Family Planning Association began to open clinics in various island towns, arousing criticism from the Roman Catholic Church. Eight years later—in an unpublicized experiment—836 Puerto Rican women became the first humans to take oral medication (Enovid pills) for birth control. By 1960, when the Popular Democratic Party began to offer birth control information at government health clinics, the island's Catholic bishops declared it a sin to vote for the PDP. They even formed a Christian Action Party to compete in the elections, but it vanished after receiving few votes.

Since the mid-1960's, the government Health Department has quickly expanded its "family planning" services in clinics throughout the island. Pregnant women who avail themselves of government health facilities are given advice on birth control methods and offered free contraceptives, or free sterilization, if they wish. Some proindependence groups charge that these programs are tantamount to "genocide," reducing the population rather than solving the chronic unemployment problem. But the government replies that its services are "voluntary," and that sterilization clinics are operating "at a top capacity" of about 1,000 operations per month, with "long waiting lists." A recent survey estimated that more than one-fourth of the women of child-bearing age in Puerto Rico have been sterilized.

The birth control program has already had a dramatic impact. Between 1960 and 1970, Puerto Rico's population rose by 15 per cent, and some age groups rose by as much as 57 per cent. But the number of children aged five to nine years increased by only 3 per cent, and those from less than one year old, up to four years old *decreased* by 10 per cent. Government officials predict that birth control measures will greatly relax future pressures in schools and other social services.

Patterns of Living

A generation ago, when most Puerto Ricans lived in the countryside, *"el pueblo,"* the nearest town, consisted of a plaza surrounded by a church, the municipal hall, a few stores, and a scattering of homes.

As Puerto Rico became industrialized, one-family homes cropped up around the cities. Pastures gave way to tidal waves of new "bedroom communities," a short drive from town.

More than twenty thousand new dwellings are built each year, three times as many as in 1950; of these, one-fourth are low-cost homes for the poor, built by the government. Private housing investment has quadrupled in a decade, and homebuilding represents 8 per cent of the gross product, twice the United States ratio.

The new executive elite has created a demand for lavish suburban homes and luxury high-rise apartments in San Juan. The housing boom is felt everywhere, but mostly in the 70-square-mile San Juan area, the core of a megalopolis that creeps westward along the coast to encompass Bayamón, eastward to Carolina, and south to Caguas. While the island's population grew 15 per cent between 1960 and 1970, populations in suburban areas have surged upward by 200 per cent. Many of the "suburbs," known as *urbanizaciones*, have their own shopping centers, churches, and schools. Whatever planners neglect to include is quickly added by the residents. Corner homes, or those on main avenues, are soon converted into barber shops, beauty parlors, real estate offices, grocery stores, bars, and auto parts distributors. Open-air carports are soon walled in, or second floors added, to accommodate a newborn child, an elderly parent, or as a rental unit. Thanks to year-round summer weather, muddy tracts soon blossom forth lawns, palm trees and flowers.

Housing Conditions

Tremendous strides have been made in improving the quality of housing in Puerto Rico. Not many years ago, a simple wooden house, with latrine out back and a communal water spigot, was the rule rather than the exception. Many homes were mere shacks with thatched roofs.

Nearly half of the homes in use today were built since 1960. More than 474,000 of the island's 709,000 dwellings have strong masonry walls and, in most cases, a concrete slab roof. Such modern conveniences as electricity, piped-in water, indoor toilets, tubs and showers, and refrigerators are now taken for granted by the majority of the people.

But there remains a great deal of "unfinished business." According to the 1970 Census, about 25 per cent of the island's homes are still "unsound," and another 14 per cent are "substandard" because they lack some basic convenience.

For example, nearly 250,000 homes (three-fourths of them in rural areas) still have neither access to public sewage nor septic tanks. About the same number of homes have no indoor flush toilet, and some 167,000 homes have no tub or shower. Furthermore, 90,000 homes have no piped water indoors, and more than

50,000 homes have no electricity or refrigerator. Only 33 per cent of urban homes, and 3 per cent of rural homes, have telephones.

Home ownership is very high in Puerto Rico: about 63 per cent of urban dwellings and 84 per cent of the rural are owner-occupied. But more than 80,000 of these homes are valued at less than $2,000. Indeed, the median value of all homes in the countryside is a mere $3,700.

Thus we have the sad contrast in Puerto Rico of many families living in homes that are comparable to middle-class dwellings anywhere, while many others lack the most basic amenities.

Money, or the lack of it, is clearly the reason. There is an undeniable correlation between the fact that nearly 40 per cent of the homes are "substandard" and the fact that about 42 per cent of the island's families earn less than $3,000 a year.

The poor simply cannot afford to buy better homes. Part of the problem is land scarcity (land costs now represent 34 per cent of a new home's price, nearly double the U.S. average), which encourages speculation and causes housing costs to climb 7 per cent yearly.

Today, the cheapest privately built homes on the island sell for $20,000, requiring a family income of $8,000 per year to qualify for a mortgage.

This is clearly impossible for the 42 per cent of the families who earn less than $3,000 a year. Even the "low-cost" condominum apartments built by the government sell for $15,000 and require an income of $6,000 to qualify.

(Not only the poor are caught in the housing dilemma. A 1974 survey showed that 10,000 middle-class families were anxious to buy new homes, and that some 12,000 new housing units were empty, but 9,000 of these available units were condominium apartments priced between $35,000 and $50,000. The developers "built for a market that doesn't exist," said one economist.)

The Slums

In Puerto Rico, a slum is called an *arrabal*. Thousands of island families still live in *arrabales* in the midst, or on the edge, of the cities.

Despite the hardship of urban poverty, some slum founders displayed a sense of humor in naming their communities. "La Perla" means The Pearl. One of the worst-smelling slums is called Buenos Aires ("Good Airs"). Others slums are called—in translation— Good Advice, Black Ass, Boston Braves, and Vietnam.

Puerto Rico's worst slum belt is located along the banks of the Martín Peña Channel, which begins at San Juan Bay and flows eastward for a few miles, emptying into the San José Lagoon. In this area of marshes and stagnant water, 71,000 people live in 14,000 tightly packed homes. The Martín Peña slum has the city's highest infant mortality rate, the greatest number of welfare cases, the highest rates of tuberculosis, pneumonia, delinquency, and violence. The slum emerged during the Depression years, and experienced startling growth in the 1950's. Most of the homes were built illegally on public land, of scrap wood and metal, with flimsy partitions for walls. Late arrivals built closest to the water, sometimes driving wooden piles into the black muck of contaminated water. The people use outdoor privies, and sidewalks consist of crude plank bridges above the water, which is full of garbage and human waste; much of the area is inaccessible to garbage pickup trucks. A few of the Martín Peña residents own their shacks, which have an average value of $1,400, but most families rent them, for an average of $23 a month. Newcomers may buy a crumbling shack for $100 to gain the land beneath it. After paying a $25 fine for clandestine construction (which, by now, is considered part of building costs), they will slowly fix it up. Municipal authorities, in a dilemma between obvious legal violations and the plight of the poor (who also vote), provide building materials, such as planks and roofing paper, as well as light and water outlets.

La Perla slum on the Atlantic Coast in Old San Juan is elegant by comparison with Martín Peña. Located on steep seaside banks, separated from the city by thick Spanish colonial fortification walls, La Perla is a labyrinthine Caribbean Casbah of 900 houses, with a population of 3,300. The beach is filthy, strewn with driftwood and garbage, an ideal site for the pigs that some families raise there. But a constant sea breeze eliminates the stench, which overwhelms the newcomer in some parts of the Martín Peña area. Despite poverty and high levels of violence, the general mood in La Perla is one of gaiety. There is constant noise from radios, jukeboxes, and television sets. Some homes are so closely packed together that one may see an elderly woman gazing out her window and into the window of a neighbor to watch an afternoon soap opera on television. Most of La Perla is served by electricity and water, and the narrow streets permit 'garbage trucks to descend from the city above for regular pickups.

The mere passage of time is no guarantee that housing conditions will improve. In 1960, there were 147,000 families in "substandard" homes. Ten years later, while the percentage of "substandard" homes had dropped, the absolute number had risen to 163,000 homes. More than 11,000 poor families are on waiting lists for public housing apartments (known as *caseríos*), and it appears that most of them have a long wait in store. In fact, if the current rates of "substandard" housing and public housing construction continue, the number of people in "substandard" homes will not diminish within the next half-century.

There were high hopes that the Federally funded Model Cities program of the 1960's would substantially improve the lives of thousands of families in the Martín Peña slum belt and in the nearby Nemesio Canales public housing project, where unemployment was about 40 per cent. Model Cities spent an average of $13,000 per family in services to provide health, welfare, employment, education, and job sources. But, according to Howard Stanton, a social scientist who worked on parts of the plan, much of the money would be diverted to salaries for middle-class technicians to administer these services. He suggested some years ago that giving each poor family $13,000 in a direct cash grant "might work better." In retrospect, he may have been right.

Poor families have grown so desperate for housing that many have invaded public or privately owned land and set up squatters' shacks. Sociologist Marcia Quintero calculates that between 1968 and 1972 about 6,000 Puerto Rican families took such drastic action, prompting the *San Juan Star* to describe the wave of land invasions as "a new social phenomenon."

A typical squatter is thirty-two-year-old Carlos Laboy, who

lived in a one-bedroom shack with his wife and three children in the slum of a small island town. He paid $35 a month rent for this shack, which was surrounded by open sewers. One rainy night, Laboy and several other heads of families sneaked onto vacant municipal land, which was being reserved for a hospital site. They had first decoyed the police into believing that the land invasion would be staged in another part of town. By the time the police arrived, they found a small "pioneer community" of pup tents and lean-tos, already occupied by Mrs. Laboy and the other mothers, who were cooking supper on wood fires. (Puerto Rican law makes it nearly impossible to demolish a squatter home once it is occupied.) A few weeks later, there were twenty-six new houses in the community, which called itself Villa Extensión San José. Sr. Laboy had nearly finished a new three-bedroom wood house. Building materials had cost him $1,000 and labor was donated by the neighbors. His children were enrolled in a nearby public school. Negotiations were under way to "plug in" to nearby municipal water and electrical sources.

The squatters concede that their actions are illegal but claim they have no choice. "I am a decent woman," said one middle-aged mother with a large family. "I work and pay my bills. With a lot of sacrifice I could get a loan of maybe $800 or $900. But what can I do with that? A lousy little piece of land costs $4,000. So here I am, fighting for me and my children."

Income and Welfare

Income in Puerto Rico has multiplied tenfold since 1940 but is still far below U.S. levels and is less equitably distributed.

While the top 10 per cent of the island's 450,000 families earned $10,000 or more in 1970, the 25 per cent at the bottom had to house, feed, and clothe themselves on less than $20 per week.

Between 1960 and 1970, median family income rose from $1,268 to $3,063 per year, but this was still only $60 per week, and much of the raise was eroded by inflation.

In 1973, reporter Tomás Stella of the *San Juan Star* looked in on a "typical" family. The only breadwinner was thirty-one-year-old Pablo Ramos, a carpenter's helper, whose $65 weekly wage is close to the island median. The Ramos household consisted of husband and wife, two children under eighteen, and a baby on the way, also close to the average family size of 4.3 persons.

Unlike most families, however, they did not live beyond their means. Pablo and Margarita Ramos worked for four years in New York (earning $180 weekly between them) and saved $2,000, enabling them to buy their furniture, appliances, TV set, washing machine, and phonograph for cash.

Here is how Mr. Ramos' $280 monthly income was divided: $46 in rent for a three-bedroom apartment in a public housing project; $135 in groceries (thanks to Mrs. Ramos' ingenuity and bargain-hunting, the family eats well—albeit simply—on this amount); $9 for electricity (water is free in the projects); $10 for *público* transportation to work since Mr. Ramos has no car; $38 for Mr. Ramos' "only vices"—beer and cigarettes; $13 for clothing; $5 in pocket money for the children; $10 on miscellaneous; $5 for medical care (there is a free public dispensary nearby). The only installment debt: $9 a month for the next few months to pay for a large oil painting of Venice, hanging in the living room, bought from an itinerant peddler. The Ramos family can't afford such "frills" as owning a car or attending movies. Mr. Ramos takes a hot meal from home for lunch. Mrs. Ramos sews most of her own clothing. "It's not easy," she sighs, "but it can be done."

By Puerto Rican standards, the Ramos family stands squarely in the middle. Half the island's population has an even harder struggle.

Unemployment (without mentioning thousands of persons who are underemployed, working less than thirty-five hours a week, or who are permanently out of the labor force) has wavered between 10 and 13 per cent for many years. The average jobless male has only six years of schooling, and many have had no schooling at all, which indicates that a major portion of the populace will, for a long time to come, be marginal to the society and depend upon some form of welfare.

The standard of living has risen sufficiently, and items of clothing are reasonably enough priced for even the poorest man to wear shoes, a clean pair of slacks, and sportshirt. But many of these "well-dressed poor" walk around with empty pockets, and stomachs much the same.

Welfare Payments. The Commonwealth government, with limited funds of its own, plus meager supplements from Washington, must spread welfare payments thin.

More than 300,000 Puerto Ricans (about one-ninth of the island's people) receive some form of welfare payments. The majority of them—268,000 persons, including 195,000 minors—receive aid to families with dependent children (AFDC). About 30,000 elderly, blind, or disabled persons are also on the welfare rolls.

Welfare is the sole source of income for nearly half the island's recipients, but the amounts are skimpy. Although a family of four needs a "rock bottom" of $135 per month to survive in Puerto Rico, the elderly, blind, or disabled get monthly checks of from $13 to $18. The typical needy family receives AFDC checks of less than $50 per month, about $9 per person (the U.S. average for AFDC families is $188 per month).

There is a widespread impression that most health and welfare benefits are paid by the Federal government, but Puerto Rico pays the largest share. Ceilings established by Congress severely limit the total amount of aid for Puerto Rico. The island must usually match Federal aid on a 50-50 basis, while the U.S. states pay as little as 17 cents for each Federal aid dollar and have no ceiling limits.

In the states of Mississippi, South Carolina and Alabama, for example, the Federal government picks up 80 per cent of the tab for AFDC payments, but only 47 per cent of Puerto Rico's.

Since residents of Puerto Rico do not pay Federal taxes, many Congressmen feel that the island should not share in programs to which it does not contribute.

However, Santiago Polanco Abreu, who was Puerto Rico's Resident Commissioner to Washington until 1968, claims that this argument has "little relevance." He says that Puerto Rico contributes to the U.S. general welfare "in many ways," by being a major U.S. export customer, by sending its sons to fight in the U.S. Armed Forces, and "besides, welfare residents cannot pay taxes anyway. It would be a strange system that determined welfare eligibility by the amount of Federal taxes the prospective recipients were fortunate enough to be paying."

Puerto Rico was totally excluded from a 1966 amendment to the Social Security Act, which pays monthly benefits to uninsured persons age seventy-two or over. Puerto Rico was again excluded in 1967, when the amendment was reamended, to increase monthly payments up to $75 a month.

In 1969, when President Nixon announced plans for a new type of guaranteed income plan for the poor, no mention was made, at first, of Puerto Rico. When officials in Washington were pressed, they said the island would participate, but that Puerto Rico's poor would get "somewhere around 55 per cent" of the benefits per capita compared with the mainland poor.

On the basis of its per capita income, Puerto Rico devotes a large portion of its resources to welfare. It spends $6.64 per $1,000 of personal income, compared to a U.S. mainland average of $4.86. But since it is working from such a small base, its payments are scanty, especially in the San Juan area, where the cost of living surpasses that of most American cities.

A not untypical case of the meager help provided by public welfare in Puerto Rico is that of Agripina Carrión, a forty-year-old woman, interviewed recently by a local journalist. Agripina Carrión lives in a public housing project with five children; her husband abandoned her eight years ago. Her lone source of income is a $37.25 monthly welfare check. One son, eighteen years old, dropped out of school after the sixth grade and is jobless. Another son, nineteen, who is an invalid and confined to a wheelchair, suffers from calcium deficiency and is getting worse. Their home is a three-bedroom public housing apartment, which is virtually bare, except for some scattered pieces of torn-up furniture. Mrs. Carrión pays her $6.50 monthly rent without fail. She pays $4 a month for electricity. The rest goes for food and clothing. She also receives a Federal food package, which includes rice, butter, wheat and corn flour, beans, and canned meats. She buys the rest at a nearby *colmado* (grocery store) on credit and usually owes $20 by the time the check arrives. Neither she nor her invalid son eats lunch. They awaken late, have coffee, bread and butter, perhaps an egg. That is all until suppertime. Her three young daughters eat a free lunch at school, provided by another Federal program. Her typical supper is rice, beans, and, perhaps, some canned meat or sausage. Once or twice a month they have a treat of fresh meat, usually chicken.

Surplus Food Program. The food Mrs. Carrión received came from surplus commodities distributed by the U.S. Department of Agriculture, in a program costing about $20 million yearly. Twenty-two different food products are given out monthly to nearly 500,000 people at distribution centers throughout the island. This program reaches people on relief, patients in medical and mental clinics, and children in day care centers. The food packages rarely last the entire month, but the items are appreciated by the poor. Many complain, however, that they cannot stomach the canned powdered milk (a number of poor in the country, or in the slums, feed this milk to pigs they raise in their backyards). Other recipients have picketed welfare offices, showing cheese, beans, corn meal, and rice that was infested with worms and maggots.

During 1974, the surplus food program was being phased out, in favor of gradual implementation of the Federal Food Stamp program. This program enables low-income families to multiply their food purchasing power, investing their money in food coupons, which are granted on the basis of a family's net income. One man, the father of six, is a diabetic with heart problems and is unable to work. He currently receives $100 monthly in welfare aid. By spending $29 of this amount on food coupons, he will be able to purchase $210 worth of groceries. In early 1975, it was estimated that from one-third to one-half of Puerto Rico's families would qualify for food stamps. In ten island towns, the numbers of families found eligible was about 80 per cent of the families counted by the 1970 census.

Health

Probably the most dramatic change in Puerto Rico in the past few decades has been the improvement in health and life expectancy. In the 1930's, two social scientists reported:

Sanitation in small towns and rural areas was almost nonexistent, water supplies were polluted, malaria, tuberculosis, gastritis-enteritis and other diseases were endemic. The resulting mortality rate was very high and life expectancy very low . . . There were few latrines in the rural areas, with the result of a very high incidence of hookworm.

Malnutrition was an important factor in the death rate, not so much from starvation, as by lowering resistance to disease. Poor and unsanitary housing was also instrumental in fostering disease and disability. Many of these troubles were due to ignorance. Even though the government spent an unusually high percentage of its income on education, less than half of the children had an opportunity to go to school, and for the majority this meant only a third grade education.

Draft calls during World War II offered appalling statistics. Out of 200,000 Puerto Ricans called to military service, 78 per cent failed for physical reasons. This was far worse than the U.S. rejection rate, which ranged from 15 to 40 per cent, depending upon the region. More recent Selective Service figures demonstrate the improvement in health standards. About 16 per cent of draftees were refused for health reasons, although a large number failed to qualify for educational or linguistic shortcomings.

Since 60 per cent of Puerto Rico's people cannot afford private medical or dental care, the burden has fallen upon the government. The island now spends more than $100 million a year on health, with about one-fourth of this amount coming from Federal funds.

A regionalized health care system of ninety-one hospitals and clinics is operated by the insular and municipal governments. There are also fifty private hospitals and clinics. In 1940, there were only 499 doctors (about one for every 3,745 persons). By 1970, there were 3,447 doctors (one per 1,269 persons). Many work with the government at fees well below those earned in private practice.

In addition to free medical and dental care programs, the government has special hospitals for tuberculosis, leprosy, and mental illness, and programs for cancer, heart disease, diabetes, and venereal disease.

Life expectancy, 46 years in 1940, is now 72 years. Infant mortality has dropped from 68 per thousand live births in 1950 to 27 in 1972 (still high, compared with the developed nations); deaths from malaria, tuberculosis, and diarrhea have dropped from 762 per thousand in 1940 to thirty. The drop in infant mortality and in deaths from infectious diseases has shifted importance to heart disease and cancer as major causes of death. It has also accented the need for elderly care facilities. Despite shortages of funds and trained personnel, facilities are admirable compared with a few years ago. As recently as 1950, about 85 per cent of all new babies were delivered by a midwife in the home; today about 98 per cent of all children are born in a hospital. Over 7,000 of Puerto Rico's 12,000 hospital beds have been made available in the last two decades. Within the past five years, a modern Centro Médico (Medical Center) has been built on several acres just outside San Juan, where the seriously ill are referred from regional clinics and hospitals. The Center has modern equipment, including radiotherapy treatment for cancer patients.

Health care, however, remains uneven. The sprawling $55 million Centro Médico was described as "useless" by the Secretary of Health, because of its unmanageable size, resulting in lost medical records and endless red tape. Smaller towns in remote areas have clearly inferior health care. The mountain town of Orocovis, with 22,000 people spread over eighteen far-flung *barrios,* recently had only one doctor at its municipal health center. In remote Jayuya, the average life span is ten years shorter than that of urban residents because of poverty, malnutrition, and inadequate health care.

Diet

Puerto Rican teenagers are taller and healthier than their parents. Higher income, more efficient marketing, and refrigeration have put protein-rich milk, eggs, and meat within reach of the vast majority of the public. About 20 per cent of the people suffer from some form of malnutrition, but this includes a surprising number of middle-class city dwellers who "eat the wrong foods and are overweight," according to health officials.

Supermarkets and grocery stores are well-stocked with American-brand canned goods, but although middle and upper income families often eat *americano* dishes, the typical meal has a distinctly Puerto Rican style.

For breakfast, eggs (usually boiled or fried), American cereals, coffee, and toast are common. But for lunch and dinner, rice and beans comprise the nucleus of the meal, in combination with meat or poultry.

The beans (white, rose, red, chickpeas, or pigeon peas) are made with *sofrito,* a spicy sauce that includes bacon, ham, lard, pepper, tomato, garlic, and onion. The *sofrito* is mixed with the beans and poured over boiled white rice. Another favorite is fried rice with pigeon peas or chickpeas.

The *plátano* ("plantain") and the *guineo* ("banana") are also mainstays in Puerto Rican cuisine. The green plantain is sliced, flattened, and fried into crisp *tostones.* The "ripe plantain," called an *amarillo* because of its yellow color, is served boiled, as are green bananas. Typical country staples are starchy roots, such as the *batata* (a white sweet potato), the *yautía* ("tanier"), the *ñame* (also a white potato-type root), the calabash, and the eggplant.

Another traditional favorite is *bacalao,* dried salted codfish, which is served stewed with vegetables, in an omelet, or in a vegetable salad platter known as the *serenata.* Fresh fish is not too common, since the bulk of the people come from the island's interior. Some rural folk become ill when exposed to the strong odor of fresh seafood. But fish and lobster are eaten in San Juan and in some coastal towns, as are *jueyes* ("land crabs"), which once abounded in the marshlands outside San Juan, where housing developments have rendered them scarce.

Lechón asado ("roast pig") is indispensable at Christmas or for other special occasions. The pig is roasted for hours on an outdoor spit until the skin is crisp. Roadside stands sell *lechón* and large chunks of skin, called *chicharrón.* The pig, easily raised in the countryside and inexpensive in the stores, is popular in island cuisine. In addition to pork chops and pig's feet, there are: *cuchifrito,* a mixed stew of pig innards; *mondongo,* pork tripe cut into tiny pieces and stewed in a *sofrito; gandinga,* chopped pork liver, heart, and kidney, cooked with various condiments and served with vegetable or rice.

Other favorites are *arroz con pollo* ("chicken with rice") and *asopao,* a thick soup of rice and chicken or seafood. A holiday delicacy is the *pastel,* a flat cake made of meat, mashed plantains, raisins, olives, and spices. These are blended, wrapped in green banana leaves, boiled in water, and served hot. *Sancocho,* a soup with chunks of meat and vegetables, is also considered typical.

Mofango has been jocularly described as "a Puerto Rican matzoh ball." It consists of mashed roasted plantain, combined with bacon and other spices and rolled into a ball. (It goes well with chicken soup.) Puerto Rico's answer to the Chinese egg roll is the *alcapurria* (which is more submarine-shaped than cylindrical), a fritter made from tanier and banana and stuffed with crab or meat.

Among the meat dishes, a specialty is *carne mechada,* a beef roast stuffed with onion, ham, and spices. The typical *biftec* ("beef steak") is thinner and tougher than American cuts, but tasty. It is often served breaded, as an *empanada,* or fried with egg, when it is called *rebanada.*

The most popular snacks are fritters: *bacalaito* is a codfish-based batter dropped into hot oil, yielding delicious cakes; *pastelillos* are fried turnovers, filled with meat, cheese, or jam; *rellenos de papa* are mashed potato balls, stuffed with meat, covered with egg batter, and fried. Pizza parlors and hotdog and hamburger stands are also widespread in the cities, as are establishments that sell whole roast chickens "to go."

Puerto Rico's most ubiquitous dessert is *flan* ("caramel custard"). Bland, white native cheese is also favored, served with guava paste, sweetened guava shells, papaya, or orange preserves.

Strong island-grown coffee is preferred to American brands. Most Puerto Ricans order their coffee *con leche,* half a cup of black brew and half of warm milk. The *pocillo negro,* a black demitasse, well-sugared, is preferred after a big dinner.

Puerto Ricans eat American-style cellophane-wrapped white bread, but also like their own hard-crusted long loaves. These are often used to make the *sandwich Cubano,* filled with cheese, pork, pickles, salami, or turkey, which is the local equivalent of the Italian "hero" or "submarine" sandwich. (Several Italian and Chinese restaurants in San Juan do a thriving business among

Puerto Rican families, who find the prices reasonable and enjoy the rice- or noodle-based dishes.)

The poor eat much the same food, but the accent is on starchy, filling items. In the country, meat is usually obtained from what is raised on the farm: chicken, pork, and, occasionally, goat or rabbit. Rather than American breakfast cereals, corn meal is served with milk and sugar. The urban poor eat chicken, but not every day, or canned sausage, or *carne bif* (tins of Argentine corned beef) with rice and beans.

As more Puerto Rican women work, there is less time to stand over the *sofrito* or prepare the more elaborate stews. A simple *biftec* and potatoes (and, in a growing minority of cases, a TV dinner) is often the answer. Some enterprising local businessmen now offer canned *sofrito* sauce and "heat and eat" *pasteles*.

Town and Country

Puerto Ricans refer to all areas outside of the city of San Juan as *la isla* ("the island"). Specifically rural regions, however, are called *el campo* ("the countryside").

El campo, once the base of Puerto Rico's society in social and economic terms, now plays a lesser role. Despite high birth rates, rural *barrios* have lost people, as the young marry and migrate in search of a better *ambiente,* which, in literal terms, means environment or atmosphere but connotes everything from the chance for a better-paying job to the peculiar fascination and movement of the city, which attracts rural folk in all parts of the world. But the *campo* is not forgotten. City families visit their country relatives often. It is a popular form of weekend recreation—and de rigueur at Christmas—to board one's car, or hire a *público,* and head for the hills. Late Sunday afternoons, main roads are heavy with cars taking families back to suburbia after a *paseo* ("drive") to the country.

Rural Subcultures

During most of the island's history, the rural folk lived only partly on a cash economy. They grew much of what they ate and exchanged surplus crops and labor for other goods and services.

At the beginning of the twentieth century, large sugarcane plantations in coastal areas were established by U.S. corporations, who bought up and combined smaller farms owned by native *hacendados*. The landless peasants no longer dealt on a face-to-face, personal level with their *patrón,* who, for years, had been a local resident property owner. They became a wage-earning proletariat, who spent at company stores and accepted advance loans from the corporation, their sole source of income during the *"tiempo muerto,"* the dead period between harvests. Since absentee owners could not satisfy personal needs, labor unions were formed. But local issues were usually settled at some distant point, in conferences between corporate management and labor leaders. A multilevel society of small farmers, peon helpers, merchants, and native *hacendados* swiftly changed to one with a homogeneous mass of proletarian laborers, a small corps of company foremen, and absentee owners. In 1894, before the American occupation, there were 205 separate sugar *haciendas.* By 1948, there were only thirty-five—much larger—plantations, and the twelve largest were owned by four U.S. corporations.

Since it is not very profitable to farm sugarcane in rugged mountain country, change occurred mainly along the flat coastal plains that ring the island. Where tobacco, coffee, and mixed fruits and vegetables were cultivated on steep hillsides, the communities retained more of their traditional structure.

In coffee country, small and large plantations were held by local owners who employed *"agregados"* (landless peasants) or owners of small farms in need of extra cash. Part of the labor was paid for in food crops.

In tobacco and coffee regions, there are more land-owning families. This fact strongly influences the life style of the people. For example, in order to formalize property ownership and facilitate inheritance, these families tended to marry, whereas a much higher percentage of landless sugar laborers entered common-law marriage. When the children of land-owning parents marry, they can often settle in the parents' home or build their own *casita* on the land. The father is more dominant in coffee and tobacco country, particularly if he is a property owner. Among the sugar workers, the woman plays a more central role; she may be the partner in a string of common-law marriages, but it is she who houses and cares for the offspring.

Where there is a native farm owner, his workers will often seek him out as a *compadre,* and, thus, establish a personal link between people of different economic levels. Sugarcane laborers cannot become *compadres* of distant American corporate owners, and tend to seek *compadres* from among their co-workers. In the 1930's, sugar workers were selling their votes for a pair of shoes; they were helpless political pawns, delivered en masse to the highest bidder. Without land, they could not accumulate capital by selling property; wages were so low that the only way to strike it rich was to hit the lottery or enjoy a streak of luck in some form of gambling.

The poor suffer much the same plight in the tobacco and coffee regions. But the composition of the community and the lines of power and influence are far different. The community composition is "healthier" in the sense that there is more local leadership, a larger middle class, more property owners. It is probably no mere coincidence that some of these mountainous regions have, for years, demonstrated greater support for Puerto Rican independence than have the areas inhabited by the landless proletariat, or that they have enjoyed better community services in health and education than is commonly found in coastal regions, or that from them have emerged more "success stories" of the poor young man struggling his way to the top by his own enterprise.

Social Structure

The industrial revolution has changed Puerto Rico from an agrarian two-class society to one that is moving quickly toward a modern industrial system. The old Spanish and creole upper classes have made room for American corporate managers in what amounts, now, to a triumvirate, where industry and bureaucratic and commercial activity, rather than land ownership, are given emphasis. The island's "old rich," with some exceptions, have survived the impact of the new wave. But they have had to learn

English and adapt to the American way of doing business in order to survive.

For business and relaxation, the wealthy travel often to the United States. They may have a second home or small farm in the countryside; some are still involved in the fine art of raising *paso fino* horses, others maintain yachts at the Club Náutico, or swim or play tennis at private clubs, or join the clubs of the more prestigious hotels, such as the Caribe Hilton or Dorado Beach.

The children of the upper class attend private schools; many of them study abroad. They have larger church weddings and receptions, the costs of which are usually exaggerated. Since the girls often attend U.S. colleges, it is not uncommon today to marry a young American from a "good" family, honeymoon in Europe, and later settle in Puerto Rico or on the mainland. As women grow older and raise a family, they become active in civic, cultural, and charitable organizations in much the same way as their wealthy American counterparts.

The men still congregate with the same "crowd" for business luncheons at the Top of the First in Santurce or the Banker's Club in Hato Rey. If one examines their business interests and investment dossiers, one notes a complex interlocking directorate, which links a small number of families in major banking, real estate and commercial firms (industrial production has been largely the province of U.S. investment companies).

Even in government, the tiny elite nature of Puerto Rican society up until the 1940's is evident among today's major figures. In the Statehood Republican Party, the candidate for governor and the party head were brothers-in-law, uniting two prominent island families. Blood lines even cross party lines in many cases, causing statehooders and *independentistas*—both tugging in opposite directions in the public view—to socialize frequently at family gatherings, thus tending to ameliorate what might otherwise be abstract hatreds. Even where family links do not exist, the smallness of the society frequently joins together people of the same class (and/or profession). Thus, it was not altogether surprising, a few years ago, to see an independence leader and a statehood leader, both lawyers, enjoying lunch together at a "kosher-style" restaurant in the hotel district.

The Middle Class

The important social phenomenon in the past thirty years has been the creation of a substantial middle class. It would be wrong to suppose that all members of this dynamic, growing sector of the society emerged from the poor. Many came from what amounted to a submerged, impoverished middle class of the traditional era—the son of the small store owner or of the small but self-sufficient farmer—and have used the growing economy to advance themselves far beyond the scope of their parents' world. At the upper end of this class, the demand for doctors, lawyers, and other professionals has created an expanded community of people who live under conditions of modest wealth. In a survey taken in 1948, only 427 Puerto Rican families reported yearly income of $10,000. Even supposing a certain degree of fibbing on income tax returns, the real number of families cannot have been much larger. Today, there are over 56,000 families in the $10,000-plus bracket and—even more important—over 172,000 families who earn more than $5,000. There are factory and office managers, advertising account executives, salesmen, accountants, teachers, and a host of small entrepreneurs who provide services for this new wage-earning class. The island's universities have 63,000 students, most of them children of the middle class.

As recently as 1960, the largest single source of employment was agriculture, which provided about 25 per cent of the jobs on the island. By 1970, less than 8 per cent of Puerto Rico's workers were in agriculture. Manufacturing had become the major industry (19 per cent of the workers), followed by commerce (16 per cent), "professional and related services" (14 per cent), and construction (11 per cent). Together with their jobs, people were changing their life styles.

Social Mobility

Puerto Rico's upper class are known as *blanquitos* ("little whites") by the poor, many of whom are also white. Although the rigid class structure of the countryside has been relaxed, a member of the lowest class rarely makes the big jump to the opposite extreme. But it does happen. A few of the island's most prominent business and government servants have emerged from the most impoverished of circumstances. The son of a landless cane worker may go to college and become a doctor. But, more often, he will—if he is extremely well motivated and not forced to drop out due to economic hardship—finish high school, perhaps attend some night classes, and become a bank clerk, an accountant, or a draftsman.

The fast-changing structure of the economy has created some overnight fortunes in real estate. Owners of relatively modest tracts of land which have, by some stroke of luck, been proper for hotel or suburban housing or shopping center development have reaped sizable fortunes. The rapid rise in land values has also touched the lower-middle-class property owner who, unable to accumulate cash savings from his salary, often sells his home for enough of a profit to "buy up" to a better dwelling.

But even the new style of suburban living perpetuates a class structure. Housing developments range far and wide in price and quality, which means that most "upper middle" families reside in communities of their own, perhaps adjacent to a "middle middle" or "lower middle" cluster of homes, priced a few thousand dollars less, and so on down the line, unlike the traditional *pueblo,* where rich and poor lived in close proximity and mingled during the course of the day.

The Family

Upheavals in Puerto Rico's social structure have also been felt in the home. In preindustrial days, the typical family followed the Latin American (and old European) stereotype: *Papá* was boss, no questions asked. *Mamá* was the "silent partner" in the household. Although the husband trusted her judgment in important matters, he announced the final decision, while she remained quietly in the background. The children respected their father, but *la madre* was adored, and any insult, no matter how indirect, of the mother, was (and is) considered the supreme offense, to be answered by violence. Family protection of a young daughter's virginity amounted to an obsession. On the other hand, the values of *machismo* ("virility") were inculcated in young men.

After marriage, the pattern of the "worldly" husband and the wholesome, stable, home-oriented wife continued. The wife was idealized, sometimes revered, as a second mother by her mate. The husband, on the other hand, was not severely stigmatized if he carried on a discreet (sometimes blatantly open) affair with a *querida,* or "hunted" for occasional adventure.

At social gatherings in the home, after the usual salutations, males would usually congregate to discuss politics, sports, or business, while the women, off in another corner, talked about family matters. Young girls led sheltered lives; boys were more pampered and encouraged to explore. Even today, when a girl is born, although she is the light of her father's eyes, he will accept mild kidding from his friends, who call him a *chancletero* ("slipper-maker," which in some vague way means maker of useless things). They may cast mild aspersions on his virility, his *machismo,* if he is unable to produce a male heir.

These relationships have been altered with Puerto Rico's social change, but they have not disappeared. Women have been "liberated" to the extent that they travel more, contribute their wages to the household's welfare, and are more "vocal partners" than before; the image of the *madre sufrida* ("suffering mother") stuck at home is slowly fading, but working wives have managed to retain their femininity. Today, middle-class women may drive a second family car to shop alone at the market or department store, whereas this was taboo years ago, but they will rarely venture out at night without the husband. With the growth of employment in the teaching profession, in clerical and factory jobs, woman's role in the society has expanded significantly.

The man is now a somewhat tamer *macho,* although he rarely if ever attains the amiable docility depicted in the stereotyped image of the American father on some U.S. television shows. He still asserts his freedom with the ritual of *viernes social* ("social Friday"), where, on payday, he may linger with "the boys" for drinking and socializing.

There is less common-law marriage today, and divorce by a Catholic couple is rarely considered shocking, except in some smaller towns, where tradition is stronger. In the city, the custom of chaperoning has relaxed. Today, one sees teenage couples at the movies, or the beach, or—on school campuses—affectionately embracing in a manner that would have scandalized passersby a few years ago.

The Extended Family. The traditional extended family—where parents, grandparents, children, cousins, uncles, and aunts live in close proximity—is also undergoing change. The extended family guaranteed that no orphaned child of a relative would remain homeless; that, despite the extreme misfortune of some member, he would not go hungry or lack a place to sleep; that there was always someone available for an emergency trip to the hospital, or ready to dip into savings to avoid some crisis, or able to speak to someone to get you a job, or some other favor. Today, with suburbia, there is more of what sociologists call the "nuclear family," with a husband, a wife, and their children under one roof, isolated from the rest of their relatives. But the old patterns are tenacious, and the extended family provides too much comfort to discard so readily.

As the island goes rapidly urban, geography tends to loosen the ties of the extended family, but relatives still try to live near each other, and their social life largely consists of visiting each other on weekends. Many elderly parents, unable to fend for themselves, can still count upon a married son or daughter to make space for them; the living room sofa is also there for young brothers, cousins, nephews, and nieces, perhaps from the countryside, who come to town seeking higher education or a first job.

Despite the increase in "nuclear families" and the multiplication of services provided by government in health, welfare, and employment, the extended family, and the parallel network of *compadre* relationships, still comprise an effective form of social security. This traditional pattern is now being augmented by new friendships—beyond family and *compadre* lines—which are established among one-time strangers, often from different towns and ways of life, who now meet on the common ground of the factory, or labor union hall, or school, or office.

In many respects, particularly in the growing middle class, the options have expanded for Puerto Rico's men and women, who have one foot planted in tradition and the other probing gingerly for new pathways.

8 The Diaspora

This Puerto Rican is silent
This Puerto Rican is sad
    to be silent and sad
    I feel something big
       or low
       or dark
       is going on
       in the back
       of the mind man.
This Puerto Rican is silent and sad.
The color no white man dares to ask.
       —From a bilingual poem,
       "Jet Neorriqueño/Neo-Rican
       Jetliner," by JAIME CARRERO

No book on Puerto Rico can ignore the more than 1.5 million *puertorriqueños,* by birth or parentage, who live on the United States mainland. More Puerto Ricans live in New York City than in the island's capital, San Juan. More live in Hartford or Chicago than in most cities of the island. With about one-third of its people living "in exile," Puerto Rico is indeed a divided nation.

There were small, scattered Puerto Rican communities on the U.S. mainland well before the turn of the century, but the trickle northward grew to tidal wave size after World War II. Thousands of Puerto Ricans boarded those $45 one-way flights from San Juan's Isla Grande airport, responding to New York City's booming job market. Back then, aboard prop planes that took eight bumpy hours, it was the equivalent of a moon voyage for the travelers, who had never seen snow, subways, or skyscrapers and knew little or no English.

In 1940, only 70,000 Puerto Ricans lived on the U.S. mainland. By 1950 the number had multiplied to 301,000, and a decade later the figure rose to 887,000. The 1970 census showed nearly 1.5 million Puerto Ricans on the mainland, including 650,000 second-generation persons born in the United States. These figures are conservative, because even the Bureau of Census concedes that it undercounted all minority groups. Nor do they reflect the tremendous volume of back-and-forth travel between Puerto Rico and the U.S. mainland. Each year, about 2.5 million passengers fly in and out of San Juan, and less than half are American tourists.

Between 1960 and 1970, while the island's population grew by 15 per cent, the mainland community expanded by 61 per cent (largely due to the birth of second generation children). At this rate, by some time in the late 1980's more Puerto Ricans might live on the mainland than in Puerto Rico.

The United States was synonymous with *Nueva York* until a few years ago, but four out of ten Puerto Ricans now settle elsewhere. New York is still the "heart" of the Puerto Rican diaspora, with about 1 million *puertorriqueños,* but more than 150,000 have moved across the Hudson River to New Jersey, 100,000 more are in Illinois, and there are large communities in California, Pennsylvania, Connecticut, Florida, Massachusetts, and Ohio. Every state has at least a few Puerto Rican families, and more than twenty-nine cities across the country have populations of 5,000 or more. A *New York Times* reporter who visited Connecticut recently said: "In New Haven, Hartford, Meriden and New Britain, the piquant smell of spices and the sound of Latin rhythms now drift out to the sidewalks where most of the signs are in Spanish."

While Europe has been the main source of newcomers to the United States during the past century, the postwar migration has had a decidedly Hispanic flavor. The 1970 census counted 5.2

million Mexicans, 1.5 million Puerto Ricans and 630,000 Cubans on the mainland; add to this a million other Spanish-speaking migrants (many of them illegal aliens) from the Dominican Republic and Central and South America.

The Puerto Rican phenomenon has been unlike any other migration in America's history. Europeans came in great waves during the nineteenth and the early twentieth century, and relatively few returned to their homelands. But the Puerto Rican migration coincided with the jet age, and, since Puerto Ricans are American citizens, travel between the mainland and the *patria* is fast, cheap, and unfettered by quotas or passport requirements. The homesick Puerto Rican, discouraged by cold weather, unemployment, culture shock—or even a broken romance—can pack up and be home in three hours. Virtually every Puerto Rican dreams of eventual return; as one teacher in New York said recently, "This is no place to raise kids; when I marry, back to *la isla* I go." Return migration is already an important statistic; in 1970, the island's population included 106,602 persons who were born in the U.S. to Puerto Rican parents—double the number ten years before. The emotional pull of the island is so great that airlines also transport numerous coffins—complying with the last wish of Puerto Ricans who insist upon being buried in their native soil.

In the early years, the typical Puerto Rican migrant fell into a classic pattern, staying with a friend or relative until he, too, found employment. Sometimes he came in response to a relative's letter, advising that a job was available in a factory or restaurant, or pushing clothesracks around the bustling streets of the garment district, which paid double the going rate of the canefields.

Other migrants were first recruited for seasonal work on U.S. farms; when the crop was harvested, they drifted to nearby towns, found year-round work, and sent for the family.

Today an estimated total of 40,000 Puerto Rican men still fly back and forth each year to work on U.S. farms, mainly in Connecticut, New Jersey, and New York. Because these workers were frequently victimized by unscrupulous growers (and were unprotected by unions), the Commonwealth government took the unprecedented step, in the mid-1940's, of opening a Migration Division in Manhattan, with regional offices in several cities. The

Migration Division negotiates an annual contract with growers, establishing minimum wages and work hours, air transportation, and insurance. Its field representatives inspect farm conditions, and its offices in Puerto Rico recruit workers. Puerto Rican law prohibits growers from recruiting noncontract workers on the island, but half of the farm workers still migrate without protection of contract.

For self-protection in an alien environment, most newcomers to the United States stick together. Recently, for example, on a street in Newark, the grocery store owner and most tenants in surrounding buildings came not only from the same island town, but from the same *barrio*.

Even in the best of times, Puerto Rican migrants are hampered by language and racial barriers; today their troubles are compounded by a shrinking demand for unskilled and semiskilled labor in the jobs that were so abundant some decades ago, when immigrants poured across the Atlantic from Europe.

The U.S. Department of Labor estimates that for every white American out of work, 1.8 members of minority groups are in the same predicament. Thus, when the U.S. jobless figure hits 7 percent, at least 13 per cent of the Puerto Ricans are out of work.

But official unemployment figures don't tell the whole story. They are based on the "labor force," which consists of adults who are either working or actively seeking work. Many Puerto Ricans, disheartened by their fruitless search for jobs, have dropped out of the labor force. This is particularly so among teenagers, who may not be the family breadwinners, but whose income represents a vital supplement. If these chronically unemployed persons were included, the "real" jobless rate for mainland Puerto Ricans would be *33 per cent,* a figure unmatched since the U.S. Depression of the 1930's.

Because of this grim job picture, only one of ten Puerto Rican families earns $12,000 or more per year (compared with four of every ten U.S. families). More than one-fourth of the mainland Puerto Rican families have incomes below the Federal poverty level and depend upon welfare payments for survival.

But despite frequently heard accusations that "Puerto Ricans come to the United States to get on welfare," the facts speak otherwise.

In the 1950's, before "Operation Bootstrap" generated a large manufacturing industry on the island, a net balance of 46,000 Puerto Ricans migrated to the U.S. each year. In the 1960's, when the island's economy improved dramatically, migration dropped to an average of 14,000 person per year.

In the 1970's the mainland economy soured, culminating in the recession of 1974–75. Times were even worse in Puerto Rico, where unemployment soared to 18 per cent, and food prices were 20 per cent higher than on the mainland. Welfare and unemployment benefits in most U.S. states are far superior to those on the island. But during the three years from 1972 through 1974 migration to the United States not only dried up but reversed itself. About 50,000 Puerto Ricans returned home, discouraged by the lack of jobs. Welfare has not been enough of an incentive to uproot Puerto Ricans from their native land. As one man said, "If I have to be poor, I'd rather be poor at home."

It was hoped that the Federal "War on Poverty" of the 1960's, which involved expenditures of hundreds of millions of dollars, would narrow the gap between America's "haves" and "have-nots." But the program appears to have done more for its middle-class bureaucrats (most of them white) than for the supposed beneficiaries. Between 1959 and 1971, median income for U.S. white families rose from $5,893 to $10,672. Black family income rose from $3,161 to $6,440, but its ratio to white income only went up from 53 per cent to 60 per cent. Puerto Ricans *fell behind* during the "War on Poverty." Family income rose from $3,811 to $6,185, but its ratio to white family income dropped from 64 per cent to 58 per cent. (The reasons for this lack of upward mobility are not only racial or cultural but also stem from the well-entrenched "class" nature of U.S. society. In 1947, the wealthiest one-fifth of America's families took home 43 per cent of the income, while the poorest fifth made do with only 5.1 per cent. Twenty-five years later, both groups were in about the same position: 41.4 per cent and 5.4 per cent.)

Puerto Rican migrants have been mainly limited to the hardest, lowest-paying jobs. Of the 194,000 Puerto Rican men employed in the United States in 1970, only 4 per cent were in professional or technical jobs (compared with 15 per cent of the U.S. white population). About 25 per cent worked in factories, 19 per cent had "service" jobs (deliveries, dishwashing, maintenance), 15 per cent were craftsmen, and 12 per cent held clerical jobs.

Among the 91,000 employed women, a slightly higher proportion (6.5 per cent) were in professional or technical careers. The largest number, 40 per cent, worked in factories, while 31 per cent had clerical jobs and 11 per cent were in "service" work.

Many workers have been hampered by language barriers and lack of skills, but they have also been held down by employers and unions who—in violation of Federal civil rights laws—resist change in the racial and ethnic composition of their work forces.

For example, while about 15 per cent of New York City's population is Puerto Rican, less than 2 per cent of the city's police force is Puerto Rican. The imbalance is even worse in some cities, where police departments disqualify Puerto Ricans because of their height or suddenly "upgrade" their standards, requiring two years of college.

In New York's schools, nearly one-quarter of the students are Puerto Rican, but only 1 per cent of the teachers are Puerto Rican. The powerful teachers' union has placed numerous obstacles in the path of Puerto Ricans (and other Hispanics) who seek certification as teachers. Only a lawsuit by the recently formed Puerto Rican Legal Defense Fund managed to win a victory for bilingual education, in a city where more than 100,000 Spanish-dominant children sorely need this type of help. (New Jersey in 1974 also approved a bilingual education program but did not appropriate funds to implement it.) In a few city school districts, Puerto Rican community members have, after much struggle, achieved majorities on school boards and begun to appoint more Hispanic teachers and administrators. But they are being fought every inch of the way. One board chose a Puerto Rican woman with eighteen years of experience for the principal's job in a Manhattan school where two-thirds of the children are Hispanic. The board's decision was challenged by the unsuccessful white American candidate for the job, who claimed that he had even longer experience and more academic credentials. The board replied that its candidate was bilingual, making her ideally suited for that particular school. But the state Human Rights Commission reversed the board's appointment on the grounds that the American candidate was discriminated against because of his "national origin."

Slowly but surely, the sheer pressure of numbers has "Puerto-ricanized" many communities in the United States. There are large Hispanic *barrios* with clothing, appliance and furniture stores, *colmados* that sell Caribbean food, *botánicas* that dispense herbs and prayer candles to ward off illness and evil spirits, and a growing Spanish-language presence in many "American" businesses.

At first, Puerto Rican migrants were an amorphous mass of humanity, linked to their *patria* by relatives, friends, and nostalgic memories. Much of that continues, but now the mainland community has created its own political, business, social and cultural institutions.

Caguas-born Herman Badillo is now a veteran of the U.S. Congress and was a serious candidate in the mayoralty race for New York City. A handful of Puerto Ricans have won seats in the New York State legislature. Hundreds of Puerto Ricans are civil servants in Federal, state, and city government agencies. Island banks now have several branches in the United States. There are associations of Puerto Rican businessmen, police officers, and army veterans. Organized crime, too, has been infiltrated by Puerto Ricans, Cubans, and other Hispanics, and, in the *barrios,* the "numbers" game is *la bolita.* Following in the footsteps of other "ethnic" Americans, Puerto Rican youths have organized into gangs for self-protection and power over neighborhood turf. One youth gang, the Young Lords, evolved into a militant political group that strongly influenced *barrio* life. There are nearly eighty *hijos ausentes* ("absent sons") clubs comprising former residents of island towns. The Absent Sons of Arroyo, of Salinas, of Arecibo, and other towns hold well-attended weekend dances, and some provide social welfare services for members. (The tiny island of Culebra, with 700 residents, has two "absent sons" clubs in New York with more than 2,000 members.) Organizations such as the Puerto Rican Forum and the Puerto Rican Community Development Project have sprouted up, offering jobs, manpower training, and political patronage. Hundreds of storefront churches, with Puerto Rican lay ministers, offer spiritual solace—and some provide child day care for working mothers. Apartment dwellers have organized into tenant groups to protest deplorable housing conditions. The Aspira agency reaches into schools, with career guidance and financial aid for further education. More than a dozen colleges now have Puerto Rican studies departments or programs.

Spanish-language television in the New York–New Jersey area offers the news *en español,* live variety shows, and *novelas* (soap operas). The Spanish-language daily *El Diario* has a large circulation, but also on sale at the newsstands is an English supplement to *Claridad,* the daily of the Puerto Rican Socialist Party. There are a growing number of community art galleries, bookstores, and theater groups. Poets and writers such as Jesus Colón, Victor Hernández Cruz, Pedro Pietri, Jack Agüeros, Piri Thomas, and Alfredo Lopez have contributed to a growing body of English-language literature about the Puerto Rican mainland experience. A bilingual magazine, *The Rican* (published three times a year in Chicago by Samuel Betances), has enhanced communications within the growing Puerto Rican intelligentsia on the mainland. A young self-styled "Hunga-Rican" (half Puerto Rican, half Hungarian) named Freddie Prinze now stars on a network television show. Puerto Ricans are still vastly underrepresented in the mass media, but the few exceptions have occurred only in the past four years.

Even more dynamic change is expected during the next few years, because the Puerto Rican community is very young. About three-fourths of the 363,000 mainland families have children under eighteen, and nearly half have children of preschool age. While the typical migrant from Puerto Rico is thirty years old (the median age for all Americans), the median age of the 650,000 second-generation Puerto Ricans is only 9.3 years. As the second generation grows to maturity, the potential repercussions—political, social, economic—are huge.

For example, while the average migrant adult has only 8.6 years of schooling (this was the U.S. average thirty years ago), second-generation Puerto Rican adults have 11.5 years of schooling, just one semester behind the nationwide figure. While only 20 per cent of the migrants have a high school education, about 45 per cent of the second-generation adults have finished high school (compared with the U.S. median of 52 per cent). While only 1.9 per cent of the migrants are college graduates, about 5.5 per cent of the second-generation have college diplomas (the U.S. average is 10 per cent).

The same pattern prevails in school enrollment. Only 28 per cent of the migrants ages three to thirty-four were enrolled in schools in 1970, largely because of language problems. But about 67 per cent of the second-generation Puerto Ricans in that age bracket were studying.

Puerto Ricans born on the U.S. mainland generally have higher incomes than migrants, and, because they speak English well, interact more with the larger society. (For example, while only 20 per cent of the migrants marry non-Puerto Ricans, about half of the second generation intermarries.)

These trends should not be misinterpreted to convey a rosy picture of socio-economic assimilation. The great majority of Puerto Rican adults on the mainland are migrants, and more arrive with each plane from San Juan. They and their children face awesome obstacles: rent-gouging landlords, dead-end jobs (when they can find them), and hostility from other ethnic groups. Many of the young are frustrated by rising aspirations, as well as a lingering identity crisis. One young Puerto Rican student at Hunter College plans to return to the island, where his parents live. Many of his friends at school are Puerto Ricans born in New York, and

. . . about one-third of them would like to go back, the others think of Puerto Rico as a place for hicks. They don't think of themselves as Americans either, they call themselves New Yorkers, and usually hang out with other p.r.'s . . . even though they're white, they call Americans "whites." Their parents speak Spanish, they speak both, sometimes together, and mix it up with Negro slang, like "*Tú sabe*, man, I can't do that, *qué tú crees?* I would like to, *pero no puedo.*"

Joseph Monserrat, former Director of the Migration Division of the Commonwealth of Puerto Rico's Department of Labor in New York City, and later president of the city's Board of Education, feels that by the year 2000, the Puerto Ricans in the States—via their experience there and, also, by return migration—will have an important hand in determining the future relations of Puerto Rico and the United States.

One problem he sees is American racism, which he calls "inherent . . . a cultural trait . . . not an aberration, but the norm." No issue, he says, "will have a greater effect upon the Puerto Rican communities of the States than the present struggle for equality that is so frequently referred to as the Black Revolution." But, he adds, the revolution is more than black, and involves many groups, including the Puerto Rican, the "only racially integrated group in the United States" who because of this "suffer the peculiar problem of not being understood either by their black brothers or by their so-called white neighbors."

Of the second and third generation on the mainland, Monserrat adds:

> . . . no Puerto Rican in Puerto Rico need constantly remind himself that he is Puerto Rican. The New Puerto Rican, on the other hand, must almost literally remind himself every minute of the day . . . if he does not . . . there are many others who will not let him forget it. . . . He does not have, as does his father and his older brothers, the knowledge of knowing what it is to be a Puerto Rican in Puerto Rico. He has been raised in a setting where he is a minority, where he is different, which in the reality of the United States has always meant to be "less than," i.e., inferior to others.

Samuel Betances, the Harlem-born publisher of *The Rican* magazine, said in a recent issue:

> Puerto Ricans are sometimes white, they are sometimes black, and they are sometimes Puerto Ricans—and so they are quite often confused. . . . The single most crucial issue burning deep in the souls of many young, second generation Puerto Ricans in the United States is that of the wider identity—the search for ethnicity.

In addition to the problem of race and ethnicity, the mainland community also suffers from a lack of political "clout." Unlike the situation on the island (where 80 per cent of the eligible voters take part in elections), most mainland Puerto Ricans don't identify with local issues, and thus remain marginal to the political process. When voter registration campaigns begin to show progress, the major political parties break up heavy concentrations of Puerto Rican voters by gerrymandering. Urban renewal projects have also razed neighborhoods where Puerto Ricans had begun to grow into a large voter bloc.

Unlike the "humble poor" of the island, some mainland Puerto Ricans have lashed out in frustration. There have been "Puerto Rican riots" in New York, Chicago, Newark, and other cities during the past decade. In 1967, rioting teenagers smashed windows and looted stores in a South Bronx neighborhood scarred by ugly tenements, addicts, and hookers. A dazed storekeeper said, "It's usually peaceful in a Spanish neighborhood; in eighteen years until now I've never been robbed." He shook his head as two Puerto Rican adults stood guard outside his looted store. "It's the teenagers without jobs that we have to watch," said one neighbor.

But young and old alike took part in the Newark riots of 1974, which erupted when police tried to break up a gambling game at an outdoor festival. A mounted policeman's horse trampled a young girl, and the angry crowd immobilized the city for a few days. "What the newspapers didn't mention," insists one Puerto Rican resident of Newark, "is that the cops would've gone away if we'd paid them off; they never care about gambling when they get their share."

Puerto Ricans have learned, from the Black Power activism of the 1960's, that militance often wins concessions from "the establishment." In fact, blacks and Puerto Ricans have sometimes formed coalitions. But there is sometimes open hostility over their respective shares of antipoverty funds. One Puerto Rican official in New York complains that "we are at each other's throats, fighting for the crumbs."

Reverend Joseph Fitzpatrick of Fordham University, a sociologist who has studied Puerto Rico for many years, feels that the mainland community will eventually "integrate from a position of strength, by Puerto Rican Power," forging a third movement neither white nor black, which promotes the specific interests of the Puerto Rican and has sufficient solidarity to pursue group interests in the political arena. But this process will take a number of years.

Puerto Rico's political status controversy frequently worms its way into mainland issues. In the *barrios* and on college campuses, activists will demand that Puerto Ricans, as U.S. citizens, play a greater role in the mainland political process. They will also demand independence for Puerto Rico. Both demands are valid but, when uttered simultaneously, they often confuse the public. During one Puerto Rican rally in New York, an American bystander commented: "I can't understand these people; do they want in, or do they want out?"

In reply, Puerto Rican scholar Frank Bonilla has said. "When people ask in what way Puerto Ricans differ from earlier migrants, we must be ready with the true answer, which is that we are a displaced offshoot of a people and a land that have yet to be liberated, and whose freedom is our own."

9 Education

I am conscious of a wide world inhabited by millions of humans, but each of us needs a friendly place to stand upon . . . the years of one's life are not many; it is painful to waste a major part of the short time at our disposal trying to escape from the labyrinth of a confused education.

—Puerto Rican novelist
ENRIQUE A. LAGUERRE

Education in Puerto Rico has been completely transformed in the past few decades. Despite all manner of obstacles, the island now gives every young child the chance to study and has achieved a high degree of enrollment in its universities.

This was done by assigning the highest priority to education. Puerto Rico's may be the only government in the Americas that spends one-third of its budget on education. It is one of only six countries in the world that spends from 7 to 9 per cent of national income on its schools. The island's school system employs more people and spends more money than any other sector of government.

Between 1960 and 1970, the median of school achievement for Puerto Rican adults rose from 4.6 years to 6.9 years. Persons with no formal education at all diminished from 23 per cent to 14 per cent of the population. At the same time, the proportion of high school graduates doubled, from 7.5 to 15 per cent of the adult population.

Puerto Rico still lags far behind the United States, where adults have a median of 12 years of schooling, and 52 per cent have finished high school. In fact, the level of education of Puerto Rican adults today is nearly two years lower than the U.S. average in 1940.

However, during the past two decades the rate of educational improvement in Puerto Rico has been greater than on the U.S. mainland.

For a better appreciation of the island's accomplishment, one can glance "next door" at its neighbor, the Dominican Republic, held stagnant for thirty years by dictator Rafael Leonidas Trujillo, the self-styled Great Benefactor of his nation. In 1920, 10 per cent of Dominican children were in school; by 1964, this was only up to 16 per cent, and 300,000 children, mostly rural, went without school. Only one-tenth of the country's $160 million yearly budget went to education, less than many small U.S. colleges spend. Teachers there earn from $60 to $150 monthly, and half of them have less than junior high school training. This is more or less where Puerto Rico stood thirty or forty years ago.

In contrast, the picture in Puerto Rico is one of spectacular change.

At the beginning of this century, only 14 per cent of Puerto Rico's 320,000 school-age children were studying, and most failed to reach the third grade. One person in four could read and write.

By 1940, still only half of the 600,000 school-age children were receiving any education. Two people in three were literate.

The process of change quickened after World War II. By 1954, for the first time in island history, almost every six-year-old Puerto Rican child was registered in the first grade, although teacher and classroom shortages required half-day sessions for many groups.

The school budget has more than tripled in the past decade. Literacy has climbed to 89 per cent. The schools now enroll more than 800,000 students (over 27 per cent of the island's population), and more than 91 per cent of the children from age seven to thirteen are studying.

The Department of Education in San Juan has island-wide authority. The school system is subdivided into six regions, each of which is composed of districts that roughly correspond to the various municipalities. There are about 3,500 public schools, including elementary (grades one to six), intermediate (grades seven to nine) and high school (grades ten to twelve), which vary from small wooden structures surrounded by fields of planted crops to multibuilding complexes in the midst of the cities.

Students have many incentives to study, including small scholarships ($40 to $60 a year) to encourage poor families to keep their children in school, shoes for needy children (at $.50 a pair), free lunches, free transportation for rural children who live far from school, and cut-rate bus fares for urban students. All children wear similar, attractive uniforms in order to diminish economic class-consciousness.

Puerto Rico's 24,000 teachers (three out four are women) are now younger and better trained and paid than those a few years ago. More than half the teachers now have bachelor's degrees, all but a few hundred have at least normal school training, and many take summer or evening courses to advance themselves. Salaries for public school teachers with bachelor's degrees range from $500 to $800 per month, depending upon experience.

Major Problems

Progress has engendered new goals. Educators are now more aware of the need for qualitative improvement. Many of Puerto Rico's education problems are symptoms of the fever in all developing countries, which try to accomplish in decades what other nations have wrought during centuries.

Seven out of ten children who entered the public schools twelve years ago failed to graduate from high school. This is better than 1948, when six out of seven were dropping out, but far behind the U.S. average, where two-thirds of the first graders earn a high school diploma.

The drop-out rate is most serious in the teen years. More than one-fourth of the 358,000 youngsters age fourteen to nineteen are not in school, and many of the dropouts are chronically unemployed. Undermotivated and undertrained, their futures appear bleak in a society of soaring aspirations.

The still "thin" quality of island education is evidenced by the island's libraries. Optimistic press releases from the Department of Education speak of "615 public libraries." But there are really about 250 small libraries (with 1,500 to 2,000 books apiece) in schools, municipal buildings, housing projects, and mobile truck units, which serve rural communities. The other 300-plus "libraries" are wooden boxes, each containing 150 books, which are circulated in rural *barrios*.

Although nearly one of every three government dollars goes to education, 80 per cent of the school budget is spent on the salaries of teachers and other personnel; little is left over for construction, maintenance, and learning materials. Thus, expenditure per student is less than half the U.S. figure. (This is so not only because the island is poorer, but also because Puerto Rico, with a median age of twenty-one, has proportionately far more school-age children than the United States, where the median age is thirty.)

Scarce education resources are not always spread evenly. A university graduate receives fifteen times more financial aid from the government than a fifth grade dropout. Rural and slum schools often have the skimpiest facilities and least-prepared teachers.

Although the government has increased the number of school rooms from 17,000 to 21,000 in the past five years, budget problems have allowed many of them to lapse into disrepair. Rapid population shifts to new suburbs have also spawned crises. The Levittown development, for example, was recently faced with the dilemma of 900 children entering kindergarten, with classroom space for only 50 of them.

Curriculum content is another cause for concern among education planners. On the one hand, it is not "modern" enough to help students cope with today's technology. On the other hand, it "lacks a Puerto Rican orientation" to make the child more aware of his island's history, its place in the world, and its unique problems. The confused political status has, of course, not helped things.

Who, for example, is George Washington to a young student in San Juan: "our" first President or "theirs"?

Spanish and English

In 1898, the United States tried to convert Puerto Rico as quickly as possible into an English-speaking, or at least bilingual, society. English was made the sole language of instruction in all grades.

Some older people remember with resentment, or at least incredulous amusement, the way English was figuratively crammed down their throats in those early days. Arturo Morales Carrión, a Puerto Rican historian and former special adviser to the Organization of American States, has written that in 1898, the "U.S. considered itself the Promised Land. Once the smoke of war was cleared . . . the task was to Americanize the island. Puerto Ricans were to shed their Spanish culture as one sheds an old coat."

But in 1948, pedagogy prevailed over politics, and Spanish was established as the medium for classroom teaching, with English a required second language. English has made strong inroads: In 1910, an estimated 3.6 per cent of the people spoke it, but now about 45 per cent can understand, or make themselves understood, in English, although only a small group is fluent. Most Puerto Ricans today view English as an essential tool for economic advancement. The schools try to satisfy this need, but a good deal more of the language is learned outside the classroom. The public schools have the added dilemma of teaching Spanish to many Puerto Rican children whose families have back-migrated from the United States.

The Private Schools

Private schools enroll about 12 per cent of the island's students. Many teach English as a first language. Since they generally attract children from upper-income families, this tends to cause a dichotomy, where the island's leadership class is being formed into an English-speaking elite. In the wealthy suburb of Guaynabo, for example, one-third of the children attend private schools, compared with 2.6 per cent of the children in the blue-collar town of Cataño.

University of Puerto Rico records show that applicants from private schools score higher than public school students in every area tested. During one recent year, the University of Puerto Rico accepted 82 per cent of private school applicants, compared with 61 per cent from the public schools.

Since tuition costs at the University of Puerto Rico are only about one-fourth of the costs at the less stringent, and private, Inter-American University, this means that private school students from more affluent homes can receive a low-cost college education, while many public school students must pay heavier tuition costs elsewhere. It is paradoxical that many middle-class parents reject public schools but favor the government-run university, which is considered the island's best college-level institution.

The University

In 1532, more than a century before Harvard was founded, the Saint Thomas Aquinas University of General Studies in San Juan was authorized and accredited by Pope Clement VII, becoming the first center of higher learning in the New World.

Its main function was to serve as a seminary for the entire ecclesiastical province of Santa Cruz de Las Indias, which included much of Central and South America. The founder of this university was the famous Fray Antón Montesino, who later pioneered the defense of the Indians against enslavement by the Spanish colonists.

For some time the university trained and ordained priests (including some native-born Puerto Ricans) but its importance faded as the Spanish Conquest shifted it attention to Central and South America. When the Dutch laid siege to San Juan in 1625, they burned most of the school buildings, and the university was transferred to Santo Domingo. The chapel of the seminary, the present San José Church in Old San Juan, is considered one of the finest examples of Gothic architecture in the Americas. The other buildings have also been restored and serve as the head-quarters for the Institute of Puerto Rican Culture.

During the next three centuries, higher education in Puerto Rico was neglected by Spain, and students went abroad for their training. It was not until 1903 that the University of Puerto Rico was established in Río Piedras, a suburb of San Juan, with 173 students.

Today nearly 80,000 students cram the island's college campuses, compared with 56,000 in 1970.

Enrollment at the government's University of Puerto Rico has jumped from 18,000 in 1960 to a present figure of 48,000. Private colleges have seen even more spectacular growth; they now have 33,000 students, compared with only 6,000 in 1960.

The largest concentration of college students is at the University of Puerto Rico's main campus in Río Piedras. UPR's Medical School, School of Tropical Medicine, and Dentistry School are a few miles away in Old San Juan. The College of Agriculture and Mechanical arts (founded in 1911) is on the west coast, in Maya-güez. In 1957 the university began to administer a new Nuclear Center, (devoted to peaceful uses of the atom) for the U.S. Atomic Energy Commission. Two-year regional colleges have been opened in small towns such as Humacao and Cayey, and others are planned for the future.

Inter-American University (founded in 1912) is the largest private school on the island, with major campuses in San Germán and Hato Rey. Other schools are Catholic University in Ponce (founded in 1948), Puerto Rico Junior College in Río Piedras (1950), the College of the Sacred Heart in Santurce (1935) and the World University in Hato Rey (1966).

University Problems

A few years ago, a Puerto Rican economist said that "we shall require by 1975 about 60,000 more persons with college degrees than were available in 1960," in order to meet the society's develop-ment needs.

Puerto Rico has fallen short of this goal, but the number of college graduates did increase remarkably—from 32,000 to 72,000

—in the past decade. This is still just 6 per cent of the adult population, compared with more than 10 per cent in the United States. The island is far ahead, however, of the English-speaking Caribbean islands, where a combined population of 3.5 million people had only 10,000 university-trained personnel.

As in the case of the public schools, the key problems are quality, not quantity. One social science professor said recently, "The UPR is a large, but not a great institution of higher education." Most students, typical of those in a poor society with high unemployment, view the college diploma as a magical "union card," which assures a decent job.

Apathy among the students is widsepread. Few take part in the free cultural activities program. Few vote in the student council elections. There is no campus newspaper, mainly due to the administration's fear that it will be dominated by students who favor independence. In the classrooms, few students ask questions or seek discussion with their professors.

One professor complained recently that "students drop classes in ever larger numbers, offering such reasons as 'I don't understand the professor, his vocabulary is too advanced,' or 'we have to write papers and essay exams in that course,' or 'the subject matter is too deeply explored.'"

One very bright student told the same professor, "Don't give explanations and derivations. Just give us facts and formulas to memorize."

Attitudes are not much better among many of the 2,000 faculty members of the University of Puerto Rico, whose output of scholarly research is small in relation to its size. The faculty is also part of the reason why few graduate level programs are offered. And, since salaries are rather low, many professors teach a minimum of hours on campus and "moonlight" in full-time jobs elsewhere.

While Vietnam and civil rights for minorities were the stimuli for campus activists in the United States during the 1960's, the question of independence has almost invariably been the rallying cry among Puerto Rican activists. Sometimes their protest also touches "bread-and-butter" issues, and they gain broad support from the largely apolitical student body. This occurred in March,

1969, when the classrooms of the Social Science School were emptied for a day, as hundreds of students demanded curriculum reform. Key points included that all courses and textbooks be in Spanish and that all professors who sought tenure should speak Spanish (about 10 per cent of the classes are taught in English and half the texts are in English). These demands caught on, since, as one professor put it, "Many students know English, but having to study college-level text material in English is a handicap."

Perhaps the best illustration of the mixed feelings of the students toward American culture and English was the largest sign in the Social Sciences lobby. It was a cartoon of Snoopy lying atop his doghouse, staring at the sky, and saying, in Spanish, "No more barking in English. I'm going to protest."

Not all protests have been so peaceful. The University of Puerto Rico has had seven violent disturbances in its history, five of them since 1964.

In 1970 a riot was triggered by the ROTC issue; proindependence students demanded that the program be removed from the campus, and prostatehood students demonstrated in support of the program. During one chaotic moment, students heaved stones at police, who opened fire. A girl student, Antonia Martínez, who stood on a balcony overlooking the scene, was killed by one of the police bullets.

The girl's death shocked the student body. A general assembly shouted down student council calls for a strike but agreed to a referendum on "key issues." About 80 per cent of the students at the Río Piedras campus voted, and more than half favored removing the ROTC program. This shocked some government officials, who had claimed that "only a strident minority of radicals oppose the ROTC." The referendum was probably the first time in the university's history that so many students had joined in a single activity.

Some campus activism has also filtered down to the high school level, where FUPI (the Federation of University Students for Independence) has spawned FEPI (the Federation of High School Students for Independence).

In August, 1971, for example, the senior class in the small town of Vega Alta organized a graduation program with a highly political content in defiance of the school administration, causing some parents to walk out in protest. There were loud boos when the U.S. national anthem was played. The president of the graduating class, in his speech, urged his fellow students "not to forget those young men who won't be able to enter the university and will be forced to join the ranks of the unemployed," or will join the army and "be used as cannon fodder by the forces of imperialism."

10 Culture

This is really a schizophrenic society. Puerto Ricans have two languages, two citizenships, two basic philosophies of life, two flags, two anthems, two loyalties. It is very hard for human beings to deal with all this ambivalence.

—Puerto Rican writer RENÉ MARQUÉS

My idea of a "teenager" is a kid who dresses real wild, who has pretty clothes, whose shoes are shined, and whose pants are well pressed, whose shirts are in style, Ivy League, and who's got a real sharp belt. Others say a "teenager" is a young guy between 13 and 19, what they call an *adolescente*. I think that people who dance real sharp are "teenager." Right now I'm smothered, and don't have much clothes, so I'm not really "teenager." When I have clothes, I'll be more in orbit.

—Young resident of a San Juan public housing project

What is Puerto Rican culture? *Is* there a Puerto Rican culture? Because the island lacks an easily defined political identity and, in recent years, has undergone radical social change, the issue of culture is hotly debated by Puerto Rico's opinion-makers. In the meantime, the people (the alleged victims of this cultural confusion) continue to operate somewhat like the fellow born with a nervous tic, who is *used* to blinking.

Those who employ the narrow meaning of the word culture (the fine arts and folklore) conclude that Puerto Rico has little or none of its own because traditional music, dance, and art forms have been eclipsed by change (this is somewhat like claiming that America has no culture because people no longer dance the Charleston or gather in barber shops to sing "Sweet Adeline"). Others, who view culture in the slightly broader context that encompasses leisure and recreation, warn that Puerto Rican culture is on the wane, because the car has replaced the horse, the hamburger has nudged aside the *pastel*, and the transistor radio or television drowns out the night call of the *coquí* (which implies that these mechanical gadgets and food fads have existed in America and other modern nations since the Great Flood).

But culture can be a far broader concept. The *American Heritage Dictionary* calls it that "totality of socially transmitted behavior patterns, arts, beliefs, institutions, and all other products of human work and thought characteristic of a community or population."

Thus, even the color and size of car that a man prefers, the way he drives it, and the stations that he tunes in on his radio or television all have something to do with culture.

The one generalization we can risk when trying to define Puerto Rican culture, or any other, is that it is very complex and very much change-oriented. Perhaps, the way to view culture is as a large stew, composed of multiple ingredients, which has a unique flavor. No matter how many new ingredients are added to the stew, no matter how much they change the flavor, the combination of old and new retains a certain uniqueness. No other stew (national culture) will match it, because it cannot have identical ingredients in exactly the same proportion. If Puerto Rico "tastes" different from anywhere else in the world—and it emphatically does—then it has its own culture. (Whether the new culture is to the liking of a country's elite, or of those who yearn for the way the "stew" tasted thirty years ago, is another problem entirely).

A chapter, even a book, is hardly enough to define the culture of a people. But we can sketch in a few common patterns; we can look at formal expressions—such as literature and art—at holidays, at modes of leisure and recreation, at customs and dare a few conclusions. "Dare," because such general comments run the risk of reinforcing stereotypes. We've all heard of the "happy-go-lucky, hard-drinking" Irish, the "business-oriented" Jews, the "mechanically inclined" Germans. And we know how such broad brushstrokes fail to account for the complexity and diversity of people.

With these limitations in mind, we can list a few "official" values shared by enough Puerto Ricans to give them island-wide scope and to make Puerto Rico's culture "taste" different from others.

Some of these values can be traced directly to the island's Hispanic heritage. Others also arrived via Spain but are shared by many traditional, farm-based societies. It is also worth remembering that some of these "official" values are being challenged and modified as Puerto Rico's traditional society is edged into the wings by new, dynamic forces.

Official Values and Traits

Some of the "official" values long attributed to Puerto Rican society are a fatalistic outlook, an assumption of male superiority, a strong emphasis upon respect and dignity, and a humanistic view of the world. Some consequences of these values have been political conservatism, a tendency toward individualistic action, an easy-going manner in social affairs, love and tolerance for children, hospitality, a willingness to break small rules in order to do favors for sentimental reasons, and a form of humor that reflects these values and traits. Puerto Ricans are, also, emphatically gregarious, to the point that a "loner" is looked upon as somewhat odd.

The typical Puerto Rican adult was raised in a traditional, firmly structured world, based on respect for a supreme being, for the hierarchy of the community, and for parents. There was a promise of life after death, an established order among living men, and a tacit recognition that each man has his "place" in that system. Catholic dogma cannot have been the sole cause of such a well-ordered universe, but it tended to reinforce it.

Thus, one value ascribed to Latin cultures is "fatalism," the belief that life is controlled by supernatural forces, that one should be resigned to misfortune, and rejoice when some divine decree, perhaps in response to prayer, brings good fortune. The impoverished (and sometimes the wealthy) Puerto Rican will often say *Acepto lo que Dios me mande* ("I accept whatever God wills for me"). This stoicism chains a man to his destiny. For the poor man, it also serves as a balm against frustration after he has examined the scarce options at hand to bring about change.

"Machismo," the importance given to being a "he-man," is another trait commonly ascribed to Puerto Rico and other Latin societies. It is sometimes narrowly linked with sexual potency, or physical courage, but it extends beyond that. It includes the belief that man is innately superior to woman, and it affects the whole pattern of family relations. Boys and girls are raised mainly apart, and communication between husbands and wives is limited in later years. Women are brought up to be responsible, to seek a man who is *serio* ("serious"), while the value of *machismo,* although it suggests a protective attitude toward women, also tends to condone male promiscuity. A girl rarely has more than one or two *"novios"* (steady boyfriends) before marrying, while a boy may have an unlimited number. The *noviazgo* (formal courtship) is quickly established by the girls' parents, who frown upon her frequent dating with different boys. In traditional families, if a young couple date each other several times, it is assumed that *noviazgo* and *la boda* ("the wedding") will inexorably follow. Indeed, the words *"novia"* and *"novio"* can mean both bride and groom, or girlfriend and boyfriend, which shows the short bridge between friendship and marriage. Once married, the women avoid being seen alone with other men, because for a husband to be cuckolded—to "have horns put on him" as they say in Puerto Rico—or even for there to be suspicion of such a thing, is a serious affront to his *dignidad.*

A man, any man, despite his situation in life, is thought to be worthy of *respeto* ("respect"). Even in modern Puerto Rico, men treat each other with more formality than one finds in the United States. Any *falta de respeto* ("lack of respect") toward a man violates his dignity. The poor man who stoically accepts God's will does so not only because he is resigned to his fate, but also because to whimper and whine is undignified. Involved here, too, is the concept of *vergüenza* ("shame"). One of the supreme insults to a traditional Puerto Rican is to call him a *"sinvergüenza"* (a man without shame), implying that he lacks moral standards and dignity. Of course, one can say this with a smile to a friend (just as one says "s.o.b." in America) and get away with it. Thus, the symbols intertwine: The real *macho* accepts his destiny, in part to affirm his dignity. The *hombre vertical* ("upright man") is the man who has *vergüenza*, who is upright, honest, and dignified. Two of the most pejorative terms are *"ñangotado"* (to be in a stooped, kneeling position) and *"aplatanado"* (to be flattened out), meaning the man who endures stress not with stoicism, but with docility, and, thus, lacks dignity.

Perhaps for this reason, there is little self-deprecatory humor in Latin societies, nor will one Puerto Rican risk openly ridiculing another to the point where it strips him of his dignity. Long before America's publicists coined the term "disadvantaged" to describe the poor, wealthier Puerto Ricans called their poor *los humildes* ("the humble people"), a way of sugarcoating the issue, since humility is a Christian virtue and does not imply a lack of dignity.

"Personalismo," a belief in the innate worth and uniqueness of each man (not necessarily the equality of all men), is another traditional value. The old-time individualist resists joining groups or merging his personality in committees. He is often willing to trust *his* destiny to the judgment of some other strong-willed "father figure" who is more charismatic than he. This involves a strange pecking order that demands obedience from one's inferiors (children, employees, servants) but also permits the "master" to obey his own superiors (the boss or the policitian). The fact that Rotary Clubs, Lions, and other voluntary associations flourish today among members of Puerto Rico's new indusrial-commercial middle class indicates that the old-fashioned "antijoiner" *personalismo* may be bending, but the residue of tradition also suggests that the power structure in the Mayagüez Lions Club may be different, for example, from the Lions Clubs in Seattle or Cleveland.

A strong faith in person-to-person contact and skepticism as to the value of impersonal procedures is another aspect of *personalismo*. Puerto Ricans use the telephone and the mails, but to "really get things done," there is no substitute for a face-to-face meeting. Thus, the phone is not an extension of the ear, it is an impediment to the intimacy between two individuals. For this reason, Puerto Ricans are in unanimous agreement that the *americano* ("North American") has a "colder" personality, because of his penchant for mechanical communication and for "going by the book."

Humanismo ("humanism") is another trait associated with Puerto Rico's Latin American roots. In Latin America, nations have been led by either strong-armed military *caudillos* (the *macho*) or eminent intellectuals (the humanist) such as Gallegos of Venezuela, Sarmiento of Argentina, and Bosch of the Dominican Republic. Muñoz Rivera of Puerto Rico was a journalist and poet, and his son Muñoz Marín followed this classic pattern. Thus, Puerto Rico, like other Latin American nations, has traditionally prized the man who combines dash with intellect. A glance at the list of Puerto Rican holidays later in this chapter shows that most of the men whose birthdays are honored have been not only political activists but also men of letters.

An interesting barometer of cultural change in Puerto Rico may be the fact that none of Muñoz Marín's three successors is a literary man. The present governor, Rafael Hernández Colón, is a lawyer by profession. The two men before him—Roberto Sánchez Vilella and Luis A. Ferré—are graduate engineers. But Ferré is still "cultural" in the sense that he founded the Ponce Art Museum and is active as a patron of the arts. (One evening a few years ago at La Fortaleza, while arguing the virtues of statehood among a circle of visitors, to "convince" them, Ferré retired to his library and brought out a dogeared copy of essays by Ortega y Gasset, with relevant sections underlined. As an interesting exercise in comparing Puerto Rican and North American cultures, try to envision Lyndon Johnson, Richard Nixon, or Gerald Ford in a similar scene.)

Perhaps because of the values of respect and dignity, Puerto Ricans are sensitive and avoid direct confrontations if someone's feelings may be injured. Doing things *a la buena* ("in a nice way") is the preferred method to settle any dispute. Resistance to someone else's views is usually via the *"pelea monga"* (literally, a relaxed fight) of passive noncooperation, rather than a direct counterattack. A directly negative reply to some request is also avoided when possible. One rarely says "no" or "yes." Instead, one says, "Let's see" and lets the matter drop, trusting that the hint has been caught. There is also a soft-hearted sentimental attitude, which some people call the *ay bendito* complex. *Ay bendito* is short for "blessed be the Lord," but its meaning is closer to "ah, woe is me," and it serves as a handy lubricant for potentially abrasive situations. The university student who has received an "F" in his final exam will sometimes employ the *ay bendito* to get a passing grade, explaining that he works nights to support his family and barely has time to study. The teacher, not immune to the *ay bendito* complex herself, will often feel moved to comply. The *ay bendito* is also a favorite tactic employed with traffic policemen, who are far more sentimental than their counterparts in New York State. Jaime Benítez, former university president and now Resident Commissioner, says: "Some call it [the *ay bendito*] in jest our categorical imperative. For myself, I regard it as our outstanding contribution in social wisdom."

This does not mean that Puerto Rico is a paradise of soft-hearted saints. But the sentimentalism of the *ay bendito* ameliorates much personal conflict and makes possible many small favors and amenities, which people rarely seem to find time for in the "developed" nations of the world.

If one searches back into the earliest chronicles by Spanish visitors to their colony in Puerto Rico, the word "hospitality" is mentioned time and time again. *Esta es su casa* ("this is your house") is the common greeting when a visitor arrives. When two men strike up a friendship and exchange home addresses, it is also common to conclude with *a la orden* ("at your service"). These courtesies may be mere reflex actions among some Puerto Ricans, but they are usually sincerely felt. If the visitor has come from afar, the hospitality flows like Niagara.

Puerto Rico's small size and impoverished condition have nurtured other values or traits, not all of them necessarily positive. For example, one suspects that what writer René Marqués refers to as the "docility" of many Puerto Ricans emanates from the mix of respect for order, the smallness of the island (which decreases the options available to change that order by force), and a long-time colonial dependency. In the old rural society, the *hacidena* owner enjoyed tremendous power over his *agregados*, the landless peons on his property. Such dependency calls for revolt, but more often breeds assent. On a larger scale, Puerto Rico was run by an authoritarian Spanish colonial regime. It had the option of revolting, as Cuba did, or—perhaps because of its size and other factors—remaining under Spanish influence, making moral pleas for more liberty. When the United States replaced Spain as Puerto Rico's colonial *patrón*, the same power relationship prevailed, although more stress was given to participant democracy at the local level. Even today, the crucial role that American-owned factories and legislators in Washington play in determining Puerto Rico's economic fortunes nourishes a certain feeling of dependency and apparent docility.

However, "docility" may, in some cases, be the result of a "practical" decision after examining other choices and finding them either suicidal or wanting in efficacy. In 1891, when Luis Muñoz Rivera proposed a pact with Spain, he wrote: "We are not bent on fighting useless battles or pursuing the impossible."

This "practical" approach—this "art of the possible"—has characterized insular politics for the past century.

On the other hand, tactics may change with conditions. Changes have taken place in Puerto Rican society. The disintegration of the *patrón-agregado* relationship has been slowly replaced by that of manager-employee. There is far more private ownership of land. Options for other jobs are available. Unions are quickly increasing in strength, not without resistance from within and without. One suspects that, little by little, on an individual basis, the Puerto Rican is acquiring more mobility, more options, and a shade more militancy than his parents had.

Puerto Rico's smallness also gives it a certain comforting *ambiente,* which has disappeared in the world's major metropolises. Most island cities are small enough for "everyone" to know "everyone else." Even San Juan, with nearly 1 million people in its metropolitan area, began with a small enough nucleus so that in certain professions a man can still (well, almost) "know everyone" among his colleagues. This smallness nourishes the individual, who is rarely anonymous. The lack of anonymity also tends to reinforce traditional customs and conventions, which are sometimes observed, not out of conviction, but because of "what people might say." (The discreet keeping of a mistress, for example, according to those who still practice this time-honored Latin tradition, often requires the most elaborate feats of rendezvous-making, and hasty disappearing acts that would be the envy of the most accomplished magician.)

One of the most serious social problems in Puerto Rico has been caused by the mass migration of the rural poor to the cities, where they live in slums or housing projects. The poor, uprooted from a strongly structured environment where one "learned" how to act by conditioning since infancy, have been thrust into a new situation, without the *patrón*, without the neighbors who lived nearby for generations, without the old taboos, and *with* a frightening dose of anonymity.

It is bewildering for any adult to have his cultural underpinnings removed without having something equally strong put in their place. He may buckle under the strain or cling desperately to the old ways. The real trouble comes when he tries to transmit the old ways to his children, in an environment where these ways make little sense or cannot be enforced. The hostility and rambunctiousness of many of the children of the urban poor appear to be a direct consequence of the landslide of the old values; case histories can be cited not only from San Juan, but Detroit, Watts, Chicago, Newark, and New York. The city child soon learns that, while docility and respect may work in the hills, to survive in the slum one must be tough and brash.

El Jíbaro

Every country has its idealized folk hero. In Argentina, it is the gaucho. Cuba has its *güajiro,* and Puerto Rico has its *jíbaro.*

By the eighteenth century, the rural people of Puerto Rico were called *jíbaros.* The root of this name is uncertain, but Indians of South America's interior are also called *Jíbaros*, and it may have emerged in the early days of the Spanish colonization, when Indians fled to the mountains to escape slavery. The *jíbaro* lived with his family in the isolated hill country and led a hard but independent life. A Catholic, he worshiped in his own way, praying to rustic carved saints in his small home, which usually had a straw-thatch roof. The main piece of furniture was a hammock, part of the Indian heritage. The *jíbaro* rarely visited town, except for holiday festivals. He treated illness with prayer and herbs that grew around him. He had learned to roast pig, as did the buccaneers of the epoch. He liked to dance and sing *décimas* and songs, often of medieval Spanish origin. His calendar was kept by counting the moons and the hurricanes. He worked cooperatively with the families of his *barrio* and was a man of his word. He was also ready to defend his dignity in combat, and a fight often involved total destruction. He was tanned by the tropical sun and, in some cases, by an African or Indian ancestor who had sought refuge in his hills. He wore a broad straw hat, a *pava*, a simple rough shirt and trousers, and, usually, went barefoot. His right hand was the machete, a long sharp weapon, for cutting through the thicket, for farming, and for defense. He was a good horseman.

This is an idealized image of a vanishing breed. The vast sugar-cane monoculture, established in the early twentieth century, drew many *jíbaros* from the hills and turned them into a landless, wage-earning proletariat, stripping them of their solitary independence. Today, the typical *jíbaro* is in late middle age, and his son has migrated to America or San Juan, and will likely never return to farm work.

Today, the word *"jíbaro"* has two meanings. Among the urban poor, who strive to move up the socio-economic ladder and who do not wish to look back, the *"jíbaro"* is a hick, an ignorant, naive man, not to be emulated. But the Puerto Rican who has "made it," or who always "had it made," often likes to describe himself as a *jíbaro* at heart. He is saying, in effect: "I may wear a tie and shuffle papers, but I am still a solid person, with the stain of the plantain indelibly printed on my soul."

The Puerto Rican who has successfully moved to the city realizes, with some nostalgia, that he has lost something by gaining something else. To him, the *jíbaro* is the "salt of the earth," the honest man, the man with both feet firmly planted on the soil, the man whose lack of schooling does not deprive him of a native shrewdness and wisdom that has something to do with the timelessness of nature.

Artists and poets, some of whom have never muddied their

shoes in the countryside or cut a stalk of cane, still harken back to the *jíbaro* as someone ideal, someone lost, in Puerto Rico's collective soul. This idealization of rural ways does not occur throughout the United States. The New York businessman does not reminisce about the countryside or put "hillbilly" music on the phonograph at Christmastime. But, in some regions of America, such as the South, there is a similar phenomenon, a sentiment for the innate goodness of "country folk," a tendency for the urbane Georgian or Texan to say "I'm just a country boy m'self," to reinforce the wisdom of some statement.

The *jíbaro* is often present in Puerto Rico's popular entertainment media, sometimes in the form of the "citified" *jíbaro*, who still speaks a pungent country twang. He is, often, the target of some joke or plot, but his innate goodness and shrewdness pull him through. The *jíbaro* is the man who, when asked to buy the Puerto Rican equivalent of the Brooklyn Bridge by some city slicker, will nod politely, never say no, but in the end excuse himself and walk away, unconvinced. These qualities are projected in some of Puerto Rico's most popular television comedians. One is the *pava*-hatted "Machuchal" (Adalberto Rodríguez), mayor of a fictitious island village, a good-natured, lovable man, with a touch of innocent mischief. The other is *don* Cholito (José Miguel Agrelot), who is probably as well-known as any politician in Puerto Rico, and far more trusted. *Don* Cholito appears daily on television, a chubby, good-natured man, also often wearing a *pava* hat. His daytime show, where he comments upon topical affairs, is funny, sometimes earthy, and immensely popular. Sometimes he plays *El Soldado Manteca* ("Private Butterball"), a countryish "mama's boy," stationed at a U.S. Army base in Puerto Rico, ever homesick and always, in a gentle, good-natured way, getting the best of the not-too-bright U.S. Army officer, who speaks Spanish in a funny *gringo* accent.

While on the subject of humor, it is important to mention the word "*relajo*," which in formal Spanish means relaxation or loosening. But in Puerto Rico and Cuba, "*el relajo*" means joking, goofing-off, fun-making, disorder, a tendency not to take "serious" things seriously. A sedate party can turn into a *relajo* with boisterous music and dancing; a classroom can become a *relajo* if the students turn the professor's serious lecture into a source of wise-cracks.

A mild form of *el relajo* occurred in 1969 when Governor Ferré visited the state penitentiary and a pickpocket deftly stole his handkerchief. A week later, the Governor's handkerchief was returned. It was embellished with drawings of seven coconut palm trees (his party's symbol), three United States flags, and two of Puerto Rico's. A card accompanied the stolen object, with a poem from the prison's drug addicts, thanking him for the visit.

Juan Bosch once wrote that the Cuban's sense of *el relajo* would never allow a "textbook form" of Communism to take hold in Cuba. In Puerto Rico *el relajo* is a strong form of defense, not against Communism but against the grayish color that often permeates life in the "developed" countries.

Holidays

The calendar in Puerto Rico is liberally sprinkled with holidays. In addition to eleven religious or patriotic holidays commonly celebrated in the United States, nine others are local in nature. During some local *días de fiesta*, Federal agencies, such as the Post Office, remain open; private banks and businesses close at noon; and Commonwealth government offices and schools close the full day. The U.S. holidays are well known to the reader, but the Puerto Rican celebrations merit a few remarks:

January 6 marks the Epiphany, a Christian festival that celebrates the manifestation of the divine nature of Christ to the Gentiles, as represented by the Magi. It is known here as *Día de los tres reyes* ("Three Kings Day").

January 11 is the birthday of Eugenio María de Hostos (1839–1903), a writer, abolitionist, and educator, who is admired throughout Latin America. De Hostos was exiled from Puerto Rico because of his separatist ideals and lived a number of years in the Dominican Republic, where he was instrumental in strengthening its school system.

March 22 commemorates the day in 1873 when slavery was abolished in Puerto Rico (see chapter on history).

April 16 is the birthday of José de Diego (1866–1918), a lawyer and eloquent orator and writer, who was Secretary of Justice in the short-lived autonomous government in 1897. After the U.S. occupation, de Diego became the first President of the insular House of Representatives and, in his later years, devoted his efforts toward gaining independence for Puerto Rico.

July 17 marks the birth of Luis Muñoz Rivera (1829–1916) who, together with his son Luis Marín (1898–   ), dominated island political life during much of the past century. Muñoz Rivera negotiated the Charter of Autonomy with Spain and later served as Puerto Rico's Resident Commissioner in Washington. He was also a prolific writer and poet.

July 25 is Puerto Rico Constitution Day, marking the occasion in 1952 when the Commonwealth government was formalized, ending the island's status as a U.S. territory and granting some measure of home rule. The constitution went into effect exactly fifty-four years to the day after the American troops landed at Guánica and wrested the island from Spain.

July 27 honors José Celso Barbosa (1857–1921), who studied medicine at the University of Michigan in the late nineteenth century and was later named Undersecretary of Education in the autonomous government. In 1900, he founded the Republican Party which, for sixty-four years, was the island's strongest prostatehood political movement.

September 23 was proclaimed a holiday by Governor Ferré, in 1968, to mark the centennial of the *Grito de Lares,* when a band of patriots in the mountain town of Lares rebelled and declared the Republic of Puerto Rico. The insurrection was quickly crushed by the Spanish colonial authorities. (The bill was introduced into the Senate by a prostatehood legislator, Justo Méndez, one of whose ancestors fought in the Lares revolt.)

November 19 is Discovery Day, recalling 1493, when *Cristobal Colón* (Christopher Columbus) first saw the island, which the Indians called *Borikén.*

In addition to these official holidays, each town celebrates an annual festival, often lasting a week, to honor its patron saint. Once of a religious nature, most of these festivals now emphasize recreation; games of chance and music are set up in the plaza, attracting the counry folk from miles around.

What remains the most religious festival is celebrated each September in Hormigueros, a small town 100 miles southwest of San Juan. Pilgrims visit its church to honor *Nuestra Señora de la Monserrate,* and often inflict punishment upon themselves, climbing long flights of hard stone steps on their knees.

Even better known is the Fiesta of Santiago Apóstol (St. James the Apostol) in Loíza, a coastal village just east of San Juan with a large population of African slave descendants. This fiesta, which begins July 25, retains much of its original religious content, with saint-bearing processions, vows, and prayers. It is also a time for secular fun, highlighted by gaily dressed masqueraders.

Las Navidades. By far the most important holiday of the year is the Christmas season (*las navidades*). America's Santa Claus has diluted, but by no means erased, the special flavor of the occasion. The Christmas spirit begins to effervesce early in December and bubbles on through to January 6, Three Kings Day. In parts of the countryside, it extends a week or two for the *octava de reyes* and the *octavita,* when rosaries are sung and recited and parents and godparents exchange visits.

Puerto Rican hospitality glows brightest during the Christmas season; it is a time for visiting and eating and drinking heartily. *Villancicos* ("carols") are sung; friends organize *parrandas,* groups of roving merrymakers who go from house to house with *asaltos* (attacks or surprise visits) until all hours of the morning, waking their friends with boisterous singing and noisemaking. Small boys knock on a stranger's door, smile shyly and immediately break into a raucous song, rapping on tin cans with sticks, scraping *güiro* gourds, and ask for a small *aguinaldo,* or Christmas gift. Older men from the country, who come into San Juan with guitars, *cuatros,* and vibrant voices, stroll through the shops and restaurants, singing typical *música navideña,* some of it gay, some of it evoking nostalgia for the rural past.

Christmas officially begins the Night of December 24 (*nochebuena*), with a midnight mass (*misa de gallo*) and a late supper of roast pig, pigeon peas, native sausage, and other delicacies, and *coquito* (eggnog made with coconut milk and rum, usually the bootleg variety known as *cañita*). In the country, some people break out exotic homemade beverages, such as orange wine or glowing red anise-rum, or a type of brandy made by soaking raisins, prunes, and other ingredients in rum.

December 25 is now the major gift-giving occasion, and Christmas trees brought from the mainland adorn many homes, but most families reserve a small gift or two for Three Kings Day. The night before, children fill small boxes with grass for the king's horses, and place them beneath the bed; while they sleep, the parents remove the grass and substitute the gifts.

Sports and Gaming

Puerto Rico—along with Japan, Cuba, and a few other nations —has adopted baseball as its "national sport."

Although Abner Doubleday's invention might be called "foreign," since it was introduced here after the turn of the century, ball-playing is a venerable tradition in the Caribbean. Games using a rubber ball probably originated near the Amazon Valley, where trees give forth an elastic gum. Ball games were popular with the Aztecs and Mayans, as well as the Arawaks, the parent tribe of Puerto Rico's Taínos. About 400 ancient ball courts, including dozens in Puerto Rico, have been unearthed. The largest ball court (known as a *batey* to the Taínos) yet found in the Caribbean is in the mountains of Puerto Rico, near Utuado, and has been carbon dated to nearly three centuries before Columbus reached the island.

The Taíno courts were fields, walled in by rows of tall, flat stones. Some of the Mayan courts, where the technique of masonry had been developed, are massive. Friezes decorating the court at Chichén-Itzá show the captain of the losing team being beheaded. The court there is an H-shape, 500 feet by 207 feet over all; set 30 feet high in one central wall is a stone ring 18 inches in diameter. Early accounts say that if the ball was knocked through the ring, the game was won. The player who achieved this was permitted to pursue the fans and strip them of their robes and jewels. The dimensions of the courts and the rules of the games varied widely in different parts of the Caribbean and Latin America, but it was usually forbidden to hit the ball with the hands (much as in modern-day soccer). A few years ago a group of athletes in Yale University's gym conducted an experiment with large, prehistoric stone rings found in the Caribbean that were apparently used as a form of "belt bat." According to *New York Times* science writer Walter Sullivan, the athletes slipped the rings over their heads and let them rest on their hips, whereupon they

> . . . grasped the rings with their hands and, as a basketball came within range, whirled the stone around their hips, striking the ball with a knobby protuberance on the ring. The results were spectacular. The ball flew across the court at devastating speed . . . one of the rings had two knobs enabling the player to wing his belt either clockwise or counterclockwise and still hit the ball. It was a massive object, probably intended for a fullback or goalie.

Other games played by the Indians made use of the body, as in soccer, but the ball must have been quite hard. A sixteenth-century friar told of seeing players carried dead off the field after being hit in the pit of the stomach with the ball. The players would propel the ball with "extraordinary velocity," using their knees or buttocks; "they suffered great damage on the knees and thighs, so that those who used trick shots too much got their haunches so mangled that they had to have the accumulations of clotted blood cut out with a small knife."

Baseball became popular in Puerto Rico after the Spanish-American War. The first official game is said to have been played around the turn of the century, when the local Boriquén nine took on a visiting team from Almendares, Cuba. The home team pitcher that afternoon was young Amos Iglesias, the offspring of Spanish and American parents. There soon emerged a constellation of Puerto Rican baseball stars, including the Faberllé brothers (Fabito and Ciquí), Cosme Beitía, José "Gacho" Torres, Pancho Coimbre, and Perucho Cepeda (who was said to be an even more ferocious batter than his son Orlando, a major league star).

Hiram Bithorn, who pitched for Chicago during World War II, was the first Puerto Rican to make the big leagues. Luis Rodríguez Olmo played for the Brooklyn Dodgers during that period. Later came Victor Pellot Power, the flashy fielding first baseman, pitchers

Rubén Gomez and Luis "Tite" Arroyo, slugger Orlando Cepeda, and (the island's biggest star to date) Roberto Clemente, who at the age of thirty-eight died in a plane crash on December 31, 1972. (Clemente, only the eleventh man in the history of major league baseball to achieve 3,000 hits, became the first Latin American to enter the Baseball Hall of Fame.)

Today, Puerto Rico has a six-team professional Winter League, with stadiums in Arecibo, Ponce, Mayagüez, Caguas, and San Juan (the San Juan and Santurce teams share the last). The league is well supported and comparable in quality to a strong minor league on the mainland. Each team has a number of local players, as well as a quota of North American "imports." Today there are several Puerto Ricans playing in the U.S. major leagues. During a recent spring training game in Florida, the three Cruz brothers of Arroyo (Cirilo, Hector and José) made baseball history when they took charge of the entire St. Louis Cardinal outfield. Later, Cardinal manager Red Schoendienst said, "They have six brothers back home, and if they come to town I'll play them, too!"

Among the team sports, basketball ranks second in popularity to baseball, with a number of amateur leagues. Since 1930, Puerto Rico has won numerous gold medals at the Central American and Caribbean games, against teams from larger countries. At the 1966 games held in San Juan, the island's basketball team was unbeaten. Also popular are volleyball, track and field, swimming, boxing and weightlifting. In 1969, Fernando Báez, a bantam-weight, won a world's title in weightlifting. Football has never caught on as a major sport, although a few high schools compete.

Tennis, golf, and swimming are not mass-scale competition sports; most of these facilities are at the luxury hotels or in private clubs. But the island has achieved some distinction in these activities. Charlito Pasarell is one of the world's leading tennis players. Diminutive "Chichi" Rodríguez, a former caddie, is a leading U.S. golf pro. Amateur swim teams have won medals in international meets. Surfing has grown in popularity; the 1968 World Surfing Championship was held at a beach along the west coast, and, in front of San Juan's capitol building, young Puerto Rican surfers ride the waves in, drawing crowds of passersby.

Boxing is also popular, perhaps because the island has had three world champions: Sixto Escobar during the 1930's and, more recently, José "Chegui" Torres and Carlos Ortíz.

Among the traditional sports is the raising of *paso fino* horses by some of the wealthier families. The *paso fino* is a small horse, bred over hundreds of years in Puerto Rico, whose mincing, delicate gait is suitable for the rough terrain of the interior. The Paso Fino Federation of Puerto Rico gives annual shows, and interest in this unusual horse has extended to the United States and elsewhere in the Caribbean.

The major sedentary sport is dominoes, which is played here with great skill and zest. Former Governor Roberto Sánchez Vilella is said to be one of the island's best domino players. The game is the gin rummy, or poker, of the island, and although the basic rules are simple, connoisseurs matched against each other can make it appear to be as complex as chess. In open-air plazas, factory cafeterias, bars, and elegantly furnished club rooms, men sip drinks and slap the black rectangles loudly to the table. Dr. Salvador Arana Soto, founder of the Association of Dominoes Clubs of Puerto Rico (there are more than 100 clubs), describes the game as being "more attuned to our psychological makeup than chess; the combination of luck and skill that is needed to win appeals to the Latin character." He has written one book on dominoes and is at work on another. Chess, too, enjoys prestige in the Caribbean, at least since the 1920's, when Cuba's José Raúl Capablanca won the world championship. Puerto Ricans have competed in matches abroad, and the island's chess association has hosted important international tournaments in recent years.

Cockfighting ranks with baseball as a major spectator sport, especially in the countryside and urban working class districts. Puerto Rico's 139 *galleras* (cockfight arenas) are open weekends from November through August and draw more than a million spectators a year. Even this ancient sport has been modernized; the island's newest arena is carpeted with Astroturf.

Another favorite sport is horseracing. Angel Cordero and other Puerto Rican jockeys have won fame in the racing world. The island's only track is El Comandante, which has held an exclusive franchise since it opened in 1956. Its racing meets, three times a week throughout the year, amount to a $50-million-a-year industry, including the legal operation of offtrack betting parlors, where for a few cents one may play the *cinco-seis pool,* which sometimes pays thousands of dollars.

Millions are also spent yearly on the government's weekly *lotería,* which was founded in 1814. The 2,000 winning numbers offer prizes of from $80 to $100,000, with an occasional *extraordinario* first prize of $400,000.

Despite all this legal access to betting, Puerto Ricans also play clandestine games of chance, such as *"la bolita,"* the small-time version of the lottery; it is similar to the "numbers" game in the United States, with small wages and prizes of a few hundred dollars. There are many regional *bolita* games throughout the island. In some northwest *barrios* of Puerto Rico, the winning number is determined by the last three numbers of the racing attendance at Santo Domingo's track, across the Mona Channel, which are announced on Dominican radio.

From reading the last few pages, one might assume that sports and gaming are so popular in Puerto Rico that they form part of the national character. It seems that this is a valid assumption. Writer Abelardo Díaz Alfaro once observed that "Puerto Rico is a land of horseplayers and politicians."

Communications

Puerto Rico has an extensive web of radio, television, and other media. In the tranquil countryside, roof antennae snatch from the air exotic images of roller derby, wrestling, lovers petting in parked cars, subway murders, and other scenes of modern industrial culture. To watch a married couple in the parlor of their La Perla slum home, as they observe a televised film of snarling American wrestlers, and to hear them boo the black-bearded villain and cheer the hero with the peroxide curls is proof of the awesome power of celluloid and electronics.

Since the coming of satellite TV, Puerto Rico has really been "plugged in" to the rest of the world. When Astronaut Neil Armstrong took his "one small step for a man" in 1969, Puerto Rican families shared the moment with those in New York. Since then, island sports fans have seen live telecasts of World Series baseball and football bowl games. In 1974, they crowded local theaters to watch the closed-circuit transmission of the heavyweight championship fight between Muhammad Ali and George Foreman, from Zaïre in Africa.

Radio and Television

The island's first radio station, WKAQ (a CBS affiliate), went on the air in 1923, soon after radio grew popular on the U.S. mainland. Today, nearly one hundred AM and FM radio stations serve a listening audience that owns one million home, car, and portable radios, many of which are played at near-maximum volume. ("Noise seems to be our national manner of expression," one local professor grumbled recently.) There are a few English-language radio stations on the island (some of which specialize in rock music for a growing teenage audience), but since their audience is largely bilingual, one commonly hears spot commercials in Spanish.

Radio offers a heavy dose of soap opera and pop music, as elsewhere in the world, but on an island where actual (as opposed to functional) literacy is still quite low, news broadcasts keep the populace reasonably well (although superficially) informed of local and international affairs. The stations buy their newsbriefs from the Associated Press and United Press International, which maintain offices here and whose capital and competition have nudged aside the small local news services. Sports programs are also very popular. One of Puerto Rico's best-known personalities is "Pito" Rivera Monge, the voluble announcer of horseraces from the El Comandante track. A fellow who enjoys his work immensely, "Pito" cracks nonstop jokes before the starter's gun is fired; during the race, his excited staccato delivery (unintelligible to even the best Berlitz student) sounds roughly like a man having a nervous breakdown in the midst of a thunderstorm. Three times weekly, his effusive shouts are heard everywhere, in barbershops and bars, on construction sites, and, even, from crackly, palm-sized transistors aboard buses.

Television has become Puerto Rico's most important communication medium. WKAQ-TV, a subsidiary of the newspaper *El Mundo,* opened the first television station in 1954, but it was not until the late 1960's that television became relatively common in rural areas. (Ever since the 1968 elections, political candidates have spent more of their advertising budget on TV "spots" than on any other medium.) By 1970, more than 82 per cent of Puerto Rico's 632,000 occupied dwelling, had a TV set, and nearly 43,000 homes had two or more sets. There are also large-screen sets in the public squares of many towns; a few years ago, the Mayor of San Juan installed color sets in the city's four main plazas, where the benevolent climate and numerous benches attract evening idlers to chat, play dominoes, watch a favorite program, or all three simultaneously.

San Juan has four commercial TV channels (2, 4, 7, and 11) and a government TV station (Channel 6), all of which reach other parts of the island either directly or through affiliates. An English-language station (Channel 18) recently went out of business, but there is English cable television available to subscribers in the San Juan metropolitan area, and most stations have some English content. (As a concession to the growing audience of bilingual Puerto Ricans, new major films, the World Series, and other events, although broadcast in Spanish, are also available simultaneously in English by tuning in to a local FM radio station.)

A typical morning's television fare will include the Spanish version of *Sesame Street* (the English version is offered on another channel), a *"novela"* (soap opera), or a melodramatic Mexican film, which features plenty of shooting, guitar-strumming, tears, and soulful stares. Noontime is "live," as local *comediantes* take over with variety shows that mix music, many commercials, and topical humor, often bordering on the risque. (Some of the skits satirizing the Jacqueline Kennedy–Aristotle Onassis honeymoon, for example, would have gotten no closer to a U.S. network than the corner burlesque theater.)

Late afternoon shows are aimed at schoolchildren. The top-rated "kiddies" show is live and stars an elfin Spaniard named Pacheco who wears a straw hat, bow tie, and doleful countenance. Between cartoons and commercials for toys and cereals, Pacheco reads letters from parents, such as: "My Emilio isn't eating his dinner." Gently, but firmly, he stares into the camera and tells Emilio to eat. Pacheco also warns that his helper, the *pajarito investigador* ("the little snooper bird") will be around to check on him. The tactic often improves Emilio's appetite for weeks.

As suppertime approaches, Tarzan battles wild African tribesmen who speak broken Spanish, and also competes with Spiderman, Batman, Popeye, and the Flintstones.

The evening offers local musical variety programs and popular U.S. shows such as *Ironside, Columbo, Kojak, Gunsmoke,* and *M.A.S.H.* The night ends with the late movie starting about 11 P.M.

With the exception of the lengthy supper hour news show on Channel 6, television news shows offer only tidbits of world events. Films of the bloody Vietnam conflict, for example, which caused such an impact on the U.S. mainland, rarely appeared on island television.

The only exception to what might be called the "wasteland" level of television here is the government's low-budget educational station, WIPR-TV, which takes good advantage of local writers and performers for occasional dramas, forums, poetry readings, and the like. During the day, its time is used for didactic programs, piped into the island's public schools. On evenings and weekends, it shows good documentaries produced by National Education Television, which, unfortunately, do not attract the widest audience, since they are in English, and also telecasts "live" performances of the Casals Festival and other worthwhile events.

The Press

Printing came late to Puerto Rico—the first press was installed in 1807—but the papers now have plants as modern as anywhere in the United States.

El Mundo, the largest daily, with more than 100,000 circulation, follows a staunchly conservative line. The Knight Newspaper chain indirectly controls the paper through an employees' cooperative that theoretically holds ownership. *El Imparcial* for years followed the tabloid format and sensational style of the *Daily News* of New York and, until the early 1960's, was the island's most widely circulated daily. Its owner, Antonio Ayuso, was a leader of the Nationalist Party until 1930 and, for years, wrote fiery proindependence editorials above his signature. When Ayuso was taken ill, the paper began to founder, and when he died in 1970, *El Imparcial,* closed for bankruptcy, was sold to a former leader of the pro-state-hood Republican Party. The third Spanish-language daily is *El Día,* owned by the family of Governor Ferré. *El Día* has taken away *El Imparcial*'s mass readership in recent years, thanks to its striking graphic design, lively headlines, and thorough coverage of sports.

Claridad, the weekly tabloid of the Puerto Rico Socialist Party, has recently blossomed into a daily. It also offers an English-language edition on the U.S. mainland. While obviously partisan, *Claridad* has earned a large reading audience because of its exposés of scandals in government and private industry, some of which have prompted legislative investigations.

The fifth daily is the English-language *San Juan Star,* founded in 1959 by Cowles Publications and now part of the Scripps-Howard newspaper chain. The *Star*'s circulation has spiraled to about 50,000, and it reaches a high-income reader market, including the resident American business executive community. The *Star*'s editorial policy mildly favors statehood, and, at times, its liberal North American viewpoint seems curiously detached from what is really going on in the community. In 1961, the *Star* won a Pulizer Prize for its crusade against church opposition to goverment birth control policies.

American newspapers such a the *New York Times, New York Daily News, Miami Herald, Chicago Tribune,* and the *Wall Street Journal* are flown in daily and home-delivered or sold at many San Juan stores. No paper from another country is imported, except for two Santo Domingo dailies, *Listín Diario* and *El Caribe,* which are found at a few stands, for the growing Dominican exile community.

U.S. weekly and monthly magazines are sold, as are an assort-ment of Spanish-language publications. Academic magazines in-clude the *Revista da Ciencias Sociales,* the Institute of Caribbean Studies magazine, and the *Revista/Review Interamericana.*

The print media are important in Puerto Rico because they reach the elite and the middle class. But total newspaper circulation is only sixty papers per thousand inhabitants, compared with 314 per thousand in the United States. Readership is lower in Puerto Rico than it is in Costa Rica, Uruguay, Portugal, and Taiwan, to mention a few widely spaced examples.

La Telefónica

The telephone in Puerto Rico is, allegedly, a form of communication. International Telephone and Telegraph (ITT) for years held the franchise, except in a few communities served by the government-owned Communications Authority. ITT reaped handsome profits without reinvesting enough of these gains for needed improvements. Cash outlays often went for shoddy, bargain-priced equipment or for products bought at inflated prices from an ITT subsidiary. The phone company, or *la telefónica* as it is called here, has long been the target of Puerto Rican leaders, who several times tried to remove the franchise and put the service under government control (as are the light and water companies, which provide competent service). The failure to do so was evidence of ITT's powerful lobbying power in Washington. The crisis heightened in the early 1960's as Puerto Rico's demand for new phones reached unprecedented levels.

Many residents send letters to the press that liken the phone to a medieval instrument of torture. One picks up the receiver and is as likely to hear music, or a dog barking, as a dial tone. A plea to repair service often goes unanswered, and there is no number to call to say that repair service needs repair. One dials information for a number and receives a recording which says, "All lines are busy, consult your phone guide." Puerto Ricans complain of the phone service, but since they were "born into it" and are more inured to it, their outrage never quite matches that of the "my-time-is-valuable" visiting American executive. When one American tried to call the White House from San Juan, he heard a few clicks and a recorded message: "Sorry, you've reached a nonworking number." One calls New York and gets clear sound reception, but one's party in a nearby town may sound as though he were in Singapore. A number of middle-class housing developments have no phones, years after they were built. Few of the public housing projects have phones. Lucky owners of a phone usually have to call repair service at least once a month. Rates are high and charges are sometimes made for calls while families are off the island on vacation. It is common to dial three times to get a number. But the public has become more demanding. Legislative committees and the Public Service Commission began, in the late 1960's, to apply strong pressure upon *la telefónica*. The phone company pumped enormous new investments into its facilities (increasing the number of phones from 82,537 in 1960 to 405,720 in 1973) and also mounted an elaborate public relations campaign to buffer criticism. Despite these attempts, the Commonwealth government in 1974 purchased *la telefónica*. Knowledgeable critics claim that the government paid far too much for a patchwork system of secondhand equipment. But now, at least, say defenders of the purchase, "it is our *telefónica*, and we can do something about improving it." Indications that this is so occurred a few months after the purchase, when the government canceled the contract of an ITT subsidiary that was manufacturing equipment for the system and opened the business for competitive bidding.

The Movies

Puerto Ricans see mainly "foreign films," in the sense that most pictures are from the United States with Spanish subtitles. Mexican films, also popular, run a poor second and are usually confined to shabbier theaters in workers' districts or small towns. The exception is Cantinflas, the Chaplinesque Mexican comic, whose films run for weeks and weeks. The combined high cost of movie tickets (over $2 in a first-run theater), the small number of theaters outside of San Juan, and the advent of television give Puerto Rico a low attendance ratio. The average citizen sees 3.4 films a year, much lower than the United States (11.4 films) and lower than in most of Latin America.

There are 155 theaters, about a dozen of which are "first-run" and which, sometimes, show new pictures before they appear in New York. Action films rate high, but there is a growing audience for a more sophisticated cinema. Increased secularism also permits a few places "for adults only" to show "X-rated" films.

A handful of locally made films with Puerto Rican TV comedians have received popular acceptance, but there is no local movie industry to speak of. The island has attracted some American film companies in search of a tropical site and low-cost extras. The picture *Che* was filmed partly in Puerto Rico, as were *Lord of the Flies,* the film adaptation of William Golding's novel, directed by Peter Brook, and *Bananas,* the Woody Allen farce.

Literature

Puerto Rico's rapid social change in the past three decades has pressured the island's literature into a similar metamorphosis. The nature poetry and folkloric sketches of past centuries are still favored by the dilettante, but today's handful of serious writers grapple with the society's pressing concerns: a nostalgia for the rural life of the *jíbaro;* pervasive urban poverty, accompanied by the growth of a materialistic middle class; the moral issue of colonialism, and the corresponding frustration of violent nationalism; the mass migration to the United States, and the agony of alienation in a strange environment; and fighting as a soldier in the world wars of a "foreign" army. These problems are not only reflected in the positive acts of the Puerto Rican writer, but their magnitude and complexity have, in some cases, numbed the would-be author into silence or goaded him to oversimplify, to write committed works of protest in which political polemic dominates art. On balance, however, Puerto Rican writers have made a meaningful contribution to Hispano-American letters, and their work is slowly making itself known beyond the island's boundaries, in several languages.

Other problems of writers here resemble those of their colleagues in Latin America. Peruvian novelist Mario Vargas Llosa recently explained why, among other reasons, many South Americans voluntarily exile themselves to Europe:

> . . . the writer in Latin America cannot live from his writings. He must struggle desperately to find time to write. In Peru, for example, over half the people can't read. It's almost absurd, isn't it? The wealthy classes don't read either. They know how to read. They have the time. But they have chosen to be illiterate.

Puerto Rico's literacy rate is higher than Peru's but there is still not a large reading public. The typical book appears in an edition of 2,000 copies, sometimes paid for and distributed by the author. It was not until the 1950's that a few Puerto Rican writers such as René Marqués, Pedro Juan Soto, and Emilio Díaz Valcárcel broke this age-old pattern, when publishers in Latin America or Spain printed their books, although the royalities were quite modest.

The writer's linguistic isolation is another dilemma. His island is part of a huge English-speaking nation that cannot understand him. His most receptive audience consists of intellectuals from such far-off places as Mexico City, Havana, Buenos Aires, or Montevideo, and the most that one can expect in terms of "feedback" is a critical review many months later in a small literary quarterly.

The Early Literature

The first literary accounts from Puerto Rico were letters, chronicles, and memoirs by friars and Spanish government officials who took part in the island's conquest and colonization. Among the best is the *Historia general y natural de las Indias* (1535), only four decades after the island's discovery, written by Gonzalo Fernández de Oviedo (1478–1557). Fray Damián Lopez de Haro (1581–1648), Bishop of Puerto Rico, wrote a rich account of island life in 1644. Also important is the historical summary by Diego Torres Vargas (1590–1649) which appeared in 1647.

One of the liveliest seventeenth-century works (reprinted in a 1967 edition by the Institute of Culture) is the *Infortunios* ("Misfortunes") of Alonso Ramírez (1662–93), a poor carpenter's son who left San Juan at the age of thirteen, traveled the world and became involved in thrilling episodes of piracy and shipwreck. When Ramírez stopped at Mexico, he saw the Viceroy, *don* Gaspar Sandoval, who sent the Puerto Rican mariner to Mexican scholar *don* Carlos Sigüenza y Góngora, who took down the colorful narration, first published in 1690. After this, a comprehensive history of the island was published, in 1788, by Fray Augustín Iñigo Abbad.

The next prominent book to appear was *El Gíbaro,* by Manuel A. Alonso (1822–89), a young Puerto Rican medical student in Barcelona. Published in 1849 and consisting of twenty "scenes," following the style of the Spanish romantic period, this represents the first major effort by a Puerto Rican to depict the regional characteristics of the rural society. In vivid, and often quite humorous, prose and poetry, Alonso writes of dancing, cockfights, marriage, slang, music, and many other subjects. It is a picaresque, entertaining, and highly useful source for the student of Puerto Rico's past.

The Novel

Puerto Rico did not fully come of age in literary terms—that is, by producing a novel—until the 1890's which (can it be coincidence?) were when the island also "came of age" by pressing for autonomy from Spain. The island's first novelist was Manuel Zeno Gandía (1855–1930), who lived through the memorable period of the gaining of autonomy and the reversal to colonialism after the U.S. military occupation. Zeno Gandía was a prominent doctor and man of letters who traveled widely through Europe and studied several languages, including that of the Carib Indians, Italian, and Hebrew. He edited scientific and literary journals and, true to his epoch, once fought a duel when his integrity was questioned. His first, and most memorable, novel is *La Charca* (1894), a powerful document, which blended the declining style of romanticism and the realism of Zola. *La Charca* describes life in the mountainous coffee country, where nature was abundant and beautiful, and life was scarred by poverty and injustice. *La Charca*'s characters are the one-dimensional figures of allegory, such as sweet Silvina, who aspires to a Romeo-Juliet love with young Ciro, but is bound by concubinage, together with her mother, to Gaspar, a brutish scoundrel. The book also raises, for its time and place, serious questions—in long debates between a country priest and a liberal plantation owner—about the limitations of religious faith in lifting the *compesinos* from their diseased, feudal existence. (*La Charca* means a stagnant pool, symbolizing the author's view of island society.) Zeno Gandía never quite attained the eloquence of *La Charca* in his other three novels (which complete the tetralogy that he called "Chronicle of a Sick World"), but he set an imposing standard to which future island writers could aspire. The other novels are *Garduña* (1896), a drama with a sugar plantation setting; *El Negocio* (1922), on commercial life in the city; and *Los Redentores* (1925), an ironical tale about the American "redeemers" who colonized Puerto Rico.

In 1935, the first important modern novelist appeared when Enrique Laguerre (1906–), born in the countryside near Aguadilla and, today, a university professor, published his first novel, *La llamarada*. Laguerre has written eight well-received novels on historical and social themes. *La resaca* (1949), a biography of island life in the late nineteenth century, is considered, by many readers, to be his best work. Others of note are *Montoya* (1941) and *El laberinto* (1957). In the 1950's, fiction began to appear about the dolorous life of the immigrant in New York City. *Trópico in Manhattan* (1951) by Guillermo Cotto Thorner (1916–) is one of the first of this genre. At about the same time, José Luis González (1926–) wrote the short novel *Paisa,* an acerbic comment on racial discrimination in New York.

René Marqués (1919–), probably the island's best-known contemporary writer, is stronger in the theater, short story, and essay, but his novel *La víspera del hombre* (1958) won the 1962 Faulkner Foundation Prize in the United States. In 1956, César Andreu Iglesias' first novel, *Los derrotados,* dealt searchingly with the theme of frustrated Puerto Rican nationalism.

Pedro Juan Soto (1928–) has focused his attention largely upon man's dislocation in an hostile environment. Soto, born in Cataño, was raised in New York. His first book, *Spiks* (1956), is a hard-hitting collection of brief stories about the New York Puerto Rican, which employs Spanish and "Spanglish," and explores themes of family friction, mental illness, and misunderstandings with the police. This was followed by *Usmaíl* (1959), about a young man from Vieques Island, the illegitimate son of a Puerto Rican girl and an American sailor, who abandoned her. *Ardiente Suelo, Fría Estación* (1961) examines the New York Puerto Rican who feels cultural malaise, both in Manhattan and his native island. Perhaps the most prolific of island writers, Soto has since published two novels, *El Francotirador* (1969) and *Temporada de duendes* (1970). Some of his earlier works are now available in English.

The Short Story

The *cuento* ("short story") flowered as a popular art form in Puerto Rico in the late 1940's, as the newer writers abandoned the traditional style of the Spanish *estampa,* or folkloric sketch. Emilio S. Belaval (1903–   ), a former Supreme Court judge, was one of the most elequent early practitioners, with several collections of stories. The best is the ironically titled *Cuentos para fomentar el turismo* ("Tales to Promote Tourism") (1946), which describes the poverty of the countryside.

Belaval served as the link with his generation and a group of younger men, caught up in the maelstrom of Puerto Rico's social change. Before the writer's mind shifted to the city, there was one last magnificent nostalgic stab at country life, by Abelardo Díaz Alfaro (1917–   ). He has written only one book, *Terrazo* (1947), but it is one of the most popular in Puerto Rico and is used extensively in the schools. *Terrazo* consists of sketches and stories of rural life, full of vitality, poetry, humor, and poignancy. One of the most memorable is the tale of "Josco" the Puerto Rican bull, whose owner plans to put him out to pasture in order to bring in an American stud to "improve the race." It begins in a rich, stirring language, which the English translation can only hint at:

> . . . Josco's eternal shadow, cast upon the mountainside overlooking the Toa valley. Head erect, rapier-tipped horns stabbing the blood-tinged cape of a luminous sunset. Savage, dark brown, the fleshy jowls in shadows, his gait slow and rhythmic, the gelatinous slaver fell from black, rubbery lips, leaving foamy silver snails on the jewel-green grass. He was *josco* [sullen] in color and in manner, self-centered, hostile, a tireless fighter.

In the same volume, Díaz Alfaro abandons the poetic pessimism of "Josco" for hilarious tales of country school-teacher Peyo Mercé, and his bumbling attempts to introduce the English language and the concept of *Santa Clo'* to the bewildered, barefoot children of the *barrio*. Although he no longer publishes, the author of *Terrazo* has written hundreds of what he calls "autochthonous sketches" for the government's radio station.

One of the first to abandon the countryside as a literary theme was

José Luis González, whose grim accounts of urban misery in San Juan and New York are contained in short story collections, such as *Cinco cuentos de sangre* (1945). His story "There's a Little Black Boy in the Bottom of the Water," a terse, sad incident of a slum-child who leaps into the water beneath his shack after his own reflection, and drowns, has been translated into English and included in several anthologies.

René Marqués has also written two short story volumes—*Otro día nuestro* (1955) and *En una ciudad llamada San Juan*—and has edited *Cuentos puertorriqueños de hoy* (1959), the best anthology to date of the island short story, which has recently come out in a new edition.

Another fascinating writer is Emilio Díaz Valcárcel (1930–), who after serving in Korea in the U. S. Army appeared with *El asedio* (1958) and *Proceso en diciembre* (1963), some of whose stories relate the trauma felt by the Puerto Rican during that conflict in the Far East. One of the strongest, and most perceptive, accounts is that of a Puerto Rican soldier who is mercilessly badgered by his North American barracksmates, and then—frustrated—takes out his anger upon a docile Korean friend. More recently, Díaz Valcárcel has published the short story collection *El hombre que trabajó el lunes* (1966) and the novel *Figuraciones en el mes* de marzo (1972). Although pessimism saturates much of his work, Díaz is one of the few Puerto Rican writers who have been able to translate this into an effective type of "black humor." One of his most memorable stories is *La muerte obligatoria,* which has been translated to English as "Grandma's Wake." The story develops through the eyes of a young boy in the country, whose uncle, a store owner in New York, flies in to attend his mother's wake and is angered over having gone to the expense of the trip, after he discovers that the old woman is not yet dead. Undaunted, the uncle orders a coffin and arrangements for the wake, complete with paid mourners, "right now."

The boy narrator says:

My mama and my aunt had their hands to their necks yelling you're nothing but a heretic barbarian . . . Uncle Segundo's neck swelled up, he started saying things I didn't understand and he took grandma's measurements. He measured her with his hands from head to foot and went looking for Santo, the carpenter, and told him to make a coffin of the best wood there was, that his family wasn't cheap . . . Uncle moved his hand up and down and the women began to cry and shout. Mama was stretched out on the floor, howling just like the dogs; Aunt Altagracia was fanning her and sprinkling her with *alcoholado* . . . Uncle Segundo was telling grandma to shut her damn mouth, not to laugh, for this was no joke, but a wake, where she, though it mightn't seem so, was the most important thing.

Drama

The Tapia Theater in Old San Juan, where most plays are presented, is named after Alejandro Tapia y Rivera (1826–82). Tapia was an historical playwright, whose best-known works are *Bernardo de Palissy* (1857), *Camoens* (1868), and *La cuarterona* (1867); the last deals with the then—and now—topical theme of racial prejudice.

Some of the later plays worthy of mention are *El grito de Lares* (1929) by the poet Luis Llorens Torres (1878–1944), and *El héroe galopeante* by Nemesio Canales (1878–1923), a gifted humorist.

In the 1930's, Emilio S. Belaval, one of the early modern short story writers, also stirred up currents in theater when he formed a group called El Areyto. At about the same time, the Ateneo Puertorriqueño announced a contest for Puerto Rican drama and was surprised by the number of entries from writers with ideas but no place to stage them. Among the contestants was Fernando Sierra Berecía (1903–   ), who later dealt with the New York migration in an ironic comedy, *Esta noche juega el joker*. One of the young men attracted by the El Areyto group was René Marqués, then an unknown playwright.

During this period, Manuel Méndez Ballester (1909–   ), a prominent legislator, wrote a stirring play about poverty in the sugarcane country, *Tiempo muerto*. Luis Rechani Agrait (1902–   ), a journalist, produced a lively political-cultural comedy titled *Mi Señoría*. Also new on the scene was Francisco Arriví (1915–   ), now director of the Institute of Culture's drama section, who has authored several experimental plays on local themes, with mixtures of reality and fantasy.

Island theater's "heavyweight" is René Marqués, whose major play *La carreta* (1951) has been translated into several languages, produced in English in the United States, and is being discussed for a film. *La carreta* deals with the classic migration theme: the exodus from the country to an urban slum and, then, on to New York, with its promise and pain, and the resulting nostalgia for the security of rural Puerto Rico. The key figures are the heroic mother and her tragic son, killed by a machine in New York.

Marqués has been adventurous in his search for future themes and modes of expression. Following *La carreta*, he wrote *Juan Bobo y la dama Occidente* (1955), a pantomime ballet which satirizes the old academic conflict between nationalism and universalism, a much discussed topic in Puerto Rico. The same year he presented *Palm Sunday* in English in San Juan. The theme of the play—the Ponce Massacre of Nationalists in 1937—and its presentation in English provoked a controversy. Another play, *Los soles truncos* (1958), which has been translated and produced in Chicago, Madrid, and Mexico City, depicts three elderly spinsters in a decrepit San Juan townhouse, surrounded by the menace of change. His play *Un niño azul para esa sombra* won a prize in 1962. Marqués' latest work, *Sacrificio en el Monte Moriah* (1969), takes the biblical theme of a man sacrificing his son to the gods and relates it to contemporary issues. (The play's theme is close to the author's personal concerns, since his son was jailed for refusing to enter the U.S. Army.)

The number of theater performances in San Juan has multiplied in recent years. Although there is no continuous theater as one finds in New York, London or Madrid, the Institute of Culture's annual festival presents four plays for a week apiece at the Tapia Theater in Old San Juan, which is occupied for the rest of the year with a busy succession of stage classics, Spanish *zarzuela* troupes, and ballet performances.

Several independent local theater companies have also cropped up. Probably the best established is Dean Zayas' Teatro Sesenta, which offers its plays at the Sylvia Rexach Theater. There has also been much more contact with modern theater groups abroad. In 1971, the island's first festival of Latin American theater drew 30,000 spectators to see eighteen plays over a four-month period. During two weeks in 1973, a festival of experimental plays (mainly from South America) drew 20,000 spectators.

New local playwrights and directors (many of them products of the University of Puerto Rico) have emerged, including Luis Antonio Rosario Quiles, Jorge Rodríguez, Walter Rodríguez, Juan González, and Luis Torres Nadal.

Without year-round theater, however, Puerto Rico's actors and actresses (among the best are Jacobo Morales, Miguel Angel Suárez, Esther Sandoval, and Myrna Vásquez) must work in television or radio soap operas.

Poetry

Poetry is a major facet of Puerto Rican literature, as it is in other parts of the Spanish-speaking world. Businessmen and other public figures still pen romantic thoughts and publish them in small private editions. While the art of the *"declamador,"* public recital of verse, is fading, one still sees a lawyer rise in a musty nightclub in San Juan, raise his glass, and recite verse from memory.

One of Puerto Rico's most dashing poets was a woman, Lola Rodríguez de Tió (1854–1924), whom Rubén Dario called "the daughter of the islands." She wrote the lyrics to Puerto Rico's anthem, *La Borinqueña*. A fervent revolutionary, she lived in exile in Cuba for several years, where she wrote the oft-quoted lines:

Cuba and Puerto Rico are one bird with two wings
They receive bullets and flowers through the same heart.

Probably the most quoted poet is Luis Palés Matos (1898–1959), whose lyricism and gift for onomatopoeia were poured into poems that exalted Puerto Rico's African heritage. Many of these works are recorded in his own voice on records made by the Institute of Culture before his death. Palés' book *Tun tun de pasa y grifería* (which includes poems such as *"Danza negra"* and *"Majestad negra"*) is admired throughout the Hispanic world.

Other well-known poets are Julia de Burgos (1916–53), José

de Diego (1866–1918), José Gautier Benítez (1848–80), José P. H. Hernández (1892–1922), Cesáreo Rosa Nieves (1904–), and Evaristo Ribera Chevremont (1897–).

A figure in the mold of the traditional poet-revolutionary is Juan Antonio Corretjer (1908–), an adamant far-left nationalist who has spent time in Federal prison for his convictions and his ties with Pedro Albizu Campos. His Maoist political views may be viewed as extreme, but his poetry—of rural childhood, love, and the island's Indian past—is widely applauded. A recent book of his is *Alabanza en la torre de Ciales*.

In contrast with the bold majesty of Corretjer's works are the equally worthwhile bilingual poems of Jaime Carrero (1931–), a quiet, sensitive writer raised in the United States and now an art professor at Inter-American University, and the author of the play *Flag Inside* (1966) and the novel *Raquelo tiene un mensaje* (1970). Carrero's best-known poem is his *"Jet Neorriqueño*/Neo-Rican Jetliner," part of which follows. As the young man seats himself in the plane, and the "No Smoking Please" sign flashes on:

> My name is Raúl.
> From Puerto Rico?
> Jes an' now from Noo Jork
> Muee bieeen senhor
> Raúl is my name Señor
> American—you look American
>   blond
>
> You don't look Puerto Rican:
> Raúl señor my name is Raúl.
> R-A-U-L. u.u.u.
> Like the U you find in fool?
> Jes. U. U. U. foool.

The Essay

Antonio S. Pedreira (1898–1939) made a major essay contribution in 1934 with his still-quoted book *Insularismo*, which analyzes the "insularity" of the Puerto Rican people and asks searching questions: "How are we? Who are we?"

Similar concerns were expressed by Tomás Blanco (1898–),

who has also written fine sketches on island folklore, including the lovely *Los cinco sentidos,* in which he interprets the five senses in uniquely indigenous terms.

In the field of history, Salvador Brau (1842–1912), also a poet, left a treasure of material for today's scholar, outstanding among them being his *Historia de Puerto Rico* (1904). Cayetano Coll y Toste (1850–1930) also wrote important historical works and produced the detail-rich bimonthly *Boletín Histórico de Puerto Rico,* published between 1914 and 1927, which comprises thirteen volumes.

Lidio Cruz Monclova (1899–), the first professor to give a course on Puerto Rican history at the university level, is the most prominent historian in his field today and has written an exhaustive study of the nineteenth century. Another perceptive historian is Arturo Morales Carrión, who has worked with the Organization of American States in Washington and whose major published work is *Puerto Ricon and the Non-Hispanic Caribbean* (1953). Eugenio Fernández Mendez (1924–) has also contributed valuable studies, particularly in the field of cultural history.

The late Augusto Malaret Yordán made a lasting contribution to the study of language in the Americas with his widely used *Diccionario de americanismos* (1925), a massive compilation of Spanish words developed in the Western Hemisphere.

Manuel Fernández Juncos (1846–1928), born in Spain, came to Puerto Rico at the age of eleven and, in his time, was the island's leading journalist. He was also an active translator of poetry and, in several books published in the early 1900's, gave an updated, and equally fascinating, impression of the country people whom Manuel A. Alonso had described in *El Gíbaro* years before.

Leading literary essayists are Concha Meléndez (1904–), Margot Arce de Vázquez (1904–), Nilita Vientós de Gastón (1908–), Maria Teresa Babín (1910–), and Juan Martínez Capó (1923–), also a poet, whose weekly literary section in *El Mundo* constitutes the only regular newspaper coverage of island literature.

René Marqués has also authored an important book of essays (1967), which explores the island's language problem, the "docility" of the Puerto Rican, and the function of the writer in such a clime.

His essay on the coexistence of literary pessimism and political optimism in Puerto Rico surveys contemporary island writers and the forces that move them. Marqués observes that even the humorist writes with a bitter tone, and despairs that "Puerto Rico has not reached its final goal. Its unsolved political destiny is still as corrosive a cancer . . . as it was in previous decades."

He also expresses concern over the quality of island literature, commenting that the writer—spurred by patriotism—"has often been careless with the aesthetic aspect of his trade." An outspoken advocate of independence himself, Marqués warns that in the future "Puerto Rico shall be free," and the writer must seek subtler nonpolitical themes, which beg for treatment.

Although the political status issue still obsesses many island writers, the younger ones have already moved beyond what critic James A. Collins calls "a dying form, naturalist tragedy." Marqués, for example, is widely admired, but as Collins says, none of the younger writers "will attempt to eclipse [him] by taking him as model or mentor."

One of the most popular recent works on the island, for example, was *Puerto Rico Fuá,* a satirical revue that covers the island's history and takes all the "required" swipes at the United States, but does so with telling comic effect.

Music and Dance

The people of Puerto Rico like to sing and dance, and many have more than a casual acquaintance with the guitar. A party without music and dancing is described as *"demasiado hablao"* (too talky) or as a gringo fiesta.

The island's music is a blend of several influences: African, Spanish, and, more recently, from both ends of the Americas. Many years ago, the favorite dances of the upper class were the stately *danza* and *vals.* The peasants, in the meanwhile, were stepping to the *danzón* (a livelier version of the *danza*), the *bomba* and *plena* (with strong African rhythmic roots), the *polka,* the *mazurka,* the *guaracha,* and the *seis chorreao.* Argentina's tango became popular in the 1930's and later came the slow, romantic *bolero,* the gay *merengue,* which bounced across Mona Channel from the Dominican Republic, and the frenetic *mambo,* which sounds like a clash of Afro-Latin culture and the cacophony of exile in Manhattan. The *merengue* and *bolero* are still staples for most married couples today, but youth is writhing and wriggling to the latest forms of rock. Romantic youngsters still, however, *brillan la hebilla* ("polish the belt buckle") with a good old *bolero.*

The best-known early composer is Juan Morel Campos (1857–96), who is known as the father of the *danza.* Some outstanding examples of this lovely music form are Morel Campos' *"No me toques," "Laura y Georgina,"* and *"Maldito amor."* Second in prominence is Manuel G. Tavárez (1853–1925), who created a more modern version of the *danza,* with songs such as *"Margarita," "Ausencia,"* and *"Violeta."*

The giant of popular music composers is the late Rafael Hernández, who died in 1966. Hernández is idolized in Puerto Rico, and his songs are among the best in Latin music. He was an extremely versatile artist, who wrote of unrequited love, of nostalgia, of the misery of the country people, and, at the same time, composed some of the funniest, catchiest, most danceable tunes in the Latin repertoire. Any album of typical Puerto Rican music will be dominated by Hernández' songs, such as *"El cumbanchero," "Cuchiflitos," "Campanitas de cristal," "Los carreteros," "Perfume de gardenias,"* and *"Lamento Borincano."* Every day in Puerto Rico, someone, somewhere, sings his stirringly nationalistic *Preciosa,* which has become a second national anthem. The lyrics speak of an island "without a flag, without laurels, or glory," that is "mistreated by evil tyrants," but that is nevertheless "precious" to its native sons. So masterful are the music and lyrics that, despite the song's clear political message, it is sung and played constantly.

Good Puerto Rican pop musicans and singers are plentiful. The former include Tito Puente and the late Tito Rodríguez. Among the best singers are Bobby Capó, Johnny Albino, Ruth Fernández, and Gilberto Monroig. Teenage idols today are Lucecita Benítez,

Chucho Avellanet, and Nydia Caro. The blind singer-guitarist José Feliciano has become a best-selling record artist in several countries. Puerto Ricans also claim a "half-share" of Sammy Davis, Jr., whose mother (maiden name Elvira Sánchez) is Puerto Rican.

Puerto Rico has its own Symphony Orchestra and a Conservatory of Music. Both were under the direction (until his death) of world-famed Catalonian cellist Pablo Casals, who, in 1957, when he was eighty-one years old, retired to the island, his mother's birthplace. The Symphony Orchestra regularly tours the Caribbean islands. The Institute of Puerto Rican Culture also has an orchestra, which gives free concerts in town plazas. The musical event of the year is the Casals Festival each May, which attracts famous musicians and concert devotees from different parts of the world.

The best-known composers of classical music are Hector Campos Parsi, Jack Delano, and Amaury Veray. Gifted performers include pianist Elías López Sobá, who has played with the National Symphony in Washington, D.C.; Justino Díaz, a basso with the Metropolitan Opera, who, in 1966, inaugurated New York's Lincoln Center, playing "Anthony" to Leontyne Price's "Cleopatra" in the opera by Samuel Barber; the Figueroa Brothers Quintet; Jesús María Sanromá, a world-famous pianist; and sopranos Olga Iglesias and María Esther Robles.

Puerto Rico is also the birthplace of Antonio Paoli (1872–1946), a tenor whose performances in the capitals of Europe earned him decorations from the Czar of Russia, Kaiser Wilhelm of Germany, and Emperor Franz Joseph of Austria. After earning, and spending, some $2 million, the eccentric Paoli (who once showed up at a concert walking a lobster on a leash) returned to Puerto Rico in 1922 and from then on taught music to the island's youth.

In the classical dance, Ana García and Juan Anduze have, for the past several years, headed the Ballets de San Juan, a government-sponsored ballet corps and school. The Ballets de San Juan has performed at the annual theater festivals, in town plazas, and in cities abroad, and has brought to the island as guest artists some of the world's leading ballet dancers. Sylvia del Villard, a black Puerto Rican singer, has drawn upon the African heritage of the island and of the other Antilles in creating a small folkloric troupe of dancers and musicians. Miss del Villard also offers powerful interpretations of the *majestad negra* ("black majesty") poetry of Palés Matos.

Art

A vibrant art movement has emerged in Puerto Rico during the past twenty years. Before that time, a few gifted men worked alone, largely unnoticed, without galleries, museums, or formal art schools.

The first Puerto Rican painter of note was José Campeche (1751–1809), who lived in San Juan when it was a small village surrounded by thick fortress walls. He was a prolific artist, whose main works were portraits of San Juan's elite or religious themes. The whereabouts of many of the 400 oils he is said to have painted are still unknown, although infrequent discoveries are announced from Venezuela and elsewhere in Latin America.

A century later, Francisco Oller de Cestero (1833–1917), born in Bayamón, traveled to Europe and became the only Spanish-speaking artist to play a part, however small, in the French impressionist movement. He was a friend of Cézanne, Pissarro, and Manet, and a student of Gustave Courbet. In 1861, when he began to study under Courbet, nineteen-year-old Paul Cézanne arrived in Paris. Cézanne was living on a 125-franc monthly allowance sent to him from his father, a wealthy banker in Aix. Oller, who was poor, worked as a church sexton and sang baritone with an Italian opera company. Soon the two young men were studying together and often went to paint at Oller's place in the village of St. Germain-en-Laye, west of Paris.

A breach between the two friends opened when they submitted works to the jury of the Salon. Oller's was in the new realistic mode of Courbet, and it was accepted. Cézanne, whose style was even more outrageously modern, was rejected. In the ensuing years, Oller traveled back and forth between San Juan, Madrid, and Paris. In 1895, at the age of sixty-two, Oller returned to France after a long absence, bringing with him what he considered his master-work, *El Velorio,* a mural-sized canvas depicting a group of Puerto Rican country people at a wake for a young child. Oller's work, done in a strong Courbetian style, was refused by the Salon, whose stylistic tastes had changed over the years.

There are conflicting opinions about Oller's place in art. In France, in the 1860's and 1870's, his work ranked well with his now-famous contemporaries. In fact, one of his oils, *"L'Etudiant,"* is the property of the Louvre in Paris. Two others, Normandy landscapes done in an impressionist style, were unanimously praised upon their completion (they are now owned by the Institute of Puerto Rican Culture).

"But an artist must eat," says one critic, "and Oller turned to the enormous figures of *El Velorio,* destined to impress the bourgeoisie of San Juan and Ponce."

Another critic comments: "The only climate where an impressionist painter could thrive at the time was in France. Spain was far behind, and Puerto Rico was even farther."

After Oller, the horizons for the island artist slowly expanded, but it was not until the end of World War II that a sustained—and self-perpetuating—art movement appeared.

Probably the major first step occurred when a group of talented young men returned from New York, several of them veterans of the war, stimulated by their experiences abroad and eager to create in their *patria.* They flocked to Old San Juan, with its ancient cobblestones, crumbling mansions, and bars, where life had texture and there was an environment for work, argument, and camaraderie. In 1950, Lorenzo Homar, J. A. Torres Martinó, Rafael Tufiño, and Félix Rodríguez Báez founded the Center of Puerto Rican Art, a modest nonprofit workshop, gallery, and school. Soon, many of the artists were employed by the Community Education Division, and another government-sponsored workshop opened at the Institute of Puerto Rican Culture, a few blocks away in the old city. Galleries opened, exhibits were given, prizes awarded. Local newspapers began to take notice, particularly when important museum curators and critics began to visit the island to praise and acquire the work being done. Large galleries and museums opened, including the expansive Ponce Museum, built by the Luis A. Ferré Foundation (and designed by American architect Edward Durrel Stone), which includes a wing of Puerto Rican

art, along with classic canvases from all parts of the world. Special-
ization came about, and the small Galería Colibrí opened, devoting
itself to prints by island artists.

The fact that silk screen art is Puerto Rico's forte is proof that
necessity mothers invention. At the Community Education Division,
there was a need for posters to advertise films and meetings in the
countryside. Bright color and good design was sought in these
posters, which would be tacked to trees and the walls of country
stores. There were no color presses on the island in the 1950's,
and printing was too expensive anyway because of the small quantities—perhaps 500—of each poster needed. Silkscreen, with hand-
cut stencils and the fine register of a rainbow of rich colors, was
the ideal solution. Several Puerto Rican artists grew proficient in
this art; so proficient that today artists from New York send their
stencils to be cut in Puerto Rico, where the technique has reached
a master craft level.

Together with silk screen, the related techniques of linoleum
and woodcut also took hold, thanks partly to the Mexican tradition
in these media, and also because they required simple, inexpensive
materials, compared with etching and lithography. Good oils, too,
are produced but because of the higher sales price and the fact that
it is not available in multiple impressions, as are prints, the Puerto
Rican oil is not as well known abroad.

On of the best-known graphic artists is Lorenzo Homar, who
was born in the tough Puerta de Tierra section of San Juan in
1913 and migrated with his family to New York just in time
for the Depression. Homar attended night school, was a vaudeville
acrobat, and an engraver-designer at Cartier's, where he honed his
talent for meticulous craftsmanship. After being wounded in the
Pacific, he returned to Cartier's, married, studied at the Brooklyn
Art Institute under Mexico's Rufino Tamayo, and returned to his
patria, where he now directs the graphic arts workshop of the
Institute of Culture, and also designs striking posters.

Homar's equally prominent colleague since the 1950's is Rafael
Tufiño, who was born in Brooklyn of Puerto Rican parents in
1922 and came to the island at the age of ten. He, too, served in
the U.S. Army (in Panama, where some of his earliest sketches

appeared in *Yank Magazine*) and returned to New York to open a sign shop. In 1957, he studied art in Mexico on a Guggenheim Fellowship; his return to Puerto Rico coincided with Homar's and those of other founders of the Center of Puerto Rican Art. "Tefo" (his popular nickname) divides his interests between oils and graphics. His portfolio of brooding woodcuts of Puerto Rico's coffee country, done several years ago, is now a collector's item; many of his oils feature vigorous design structures, offset by tender, muted pastel shades.

Limited space prevents more biographical data on other worthy artists. Among the best in graphics are José R. Alicea, J. A. Torres Martinó, Marcos Yrizarry, Antonio Maldonado, Carlos Raquel Rivera, and Manuel Hernández. From the younger generation, a former student of Homar's, Antonio Martorell, has developed his own flamboyant style, thoroughly in tune with the pop and go-go generation. He has carried art to playing cards, with iconoclastic caricatures of island political figures, and to the design of a new subterranean shopping center for teenagers, known as The Ondergraun.

The most prominent oil painter since the late 1950's is Julio Rosado del Valle, whose quiet, introspective canvases have been exhibited in major U.S. museums. Notable, too, are José Oliver, an elder scholar who specializes in geometric, multicolored landscapes; Augusto Marín, who uses powerful lines and acrylic paints to create works of heroic theme and dimension; and Robert Alberty, Olga Albizu, Francisco Rodón, Myrna Báez, Luis Hernández Cruz, Rafael Colón Morales, to name just a few others who have won awards in recent competitions and whose styles vary widely. The most accomplished sculptors are Tomás Batista, who works primarily with wood and stone, and Rafael Ferrer (younger brother of actor José Ferrer) who welds metal (often old typewriters and junked auto parts) into fantastic shapes.

A man who deserves mention in any survey of island art is Carlos Marichal, a Canary Islander who died in 1969, and who, for two decades in Puerto Rico, was a leading illustrator of books as well as an imaginative theatrical set designer.

In early 1970, Puerto Rico, which had already earned a place on the world's culture map with the Casals Festival, made a serious bid for another spot when it hosted the first San Juan Biennial of Caribbean and Latin American Graphics, with 700 graphic works by 180 artists. Unlike the epoch of Oller, when the Caribbean artist lived in a small, insular world, the artists of the hemisphere had traveled often to the metropolis or saw its work in magazines; some lived in willing exile there; and the critics of the metropolis came to the island to look and take notice. One could see the growing internationalization of the arts. There was the lithograph of Brazil's Roberto de Lamonica, called, in English, "The Wall Street," and another called "Groovy No. 1," and the etching by Chile's Simone Chambelland, titled "Space Station." In one collage-like silkscreen print by Puerto Rico's Carlos Yrizarry, together with images of Guernica, Vietnam, and Spiro Agnew, was a rendering of the Marines of Iwo Jima, raising aloft a huge flower.

Cultural Institutions

Two Puerto Rican institutions—one private, the other public— have been vital nuclei for the island's cultural expression.

The Ateneo Puertorriqueño (Puerto Rican Atheneum) was founded in San Juan in 1876. Scholarly papers read at its public forums have covered every area of Puerto Rican life: from art, to history, to the subculture of poverty. For years, it has awarded annual prizes to artists in drama, poetry, fiction, graphics, sculpture, and music.

The government-supported Institute of Puerto Rican Culture opened in 1955 under the direction of anthropologist Ricardo Alegría. Working with limited resources, the Institute has had an important impact on Puerto Rican cultural life. It has supervised the restoration of buildings in Old San Juan, which by law is a historic zone; it has researched and published old documents on the island's history and folklore; it has restored colonial Spanish forts and ancient Indian ceremonial grounds. Each year, it offers a festival of Puerto Rican drama and awards prizes in literature, art, and music. It sponsors concerts and ballet performances. With its expanding series of books, records, magazines, and pamphlets, it has created an impressive library of Puerto Rican culture, often rescuing long-out-of-print publications. The Institute's art workshop also produces excellent silkscreen posters and offers the equivalent of an arts-oriented high school education to promising students.

11 Conclusion

The people you meet in the squares of Cidra and San Lorenzo, the people who play the horses three times a week, or shop in the new commercial centers, or visit second cousins on Sundays, or put flowers on their mothers' graves once a year may talk about status as one may talk about heaven and hell, with much conviction and little desire to get to the cross roads.

—FERNANDO PICÓ, in a *San Juan Star* column, 1970

Talk of political status is an obsession in Puerto Rico. Earlier in this book, I wrote that no man with an ounce of sense could make any confident predictions about Puerto Rico's future political status. However—because the obsession to play the prophet afflicts everyone—I would like to risk a very tentative, perhaps absurd, guess.

Divining the distant future, in any case, has a touch of the absurd, because so many variables—including The Bomb—can nudge, or bludgeon, history onto strange pathways.

In the wake of consistent pro-statehood gains at the polls, many observers assume that Puerto Rico will someday be the fifty-first state of the Union. They feel it would be absurd—even perverse— to predict any other outcome for an island where 90-plus per cent of today's voters favor permanent association with the United States and where, since 1917, every man, woman, teenager, and infant is as much of a citizen as the most blue-blooded Daughter of the American Revolution.

Former Governor Tugwell wrote in 1953 that Puerto Rico is "likely to become a state because no proud and achieving people can go on being excluded from . . . the highest political processes of the nation of which it is part." He regards the "decision against independence to be a final one" because

> . . . the well-known underlying hostility to the United States, so publicized by many observers, has proved to have an even deeper phase, closely akin to fellow feeling. . . . Puerto Ricans, somewhat to their own surprise, have discovered that after all they have become part of us. . . . Our mutual criticism is much like that which Texans and New Englanders would also feel for each other, and not the bitter xenophobia that might well have been expected in an insular people held more or less in a colonial condition for half a century.

This argument is based largely on the feelings of Puerto Ricans toward the United States. However, it seems to grant less weight to attitudes from the mainland; these may, in the long run, prove decisive, because even a cursory glance at Puerto Rico's history shows that the island has had little control over its political destiny.

Puerto Rico could become a state of the Union, but two very large obstacles bar its path: (1) the need for an overwhelming vote by Puerto Ricans in favor and (2) the agreement of the U.S. Congress.

As for the first, it will be a long time, if ever, before an "overwhelming" *sí* for statehood is possible. No one knows how large a vote "overwhelming" means. It is difficult to conceive that Congress would entertain such a petition from an island where even 10 per cent of its citizens seek not marriage but divorce, and with a hostile voice. Congress may question the convenience of statehood for other reasons, too:

1. *Economics.*   Puerto Rico is, and will be for a long time, poorer than any American state. In recent years, a cost-conscious U.S. Congress has refused to grant Puerto Rico full participation in

Federal welfare programs, because to do so might "bankrupt the programs."

2. *Language.* Congress is unlikely to accept a Spanish-speaking state where many children, tomorrow's citizens, speak little or no English.

3. *Race.* Many Puerto Ricans are considered "colored" by their fellow American citizens on the mainland. Congress may hesitate before moving to absorb an island that is not only "foreign" culturally but also "colored."

4. *Political Power.* Heavy population and a high birth rate ensure more voting strength for Puerto Rico in the U.S. House of Representatives than *twenty* states of the Union. These states may not welcome a more powerful colleague. If Puerto Rico is strongly Democratic, its admission plea may fare poorly among mainland Republicans, and vice versa.

Of course, all of these obstacles could be swept aside if some crisis affecting America's national security made it expedient to offer statehood to Puerto Rico.

If statehood wins a future referendum and Congress ignores such a petition, a disenchanted public may seek other options because, in Tugwell's words, proud Puerto Ricans will demand some form of political equality. The only other options are the status quo and independence.

Will the status quo remain the status for long? Perhaps. Autonomy has been a persistent force in Puerto Rico. It is the haven for the undecided, the conciliatory rejection of extremes, to avoid splitting island society down the middle into two irreconcilable—perhaps fratricidal—groups. Or, the autonomous commonwealth may outgrow itself. With its "semi-developed" economy, growing education, and tradition of stable government, Puerto Rico is miles ahead of many new (and old) independent republics. Commonwealth's main drawback is that it is loaded with ambiguities that perplex visitors, irritate leaders, and infuriate moral absolutists.

Luis Muñoz Marín argues that commonwealth is a status of the future, in a world growing more complex, more crowded, more independent. The concept of limited sovereignty is, in fact, one of the guiding principles of the United Nations. But the age of nationalism is still raging, with no end in sight. With Taiwanese fighting for national independence against an unwelcome Chinese Nationalist minority, with the memory of Biafra and Palestine still vivid, the commonwealth argument may be ignored for lack of visible relevance—that is, unless some exciting new mystique is created or some way is developed to "culminate" the commonwealth in a series of logical, preordained steps.

If not, outright independence may, as Ferré says, gain the upper hand. Such a statement today sounds rather absurd, but the lack of a large independence vote or of widespread nationalist violence is not the most sensitive weathervane for a people's attitudes. Nationalism cannot be defined exclusively as a group of diehards, guns blazing, invading the grounds of La Fortaleza, shooting up the U.S. Congress, or shouting *Viva Puerto Rico Libre!* or pickets denouncing *el imperialismo yanqui.*

There is a quieter, gentler nationalism, which permeates every corner of the Puerto Rican consciousness. It is not so much against America—or *against* anything—it is *for* Puerto Rico. It is why, for example, Puerto Ricans take pride in the fact that their own team participates in Olympic sports activities, rather than forming part of the U.S. delegation. This could be mere hometown, Texas-style chauvinism. But Texas is a state connected to other states by land, language, and a common history. Puerto Rico is an island—a *compact* island—of 2.9 million people who are remarkably similar, who interact daily among themselves, who share a feeling of geographical territoriality that is as basic, and ancient, in man as it is in other species.

Succeeding decades of U.S. cultural impact will surely change and "Americanize" Puerto Rico. The day may even come when all Puerto Ricans speak fluent English. But even the language issue can be deceptive. It is easier, for example, to speak English at a cocktail party of *independentistas* than at many pro-statehood gatherings.

Because Puerto Rico is populated almost exclusively by Puerto Ricans (unlike Hawaii or Alaska, where immigrant settlers from the United States quickly took the reins of political power), any cultural wave reaching its shores—be it in buying habits; tastes in food, movies, books, or television programs; even political attitudes—must pass through what amounts to a vast "human prism" of 2.9 million brains. When that wave emerges on the other side, in the cultural expressions of the people, although it may have changed Puerto Ricans in the process, it is, in itself, changed; it is "Puerto Ricanized."

As always, external factors will weigh heavily upon Puerto Rico's political status:

1. *The Cold War.* Whether or not the United States reaches an eventual *détente* with Cuba, and whether or not other revolts occur in the Caribbean, will not only affect Puerto Rican attitudes toward politics but also determine how essential the island is in the scheme of American national security.

2. *Common Markets.* Puerto Rico's tariff-free access to the mainland, although essential today, may be less attractive if common markets encompass the Caribbean, Central or South America, or the hemisphere.

3. *Latin America.* The continent to the south is in a state of economic development similar to that of the United States a century ago. South America's "great leap forward" is yet to come. When it does, the continent may prove to be a potent magnet for Puerto Rican trade and migration. If this occurs, Puerto Rico's migrants will work in a Spanish-speaking environment; growing technical expertise also ensures that most of the migrants will be factory managers, not janitors.

4. *Economic and Educational Change.* One-third of Puerto Rico's families are poor—at least partially dependent upon U.S. welfare cash and food. It is not surprising that statehood sentiment is strong in the urban slums, where knowledge of English is often nonexistent. The new middle class, too, has strong pro-statehood elements. But no one can tell what will happen a few decades hence. The children of today's middle class may be tomorrow's rebels. We have some clue, judging from the difference between mainland youth today and their Depression-scarred (and -scared) parents. Even now, most Puerto Rican children know of the sorrows of the early 1930's only through secondhand tales from their elders. They are growing up in a new, fast-changing society, where more education breeds more independence, on a personal

level at least. How, for example, can anyone calculate the changes taking place among the young, who, a few years ago, were chaperoned on their dates and who now sit unsupervised in dark balconies, calmly watching "X-rated" films?

5. *New York*. The more than 1.5 million Puerto Ricans on the mainland should play a huge—still incalculable—role in the status question. The success or failure of the statehood movement may depend on the success or failure of Puerto Ricans in the diaspora. On the other hand, a definite move for independence would require the disentanglement of a very knotty situation. Would the mainland Puerto Ricans have double citizenship? Or would families be split down the middle, into American and Puerto Rican citizens? This is just one of many mind-boggling questions. In fact, both independence and statehood require such harsh decisions for at least one portion of the Puerto Rican people that the commonwealth status may endure much longer than anyone thinks, not because of its virtues, but by default.

To repeat, trying to predict the long-term future may be absurd. However, to count out independence or the quasi-independence of autonomy is equally absurd. While the statehood argument is, to some degree, based on a search for dignity, its main thrust is derived from economic grounds.

This is paradoxical. If Puerto Rico continues to be poor, Congress may never admit it as a state. If it becomes prosperous enough to qualify for admission, the main reason for wanting statehood may have disappeared.

Over a long period of time, of course, the cultural affinity between Puerto Rico and the United States will be strengthened, but it would be one of the rarest phenomena in history—in fact, it staggers the imagination—if a people formed over half a millennium of common joy and hardship were to willingly renounce its very existence.

A Brief Chronology of Puerto Rican History

1493—On November 19, Christopher Columbus discovers the island of Borikén on his second trip to the New World and calls it San Juan Bautista.

1508—Juan Ponce de León is made Governor of the island and founds the first settlement, called Caparra.

1509—The seat of government is moved and called Ciudad de Puerto Rico.

1513—Ponce de León sails from Puerto Rico and discovers the North American mainland.

1521—The capital city is renamed San Juan, and the island takes the name of the capital: Puerto Rico.

1530—With the limited gold supply exhausted, many colonizers are attracted to Peru; others devote themselves to agriculture.

1539—Construction begins on the massive El Morro Fortress to protect the city.

1595—Sir Francis Drake's fleet attacks San Juan but is rebuffed.

1598—George Clifford, the Count of Cumberland, captures San Juan with 4,000 men and holds it from June through November.

1625—Dutch fleet attacks San Juan on September 24, but is rebuffed after its troops sack the city.

1660—Governor Pérez de Guzmán writes to the King that "eleven years have passed since the last ship came to this island."

1680—The city of Ponce is founded on the south coast.

1760—Mayagüez is founded on the west coast.

1775—Population is 70,250, including 6,467 black slaves.

1797—San Juan is attacked by the British, who retire after a one-month siege.

1812—Ramón Power represents the island in the Spanish Cortes.

1868—On September 23, patriots in Lares declare a republic, but the revolt is quickly squashed.

1873—Slavery is abolished.

1897—On November 25, Spain grants autonomy to Puerto Rico. Population is 894,302.

1898—On February 15, the battleship Maine blows up in Havana Harbor; on April 21, the Spanish-American War begins; on July 25, American troops land at Guánica, on Puerto Rico's south coast.

1899—The Treaty of Paris is ratified on April 11, and Spain cedes Puerto Rico to the United States.

1900—The Foraker Act makes the island a U.S. territory. The U.S. military government is replaced by a civil administration, headed by an American governor.

1917—The Jones Act is passed in Washington on March 2, granting U.S. citizenship to Puerto Ricans.

1930—Pedro Albizu Campos is elected president of the militant Nationalist Party.

1934—President Roosevelt visits the island and affirms support to rehabilitate the island's economy.

1935—Five people die in a clash between Nationalists and police at the university.

1936—Two young Nationalists kill insular police chief Riggs and are later killed by the police who arrested them. Albizu Campos and eight followers are jailed for sedition.

1937—On March 21, nineteen are killed and 100 injured in "the Ponce Massacre," as police open fire on a Nationalist parade.

1938—In July, Nationalists fire at U.S. Governor Winship during a ceremony to mark the fortieth year under American rule.

Two Puerto Rican bodyguards are hit; nine Nationalists are indicted for murder.

1940—The new Popular Democratic Party wins the elections. Luis Muñoz Marín becomes Senate President.

1941—Rexford Guy Tugwell is named the last U.S. Governor of the island and joins with Muñoz in an ambitious economic development program.

1944—Popular Party wins the election with 383,000 votes, compared to 208,000 of the combined opposition.

1946—On July 21, President Truman names Jesús T. Piñero as first native governor of Puerto Rico.

1947—On August 4, President Truman signs Crawford-Butler Act, permitting Puerto Rico to elect its own governor.

1948—Populars win the election, with 392,000 votes against 346,000 of the combined opposition. Luis Muñoz Marín becomes the first popularly elected governor.

1950—On July 4, President Truman signs Public Law 600, permitting Puerto Rico to draft its own constitution. On October 30, five armed Nationalists attack the Governor's mansion; uprisings erupt in other island towns, causing twenty-seven dead and ninety wounded. On November 1, two Puerto Ricans try to kill President Truman in Washington; a White House policeman and one assailant die. Albizu Campos and other Nationalists are given long prison sentences for complicity.

1951—On June 4, 387,000 Puerto Ricans favor Public Law 600, 119,000 vote against; over 200,000 registered voters abstain.

1952—On March 3, the new constitution is approved in a referendum, 374,000 to 82,000. On July 25, the Commonwealth Constitution goes into effect, after some changes insisted upon by Congress are approved in a second Puerto Rico referendum. Populars again win the election, with 429,000 votes against a combined opposition of 232,000. The Independence Party is second, with 125,000 votes.

1953—The United Nations authorizes the United States to cease transmitting information on Puerto Rico as a nonself-governing territory.

1954—On March 1, four Nationalists open fire in the U.S. House of Representatives, wounding five Congressmen.

1956—Populars win the election with 62 per cent of the total vote. The statehood Republican Party doubles its 1952 total with 172,000 votes; the Independence Party drops to 85,000.

1959—Congress rejects the Fernos-Murray Bill, which aimed to amplify Puerto Rico's autonomy.

1960—Populars win the election with 58 per cent of the 800,000 votes. The statehooders are second, and the Independence Party drops to only 3 per cent.

1964—The Status Commission begins to study the island's political status. Muñoz Marín retires from the governorship; his hand-picked successor, Roberto Sánchez Vilella, becomes the Popular candidate and easily wins the election.

1967—On July 23, in status referendum, commonwealth wins 60.5 per cent of the votes, compared with 38.9 per cent for statehood and .6 per cent for independence. *Ad hoc* committees are to be formed to work out the perfection of the commonwealth status.

1968—A rift in the Popular Party causes Sánchez Vilella to leave, and he forms his own People's Party. Luis Negrón Lopez is the Popular candidate. Luis A. Ferré and the pro-statehood New Progressive Party win by a narrow margin, interrupting twenty-eight years of Popular Party rule.

1970—Governor Ferré and President Nixon form an *ad hoc* committee to discuss the U.S. Presidential vote for Puerto Rico. Muñoz Marín retires from the Senate. The census shows 2.8 million persons on the island and 1.5 million Puerto Ricans on the U.S. mainland.

1972—Rafael Hernández Colon wins the race for governor and the Popular Party regains a majority in both houses of the legislature.

1975—The island's economy reels under the impact of the U.S. recession; unemployment exceeds 18 per cent, inflation is triple the mainland level, and the commonwealth government, for the first time, borrows millions to balance its budget.

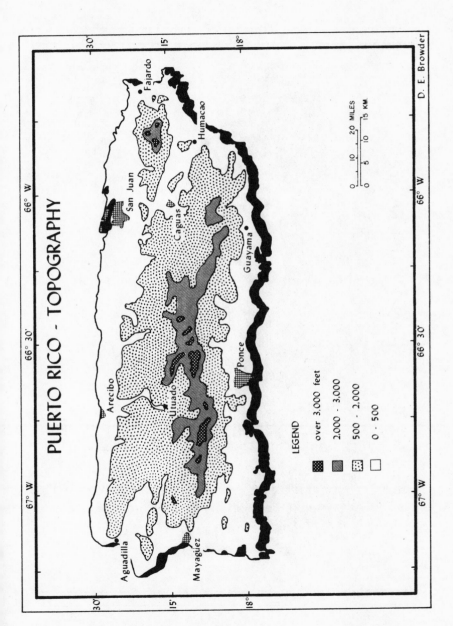

PUERTO RICO - TOPOGRAPHY

LEGEND
- over 3,000 feet
- 2,000 - 3,000
- 500 - 2,000
- 0 - 500

Aguadilla
Arecibo
Mayagüez
Utuado
San Juan
Caguas
Ponce
Guayama
Humacao
Fajardo

D. E. Browder

275

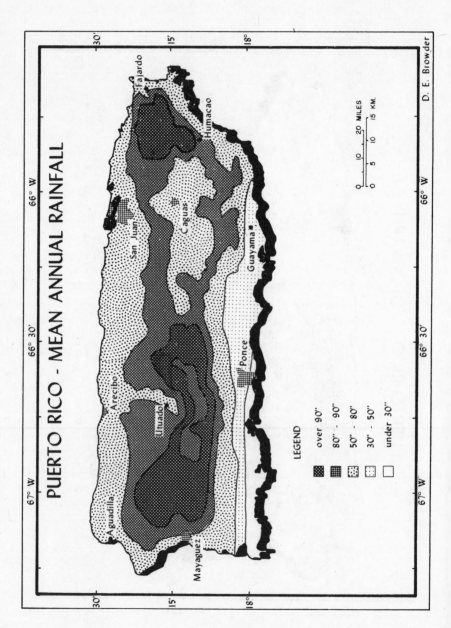

PUERTO RICO - MEAN ANNUAL RAINFALL

LEGEND

over 90"

80" - 90"

50" - 80"

30" - 50"

under 30"

0   5   10   15 KM.

0   10   20 MILES

D. E. Browder

Aguadilla
Arecibo
Utuado
Mayaguez
San Juan
Caguas
Fajardo
Humacao
Ponce
Guayama

67° W   66° 30'   66° W   30'   15'   18°

276

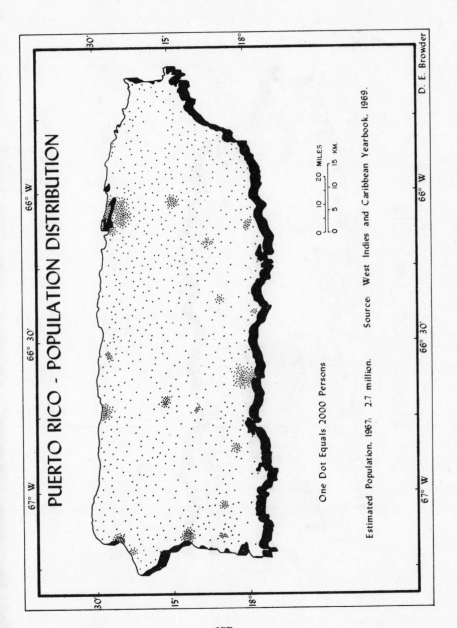

PUERTO RICO - POPULATION DISTRIBUTION

One Dot Equals 2000 Persons

Estimated Population, 1967: 2.7 million.   Source: West Indies and Caribbean Yearbook, 1969.

D. E. Browder

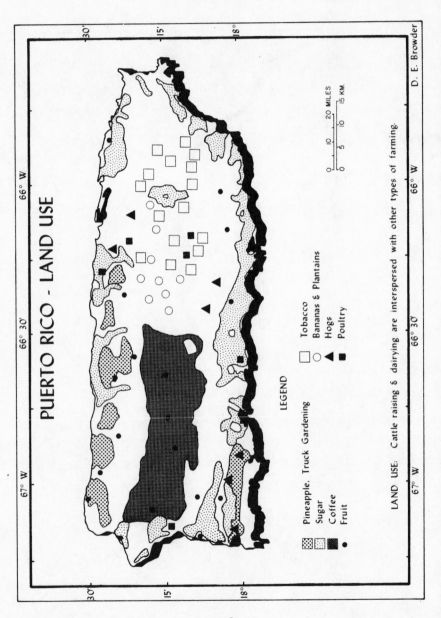

PUERTO RICO - LAND USE

LEGEND

Pineapple, Truck Gardening
Sugar
Coffee
Fruit

Tobacco
Bananas & Plantains
Hogs
Poultry

LAND USE: Cattle raising & dairying are interspersed with other types of farming.

D. E. Browder

Annotated Bibliography

Basic Comprehensive Sources

American Academy of Political and Social Science. *Puerto Rico: A Study of Democratic Development.* Philadelphia, 1953. Articles and data on the island at the time the commonwealth status went into effect; a key source, covering politics, economics, culture, demography, and the future.

Howard University. *Symposium: Puerto Rico in the Year 2000.* Washington: Howard University Press, 1968. Eleven papers by knowledgeable Puerto Ricans and North Americans about the island's past, present, and future.

Lewis, Gordon K. *Puerto Rico: Freedom and Power in the Caribbean.* New York: Monthly Review Press, 1963. A critical, indispensable study covering Puerto Rico's relations with the United States and its Caribbean neighbors.

Steward, Julian H., ed. *The People of Puerto Rico.* Urbana: University of Illinois Press, 1956, 1966. A massive, invaluable study of contemporary culture prepared by six scholars and edited by Mr. Steward, who directed the resarch project.

United States–Puerto Rico Commission on the Status of Puerto Rico. *Status of Puerto Rico.* Washington and San Juan, 1966. A valuable survey of Puerto Rican politics, education, migration, government, culture, and of other Caribbean areas under colonial control.

Wagenheim, Kal, ed., with Olga Jiménez de Wagenheim. *The*

Puerto Ricans: A Documentary History. New York: Praeger, 1973. An anthology of articles ranging from the discovery of the island to the present.

Geography, Flora and Fauna

LITTLE, ELBERT L., JR., FRANK H. WADSWORTH, and JOSÉ MARRERO. *Arboles Comunes de Puerto Rico y las Islas Virgenes.* Río Piedras: University of Puerto Rico Press, 1967. An exhaustive, well-illustrated book on trees in Puerto Rico and the Virgin Islands.

PICÓ, RAFAEL. *Nueva Geografía de Puerto Rico: Física, Económica, y Social.* Río Piedras: University of Puerto Rico Press, 1969. The most complete geography of the island; an English translation is in preparation.

History, Politics

ANDERSON, ROBERT W. *Party Politics in Puerto Rico.* Stanford, Calif.: Stanford University Press, 1965.

BAYO, ARMANDO. *Puerto Rico.* Havana: Casa de las Américas, 1966. A brief critical study.

BERBUSSE, EDWARD J. *The United States in Puerto Rico: 1898–1900.* Chapel Hill: University of North Carolina Press, 1966. A detailed study of the first two years under American rule.

BOTHWELL, REECE B., and LIDIO CRUZ MONCLOVA. *Los Documentos: ¿Qué Dicen?* Río Piedras: University of Puerto Rico Press, 1962.

BRAU, SALVADOR. *Historia de Puerto Rico.* New York: D. Appleton & Co., 1904.

Commonwealth Department of Education. *Puerto Rico y su Historia: Lectures Escogidas.* San Juan, 1964. Excellent selected readings on the island's history.

Congreso Puertorriqueño Anticolonialista. *El Caso de Puerto Rico Antes las Naciones Unidas.* San Juan, 1965.

CRUZ MONCLOVA, LIDIO. *Historia de Puerto Rico* (Siglo XIX). 3 vols. Río Piedras: University of Puerto Rico Press, 1958. A study of nineteenth-century Puerto Rican history; the most extensive contemporary source in print.

ENAMORADO CUESTA, JOSÉ. *Porto Rico: Past and Present.* New York: Eureka Printing Company, 1929.

FERNÁNDEZ MÉNDEZ, EUGENIO. *Desarrollo Histórico de Sociedad Puertorriqueña.* San Juan: Instituto de Cultura Puertorriqueña, 1959.

————. *The Sources on Puerto Rican Culture History: A Critical Appraisal.* San Juan: Ediciones El Cemí, 1967.

————. *Las encomiendas y la esclavitud de los indios de Puerto Rico 1508–1550.* San Juan: Ediciones El Cemí, 1970. A brief study of the enslavement and annihilation of Puerto Rico's Indians.

FIGUEROA, LOIDA. *Breve Historia de Puerto Rico.* 2 vols. San Juan: Edil, 1969. Historical outline from 1493 through 1898.

GEIGEL-POLANCO, VICENTE. *La Independencia de Puerto Rico: Sus Bases Históricas, Económicas y Culturales.* Río Piedras: Imprenta Falcón, 1943.

GOODSELL, CHARLES T. *Administration of a Revolution: The Development of Public Administration in Puerto Rico Under Governor Rexford G. Tugwell, 1941–46.* Cambridge, Mass.: Harvard University Press, 1965.

HANSON, EARL PARKER. *Puerto Rico—Ally for Progress.* Princeton, N.J.: Van Nostrand, 1962.

MALDONADO DENIS, MANUEL. *Puerto Rico: A Socio-Historic Interpretation.* New York: Random House, 1972.

MATHEWS, THOMAS. *Puerto Rican Politics and the New Deal.* Gainesville: University of Florida Press, 1960.

MILLER, PAUL G. *Historia de Puerto Rico.* New York: Rand McNally, 1939.

MORALES CARRIÓN, ARTURO. *Puerto Rico and the Non-Hispanic Caribbean.* Río Piedras: University of Puerto Rico Press, 1952.

Movimento Pro-Independencia. *Tesis Politica: La Hora de la Independencia.* San Juan: Editorial Claridad, 1964.

MUÑOZ MARÍN, LUIS. "Breakthrough from Nationalism." The Godkin Lectures, Harvard University, 1959.

————. "The Sad Case of Porto Rico." *The American Mercury Magazine,* February, 1929.

NIEVES-FALCÓN, LUIS. *Puerto Rico: Grito y Mordaza.* San Juan: Librería Internacional, 1971. An eyewitness account of the

University of Puerto Rico student revolt in March, 1971.

PAGAN, BOLÍVAR. *Historia de los Partidos Políticos Puertorriqueños.* 2 vols. San Juan: Librería Campos, 1959.

REID, WHITELAW. *Making Peace with Spain.* Edited by H. Wayne Morgan. Austin: University of Texas Press, 1965. The diaries of a member of the Peace Commission that wrote the Treaty of Paris, concluding the Spanish-American War.

ROOT, ELIHU. *The Military and Colonial Policy of the United States.* Cambridge, Mass.: Harvard University Press, 1916.

TODD, ROBERTO H. *Desfile de Gobernadores de Puerto Rico: 1898–1943.* 2d ed. Madrid: Ediciones Iberoamericanas, 1966. Biographical sketches of the American governors, many of whom the author knew.

TUGWELL, REXFORD GUY. *The Stricken Land.* Garden City, N.Y.: Doubleday & Co., 1947.

WELLS, HENRY. *The Modernization of Puerto Rico: A Political Study of Changing Values and Institutions.* Cambridge, Mass.: Harvard University Press, 1969. A careful analysis of the "Muñoz Era."

WILGUS, A. CURTIS. *The Caribbean: British, Dutch, French, United States.* Gainesville: University of Florida Press, 1963.

Biography

AITKEN, THOMAS H., JR. *Poet in the Fortress.* New York: New American Library, 1964. A biography of Luis Muñoz Marín.

ANDREU IGLESIAS, CÉSAR. *Un Hombre Acorralado Por La Historia.* San Juan: Editorial Claridad, 1964. Critical essays on Luis Muñoz Marín.

CRUZ MONCOLOVA, LIDIO. *Muñoz Rivera: Diez Anos de Su Vida Política.* Barcelona: Ediciones Rumbos, 1959.

GÓMEZ ACEVEDO, LABOR. *Sanz, Promoter de la Conciencia Separatista en Puerto Rico.* Río Piedras: University of Puerto Rico Press, 1965.

IRVING, WASHINGTON. *The Life and Voyages of Christopher Columbus.* 2 vols. New York: United States Book Company, 1831.

PEDREIRA, ANTONIO S. *Hostos: Ciudadano de América.* San Juan:

Institute of Puerto Rican Culture, 1964. A biography of Hostos by one of Puerto Rico's leading writers; reprinted from the 1932 Madrid edition.

Tió, Aurelio. *Dr. Diego Alvarez Chance (Estudio Biográfico).* San Juan: Institute of Puerto Rican Culture and Inter-American University, 1966. A biography of the doctor who came to the New World with Christopher Columbus.

Sociocultural Topics

Alonso, Manuel A. *El Gíbaro.* Río Piedras: Editorial Cultural, 1949. The first major book by a Puerto Rican, studying customs and traditions; this edition marks the one hundreth anniversary of the book's first publication.

Babín, Maria Teresa. *The Puerto Ricans' Spirit: Their History, Life, and Culture.* New York: Collier, 1971.

Benítez, Celeste, and Roberto Rexach Benítez. *Puerto Rico 1964: A People at the Crossroads.* San Juan: Talleres Gráficos Interamericanos, 1964.

Blanco, Tomás. *El Prejuicio Racial en Puerto Rico.* San Juan: Editorial Biblioteca de Autores Puertorriqueños, 1942.

Bourne, James Russell, and Dorothy D. Bourne. *Thirty Years of Change in Ten Selected Areas of Puerto Rico.* Ithaca, N.Y.: Cornell University Press, 1964.

Brameld, Theodore B. H. *The Remaking of a Culture: Life and Education in Puerto Rico.* New York: Harper & Bros., 1959.

Fernández Juncos, Manuel. *Galería Puertorriqueña.* San Juan: Institute of Puerto Rican Culture, 1958. The customs and traditions of Puerto Rico, by a noted nineteenth-century journalist.

Fernández Marina, R., Ursula Von Eckardt, and Maldonado Sierra. *The Sober Generation: A Topology of Competent Adolescent Coping in Modern Puerto Rico.* Río Piedras: University of Puerto Rico Press, 1969. A detailed study on the "children of Operation Bootstrap."

Granda, Germán de. *Transculturación e Interferencia Lingüística en el Puerto Rico Contemporáneo: 1898–1968.* Bogotá, Colombia: Publicaciones del Instituto Caro y Cuervo (XXIV), 1968. An important book on language and culture by a South American scholar.

LEWIS, OSCAR. *La Vida: A Puerto Rican Family in the Culture of Poverty—San Juan and New York.* New York: Random House, 1966. A controversial, highly readable book on slum culture.

————. *A Study of Slum Culture: Backgrounds for* La Vida. New York: Random House, 1968. Provides the general background data and statistical frame of reference for *La Vida,* whose 5 households formed part of the author's sample of 150 families.

MINTZ, SIDNEY W. *Worker in the Cane.* New Haven, Conn.: Yale University Press, 1960. An in-depth study of a cane cutter.

PAULAU DE LÓPEZ, AWILDA, and ERNESTO RUIZ ORTIZ. "En la calle estabas." San Juan: Editorial Edil, 1969. Studies a reform school in Mayagüez with pungent data on the life-style of island delinquents.

PEDREIRA, ANTONIO S. *Insularismo.* San Juan: Biblioteca de Autores Puertorriqueños, 1942. Important essays on the question of cultural identity.

ROGLER, LLOYD H., and AUGUST B. HOLLINGSHEAD. *Trapped: Families and Schizophrenia.* New York: John Wiley & Sons, 1966. Studies three generations of poor people living in the fast-changing slum society of San Juan.

ROSARIO, RUBÉN DEL. *Consideraciones Sobre La Lengua en Puerto Rico.* San Juan: Instituto de Cultura Puertorriqueña, 1958. A philologist examines Puerto Rico's language.

SEDA BONILLA, EDUARDO. *Interacción Social y Personalidad en una Comunidad de Puerto Rico.* San Juan: Ediciones Juan Ponce de León, 1964. Studies social change in a rural community.

————. *Los Derechos Civiles en la Cultura Puertorriqueña.* Río Piedras: University of Puerto Rico Press, 1963.

SENIOR, CLARENCE. *Americans All: Our Citizens from the Caribbean.* New York: McGraw-Hill, 1965.

TUMIN, MELVIN M., and ARNOLD S. FELDMAN. *Social Class and Social Change in Puerto Rico.* Princeton, N.J.: Princeton University Press, 1961.

VIENTÓS GASTON, NILITA. *Comentarios a un Ensayo Sobre Puerto Rico.* San Juan: Ediciones Ateneo Puertorriqueño, 1964.

Education

BENNER, THOMAS E. *Five Years of Foundation Building: The University of Puerto Rico 1924–29.* Río Piedras: University of Puerto Rico Press, 1965.

Council on Higher Education. *Estudio del Sistema Educativo de Puerto Rico.* Río Piedras: University of Puerto Rico Press, 1962. A detailed study of the island's school system.

MELLADO, RAMÓN. *Culture and Education in Puerto Rico.* San Juan: Casa Baldrich, 1948.

OSUNA, JUAN JOSÉ. *A History of Education in Puerto Rico.* Río Piedras: University of Puerto Rico Press, 1949.

Economics

ANDIC, FUAT M. *Distribution of Family Incomes in Puerto Rico.* Río Piedras: Institute of Caribbean Studies, 1964.

BAER, WERNER. *The Puerto Rican Economy and United States Economic Fluctuations.* Río Piedras: Social Science Research Center (University of Puerto Rico), 1962.

BARTON, H. C. *Puerto Rico's Industrial Development Program: 1942–60.* Cambridge: Center for International Affairs (Harvard University), 1959.

———. "The Effect of Minimum Wage Laws on the Economic Growth of Puerto Rico." *Bulletin of the Center for International Affairs* (Harvard University), December, 1959.

COLL Y TOSTE, CAYETANO. *Reseña del Estado Social, Económico e Industrial de la Isla de Puerto Rico al Tomar Posesión de ella los Estados Unidos.* San Juan: Imprenta la Correspondencia, 1899.

FRIEDLANDER, STANLEY L. *Labor Migration and Economic Growth: A Case Study of Puerto Rico.* Cambridge, Mass.: MIT Press, 1965.

GALBRAITH, JOHN KENNETH, and RICHARD H. HOLTON. *Marketing Efficiency in Puerto Rico.* Cambridge, Mass.: Harvard University Press, 1955.

GONZÁLEZ, ANTONIO J. *Economía Política de Puerto Rico.* San Juan: Editorial Cordillera, 1967. A proindependence economist, who ran for governor in 1968, discusses the island's economy.

PERLOFF, HARVEY S. *Puerto Rico's Economic Future: A Study in Planned Development.* Chicago: University of Chicago Press, 1950.

Puerto Rico Planning Board. *The Four Year Economic and Social Development Plan of Puerto Rico: 1962–1972.*

Stanford Research Institute. *Development of Tourism in the Commonwealth of Puerto Rico,* 7 vols. South Pasadena, Calif., 1968. A study made for the island's Economic and Development Administration.

Literature

ALEGRÍA JOSÉ C. *Cincuenta años de la literatura Puertorriqueña.* San Juan: Academia Puertorriqueña de la Lengua, 1955.

CABRERA, FRANCISCO MANRIQUE. *Historia de la Literatura Puertorriqueña.* Río Piedras: Editorial Cultural, 1965. The best one-volume historical survey of island literature.

———. *Literatura Folklórica de Puero Rico.* San Juan: Instituto de Cultura Puertorriqueña, 1960.

CARRERAS, CARLOS N. *Ideario de Hostos.* San Juan: Editorial Cordillera, 1966. A compilation of the thoughts of Puerto Rico's nineteenth-century educator Eugenio María de Hostos.

COOKE, PAUL J., ed. *Antología de cuentos puertorriqueños.* Godfrey, Illinois: Monticello College Press, 1956. Nine stories by six writers.

FERNÁNDEZ MÉNDEZ, EUGENIO, ed. *Antología de Autores Puertorriqueños.* 2 vols. San Juan: Commonwealth Department of Education, 1957. Writings selected and introduced by a Puerto Rican historian.

HOWES, BARBARA, ed. *From the Green Antilles.* New York: Crowell, Collier & Macmillan, 1966. Caribbean short stories, including four from Puerto Rico.

MARQUÉS, RENÉ. *Ensayos (1953–1966).* San Juan: Editorial Antillana, 1967. Twelve essays on different aspects of modern culture and politics.

————, ed. *Cuentos Puertorriqueños de Hoy.* San Juan: Club del Libro de Puerto Rico, 1959. Seventeen stories by eight authors.

MATILLA, ALFREDO, and IVAN SILÉN, eds. *The Puerto Rican Poets/ Los Poetas Puertorriqueños.* New York: Bantam, 1972. A bilingual anthology of island and mainland poetry.

MELÉNDEZ, CONCHA, ed. *El Cuento: Antología de Autores Puerto-rriqueños.* San Juan: Commonwealth Department of Education, 1957. Thirteen stories by six authors.

PÉREZ MARCHAND, MONELISA LINA. *Historia de las Ideas en Puerto Rico.* Instituto de Cultura Puertorriqueña, 1960.

RIVERA DE ALVÁREZ, JOSEFINA. *Diccionario de Literaturo Puerto-rriqueña.* Río Piedras: University of Puerto Rico Press, 1955.

Migration to the United States

BERLE, B. B. *80 Puerto Rican Families in New York City: Health and Disease Studied in Context.* New York: Columbia University Press, 1958.

CINTRON, HUMBERTO. *Frankie Cristo.* Taino, 1972. An English-language novel about *barrio* life in New York.

FITZPATRICK, JOSEPH P. *Puerto Rican Americans: The Meaning of Migration to the Mainland.* Englewood Cliffs, N.J.: Prentice-Hall, 1971.

HANDLIN, OSCAR. *The Newcomers: Negroes and Puerto Ricans in a Changing Metropolis.* Cambridge: Harvard University Press, 1959.

HERNANDEZ CRUZ, VICTOR. *Snaps.* New York: Random House, 1969.

————. *Mainland.* New York: Random House, 1973. Poetry about the Puerto Rican scene in New York.

LOPEZ, ALFREDO. *The Puerto Rican Papers: Notes on the Re-emergence of a Nation.* Indianapolis, Ind.: Bobbs-Merrill, 1973.

MAPP, EDWARD, ed. *Puerto Rican Perspectives.* Metuchen, N.J.: Scarecrow Press, 1974. Eighteen essays by Puerto Ricans about the mainland experience.

Puerto Rican Forum. *A Study of Poverty Conditions in the New*

York Puerto Rican Community. New York: Puerto Rican Forum, 1970.

ROGLER, LLOYD H. *Migrant in the City: The Life of a Puerto Rican Action Group.* New York: Basic Books, 1972.

THOMAS, PIRI. *Down These Mean Streets.* New York: Alfred A. Knopf, 1967.

U.S. Department of Commerce. Bureau of the Census. *Puerto Ricans in the United States: 1970 Census of Population.* Washington, D.C., June, 1973.

WAGENHEIM, KAL. *A Survey of Puerto Ricans on the U.S. Mainland in the 1970's.* New York: Praeger, 1975.

WAKEFIELD, DAN. *Island in the City: The World of Spanish Harlem.* Boston: Houghton Mifflin, 1959.

Young Lords Party and MICHAEL ABRAMSON. *Palante: Young Lords Party.* New York, McGraw-Hill, 1971.

Newspapers

Claridad (daily), Río Piedras and New York
El Día, Ponce
El Imparcial, San Juan
El Mundo, San Juan
The Island Times (weekly, ceased publication in 1964), San Juan
The New York Times
The San Juan Star, San Juan

Magazines

Caribbean Review, Hato Rey (quarterly)
Institute of Caribbean Studies Magazine, Río Piedras (quarterly)
Inter-American Review, San Germán (quarterly)
Revista Asomante, San Juan (quarterly)
Revista de Ciencias Sociales, Río Piedras (quarterly)
Revista del Instituto de Cultura Puertorriqueña, San Juan (quarterly)
San Juan Review (monthly, published 1964–66)
The Rican, Chicago (three times a year)

Index

70163

F
1958
W3

WAGENHEIM, KAL
    PUERTO RICO: A PROFILE.

DATE DUE

MAR 1 7 1997	
MAR 0 6 2001	

Fernald Library
Colby-Sawyer College
New London, New Hampshire

GAYLORD   PRINTED IN U.S.A.